CHILDREN AND THE INTERNET

A GLOBAL GUIDE FOR LAWYERS AND PARENTS

THOMAS J. SHAW

Cover design by Kelly Book/ABA Publishing.

Printed in the United States of America.

16 15 14 13 12   5 4 3 2 1

Library of Congress Cataloging-in-Publication Data
Children and the Internet : a global guide for lawyers and parents / by Thomas J. Shaw.
  p. cm.
   1. Internet—Law and legislation. 2. Children—Legal status, laws, etc.
3. Internet and children. 4. Internet and children—Risk assessment.
5. Internet and children—Safety measures. I. Title.
K564.C6S53 2012
343.09'99082—dc23   2012012367

ISBN: 978-1-61438-435-9

Contents

Preface

It may have been the day when my seven-year-old daughter came home from school and from memory recited the URL of an (innocent) website. I decided then it was time for a defense-in-depth approach to protect her interactions with the Internet. Up to then, although encouraging her access to approved websites, I had fastidiously allowed her to access the Internet only by utilizing her Mac user ID, which limited the applications (e.g., no email), and required pre-approval of all websites. And I kept the administrator passwords undisclosed to her. She could send emails to relatives back in the United States only from my account. I had also communicated with her school and her favorite school-sponsored websites on the issues of personal data, privacy rules, and access authorization. But with the new information coming to her from peers and online games accessible from her learning websites, with access to mobile devices (e.g., iPhone, iPad), and with her growing need and desire to try new things she had learned from friends, books, or in school, I knew I needed to expand the zone of protection around her online experiences—and fast.

This same scene has been likely played out many thousands of times across the world as parents come to realize that the Internet is now all-pervasive. There is literally no escaping its reach. If the LAN cable is disconnected, wireless access is still available. If the computer is protected, the smart phone or tablet takes its place. If home use is restricted, there is the library or a friend's house. While a child's potential access points to the Internet need to be identified and managed, controlling these will not be sufficient, because what is available on the Internet generally does not follow a child-content rating system. What is needed instead is the right combination of laws, technology controls, procedures, risk assessments, parental oversight, school guidance, and child awareness. This book addresses all of those areas.

It starts off by introducing the scope of the problem and the world of children online in Chapter 1. Chapter 2 then describes in detail the types of risks that are present when children are involved with the Internet. Chapter 3 looks at the various international conventions and agreements covering children, many of the public and public-private partnerships addressing these risks, and the problems involved with determining national jurisdiction in the global environment of the Internet. Chapter 4 presents the U.S. state and federal laws that protect children's involvement on the Internet. International laws from each major region of the world that protect children's involvement with the Internet are described in Chapter 5. Bringing this together is a best-practices approach in Chapter 6 which matches legal protections to online risks to children and describes risk assessments and treatments that are available. Chapter 7 concludes the book by providing practical examples of how stakeholders can get started. The appendices present a list of resources for protecting children in many countries around the world.

The reader should view chapters as layers building on top of each other. After the foundation is laid for why action is required and what children do online, the diversity of risks to children online is presented. Statutes that criminalize the conduct associated with those risks from countries across the world provide the layer of legal defenses sitting on top of the risks. The legal protections must be matched to the risks and with the applicable countries and their national laws. The best-practice approaches can then be designed and implemented as a layer dealing with the risks by technological, process, and awareness means. The final layer is the techniques to begin to identify risks in all the places children are online.

While this book does address the laws and risk-reduction techniques that can be used, it stops short of discussing the investigation and prosecution processes used by law enforcement, state agencies, justice departments, and other authorities involved in investigating and prosecuting crimes against children involved with the Internet. The evidence gathering, forensic analyses, chains of custody, presentation, and admissibility of gathered evidence into a criminal or civil case, and all of the respective procedural rules in the various jurisdictions, are more thoroughly covered elsewhere.

This book is written primarily for two audiences. The first is the lawyers situated globally who may need to understand the risks and the legal protections within their own jurisdiction or a foreign jurisdiction potentially and actually involved in an Internet-related matter. The second audience is the parents who are either the current or prospective clients of lawyers (or, in the best case, will never need to be). For the lawyers, the entire book is applicable, with a focus on those statutes outside their jurisdiction or laws within their jurisdiction similar to those presented. The risk assessment process is also probably new but equally important. For parents, I have excerpted a few key points at the start of each chapter, but beyond that, parents should read at least the entire introduction and the chapters on risks, best practices, and starting. The book also speaks to schools and to organizations involved with children over the Internet, in providing recommendations for their respective risk assessment and treatment processes.

This is a book about children, but it is not only about your own children; it is about everyone's children and how the Internet affects them. It is not just about the children who can sit down at a computer and utilize the Internet's capabilities, but also about the children who are victimized in some manner because of the Internet. The children who are the targets of child sex tours or the unwilling participants in child sexual abuse images (child pornography) or are the subjects of cross-border trafficking or child labor all facilitated by use of the Internet are just as much a focus here. While they will get less print than those actively using the Internet, their plights should not stray far from our thoughts.

Although this is a book *about* children, it is not a book *for* children. Beyond the obvious difficulties with understanding legal and technical terms, the need to describe some of the worst behaviors of sexual predators, child traffickers, and criminal elements that parents and lawyers must address requires the use of wording and imagery inappropriate for children. As such, while there might be paragraphs or sections that could be used age-appropriately with some older children, such as the best-practices chapter section about the roles of children and parents and getting started, in general it would be best to keep the printed book on the parent's bookshelf, situated up high, or behind a strong password for the e-book version.

I originally titled the book using the phrase "Children on the Internet" to demonstrate the use of the Internet by children. But that sounded like it was only about what happened during children's active use of the Internet, which, as you will see, is not the whole story. So I changed it to "Children from the Internet" to highlight the source of the risks and the need to be protected from them. But that sounded like the Internet itself was only about dangers that children needed to avoid. So again I changed it, this time to "Children and the Internet" to properly reflect not only children's active participation in this medium but also their passive involvement that is initiated by others. I intend this book to illustrate both roles.

I have cited many different studies in this book. It is important to understand that while I have tried to present as balanced a view as possible on what the risks are, there is also disagreement among the various stakeholders about certain issues. For instance, some studies might show that there is clearly a link between online recruitment and subsequent in-person sexual abuse between those who met online. Others might say the majority of these cases are just teenagers going through their normal growing stages. There is also some dispute as to whether the possession and use of child abuse images leads to further illegal conduct by the user. My feeling is that while all studies help in understanding the possible risks, anything bad that can happen to a child is a risk that must be taken into account, assessed, and managed, even if the odds of such a risk materializing is small. I talk about risk likelihood as part of risk management. Yet, much like the requirement to remove your shoes at airport security checkpoints, is not the less than one percent chance of losing your child to an online predator something you would want to know about and decide on how best to guard against?

I have tried to avoid sensationalizing some very disturbing stories and statistics. Some of what law enforcement and prosecutors have to look at in detail and address in some of these cases is beyond my desire to repeat. For example, reading about fathers sexually abusing their own children on video in front of live Internet audiences for profit is too appalling to think about long enough to even try to decide how to write about it. Therefore, I have simply tried to capture the essential points of the risks so that they can be understood and addressed without additional embellishment. For those who want to read in more detail of the many studies that have been done and about those carrying out the activities of law enforcement and prosecution, there are many such accounts available. In writing this book, I have not viewed a single child abuse image, believing that it is not necessary to see it to be able to understand and empathize with the horrors of the victims. My complete admiration goes to those who must do so professionally in order to facilitate the rescue of living victims and to investigate and prosecute the offenders.

A few words regarding terms: The terms "Internet" and "web" or "World Wide Web" are often used interchangeably (and may be so in this book) but do have different but related meanings. The Internet is the enabling mechanism, including network hardware, software, management software, and physical and logical connections that provide access to a common backbone and set of service, while the World Wide Web sits on top of the Internet to provide a certain set of services. While the networks used by certain service providers, such as mobile telecom providers, may technically not be part of the open Internet, for ease of discussion their services will be considered Internet services. Also, the term "child" or "children" will mean all young people up to the age of 18, encompassing such terms as "young person, adolescent, teens, young adults, minors," and the like. "Child" here encompasses both male and female children, unless specially designated. While "child pornography" and "child (sexual) abuse images" have both commonly been used, many believe the latter is the more accurate term. And there are both American and British spellings included, based on the legal influences on respective organizations and statutes.

As a parent and a lawyer whose practice is both international and focused on information law, I feel that I have the capability to get this message across to both primary audiences of this book, and I also strongly feel the mandate to do so. The use of the Internet will only increase in our children's lifetimes, so this medium will continue to grow in importance. Although I wrote this book in just two months, I hope I have covered the essence of what all of the stakeholders in the provision of children's Internet safety must know and do. With today's younger generation increasingly technology-literate, I believe there is a growing understanding globally from parents and lawyers of the need to protect children online everywhere. It is into this gap that I place this book, for the general betterment of the Internet experiences of children, parents, teachers, and their legal advisors situated across the globe.

Thomas J. Shaw, Esq.
March 2012

Dedication

My inspiration for writing this book was my daughter, Ayaka, who sat with me during much of the authoring. My little muse has only just started her journey on the Internet. May this book help guide her travels in cyberspace to be both unlimited in possibility and absent of risk.

About the Author

Thomas J. Shaw, Esq., attorney at law, CPA, CRISC, CIP, CIPP, CISM, ERM-P, CISA, CGEIT, CCSK, is a frequent author and speaker on the topics of technology and the law from a global perspective. Mr. Shaw is an attorney long based in Asia who works with organizations on Internet law (cloud computing, social networking, intellectual property, e-commerce), information law (privacy, information security, e-discovery), international transactional law, compliance, information governance, and risk assessment.

He is the author of the 2011 book *Cloud Computing for Lawyers and Executives—A Global Approach* and is the lead author/editor of the 2011 book *Information Security and Privacy—A Practical Guide for Global Executives, Lawyers and Technologists*. Mr. Shaw writes extensively on technology law and is the editor/founder of two American Bar Association periodicals: *Information Security & Privacy News* and the *EDDE Journal*.

His experience, licenses, and certifications are in law, information, risk assessment, security controls, privacy, information security, records, information systems audit, new technologies, financial statement audit, IT governance, BCP, compliance, cloud security, and cloud computing and outsourcing contracts, all from a global perspective. He runs CloudRisk Asia, which risk-assesses private and public-sector organizations and cloud service providers (www.cloudriskasia.com). He is the developer and leader of a new cloud computing risk workshop in Asia.

Mr. Shaw is also active in various certification, publishing, and leadership activities in a number of leading international professional organizations. And is a loving father.

Chapter 1

Introduction

Children around the world have always experienced life as differently as their cultures, geographies, societies, economies, and circumstances allow. But now they also are part of an unprecedented shared childhood experience, getting to interact not just with the children in their own schools and neighborhoods but with children a world apart. This is part of the new learning and communications paradigm, where young persons can use resources from around the world via the Internet to help them understand and reach out. They can find out about children and cultures geographically located far, far way and try to interact with them. They can grow their imaginations and touch such realities at a young age that were previously available only to the great explorers of yore. This chapter will introduce the dynamics of the new learning and communications paradigm and what children themselves experience in their online worlds.

Beyond how children participate more or less voluntarily with the Internet, there is also an involuntary aspect to their participation. Children are frequently the victims of illegal activity that targets them either in their role as consumers of certain Internet services, for their identities, or, more heinously, as chattel to be sold in real or represented (photo, video) form. They may be coerced into abusive situations or coerced into giving up information about themselves or their families. They may be harassed, bullied, or stalked online and offline by peers or by predators. They may be abducted or forced essentially into involuntary servitude. This book will address both of these modes of participation, voluntary and involuntary, that children have with the Internet. This will be viewed from the perspective of the child and those stakeholders in the online safety of children and will leave for others to explore the psychologies, pathologies, and motives of the criminal forces that prey on children.

The goal in creating a safe Internet experience for children is to layer multiple safeguards, building a wall so tall and deep that even the most virulent of malefactors will eventually fail. That wall is made of the legal protections; technical capabilities; processes to be followed by parents, caregivers, teachers, and children; and the education and awareness that can be a valuable last line of defense when all other techniques have been overcome. Anyone who has climbed the Great Wall of China or gazed up at the Great Pyramids of Egypt has an idea of the type of structure that will suffice. It must be something that awes and intimidates enough to encourage the bad actors on the Internet to give up and move on.

Before discussing the risks to children on the Internet and the appropriate safeguards to deploy, it is important to understand the world being discussed, from several perspectives. This includes the necessary global view, the impacts on different categories of children, the issue of consent by children, and the technologies that are involved. And mostly it is important to understand the way children see and use the various services on and access devices to the Internet. A multitude of studies make clear the trends in Internet usage by children: that Internet access is on the rise, Internet use increases with age, children start to use the Internet younger, children spend more time on the Internet than before, children have a multitude of online activities, and the devices to access the Internet are diversifying.[1] What must be made definitive is how parents, schools, organizations, and lawyers will respond to these trends.

---

1. OECD, *The Protection of Children Online: Risks Faced by Children Online and Policies to Protect Them* (2011).

POINTS FOR PARENTS
o Children have varying online experiences based on their age, genders, and locations.
o The power of the Internet is in its global character and what that exposes children to.
o There are varying rules for children's consent based on the Internet services used.
o To fully protect children, parents must understand the technologies that are used.

1.1 THE DYNAMICS

A. A Global View

The Internet is a primarily an open network that allows anyone to partake. For all participants, that means two things. First, they should be able to access it from wherever they are in the world, by whatever means and devices that are available to them. Second, because it is available to all, by definition they are connected, at least in physical terms, to every other participant. While in reality most Internet users will never know one another or in any way interact, quite a number of them will. That is both the beauty and the danger in the use of the Internet—it provides access to both the best and potentially the worst features of technology on open networks. The dangers will be discussed further in Chapter 2.

The ability of all to join allows participants the ability to go beyond their local environment and connect to those situated in places across continents and oceans very different from their own. This wider audience gives each Internet user an entry to a global stage and, at the same time, hopefully a global view that complements their local knowledge. Children using the Internet can grow up not only knowing Mary at the local flower shop and Sam who delivers the mail but Mr. Patel in India, Ms. Kim in Korea, Ms. Gonzalez from Argentina, Mr. Mueller from Germany, Ms. Tan from Singapore, Mr. Wangai from Kenya, Ms. Ozturk from Turkey, Mr. da Silva from Brazil, Ms. Johansson from Sweden, and Mr. Wang from China.

In an open and flat world, children will need to have not only the ability to connect to friends and resources from across the Earth but also the ability to understand the thinking of those on the other end of the network. Be it culture, language, custom, perspective, or humor, all will become more intertwined and globalized as the 21st century marches on. The children of today will interface as if borders did not exist, and the use of the Internet is likely to be their introduction to that experience. Because children will require the skills to live in that global village, it is important to adopt as wide an international viewpoint as possible. Trying to find the experiences of children everywhere on the Internet requires looking at the applicable laws, online habits, cultural restrictions, and type of safeguards used around the world. It is from looking through all of these diverse sets of eyes that the true power of the Internet can be fully understood and made available to children.

B.   *Consent*

Children are typically assumed not to be able to provide a legally binding consent. The judgment and wisdom needed to understand and analyze the facts and circumstances inherent in making a decision is assumed to be beyond the capabilities of most minors. While the age of consent differs based on both the jurisdiction and the statute, the basic premise applies as well to the various statutes and conventions that define the rights of children on the Internet. For example, children are allowed to consent to contracts when they are 14 years of age in American Samoa, 15 in Iran, 16 in Scotland, 17 in Gibraltar, 19 in South Korea and most Canadian provinces, 20 in Japan and Taiwan, 21 in Singapore, Egypt, and the U.S. state of Mississippi, but 18 in the majority of countries.[2] The age of majority may differ from the ages prescribed nationally or locally for consent (for sexual activity), marriage, voting, driving a motor vehicle, consumption of alcohol, criminal responsibility, and military service. And the ages of consent for disclosing personal information can vary based on the services rendered.[3]

---

2. For global ages of majority, *see, e.g.,* www.worldlawdirect.com.

3. FOUNDATION FOR INFORMATION POLICY RESEARCH (U.K.), CHILDREN'S DATABASES— SAFETY AND PRIVACY (2006).

For online services, there may be several different cases. One is in the purchase of goods and services, with a contractual relationship of offer and acceptance. Children are usually precluded from forming an executable contract, except for certain necessities. A second case may be the right to consent to provide personal information about themselves. Privacy laws do not typically provide for the protection of information based on it being about a child (instead of, for example, sensitive health or financial information). A third case might be the ability to consent to participation in online services that do not involve commercial transactions or the disclosure of data. A fourth case involves whether consent may be required for the parent to monitor the activities of the child online, as is typically the case in most parental-control software capabilities, or the location of the child, as provided for under many tracking capabilities with mobile phones.

The consent must be either obtained from the child user or the parent or both. It may then be a process of determining the dividing line specifying at which age the child may consent or the parent must consent. One such analysis for the age of consent to online activities follows:

> There is no clear-cut, legally enforceable minimum age that defines when verifiable parental consent must first be obtained. Everything hinges on the nature and complexity of the transaction and the capacity of the legal minor to understand it. . . . [I]n general, 12 is the age at which a young person might reasonably be supposed to understand enough to be able to give consent on their own behalf, at least about a range of matters. However, if the transaction is at all complex, for example if it might lead to a child's data being transferred to a third party for whatever reason, verifiable parental consent ought to be obtained regardless of the age of the child.[4]

In the European Union (EU), the Article 29 Working Party has issued several papers regarding children and consent in terms of

---

4. eNACSO, A DIGITAL MANIFESTO—AN AGENDA FOR CHANGE (2009).

disclosing personal information.[5] It recently issued its guidelines for consent.[6] In its advice on the consent from children, it first explains that across the EU there is no consistent age for consent in regards to collection or processing of data from a child, nor consistent techniques for verifying a child's age. It sees situations where a child could never consent, others where an adult would have to also consent and the requirement for online age verification mechanisms. It recommends that information be adapted to children when their consent is required. It calls for a sliding scale approach, where the proper age of consent to collection and further processing is based upon the particular circumstances, such as the age of children, "the type of processing (the purposes), whether particularly risky, type of data collected, data usages, . . . and whether the information will be kept by the data controller or made available to third parties."

C.   Technologies

Various technologies make up the infrastructure that defines the Internet. The network lines and cabling, routing and switching devices, firmware and network software, and routing and management protocols are the mostly unseen parts of the foundation upon which the Internet operates. It is the higher-layer application tools and software creating the capabilities of the Internet and the devices from which end users access these capabilities that are the focus for children's use of the Internet. While a picture can be painted of these technologies, it is important to understand that the numbers, types, and functions of these capabilities are always changing. For example, 10 years ago, social networking sites as they currently exist were barely getting off the ground. Smart phones were not yet a big part of the user experience. Ten years from now, there is no way to tell in what manner children may be accessing and experiencing the Internet.

---

5. Article 29 Data Protection Working Party, WP147 - Working Document 1/2008 on the protection of children's personal Data (General guidelines and the special case of schools); WP160 Opinion 2/2009 on the protection of children's personal data (General Guidelines and the special case of schools).

6. Article 29 Data Protection Working Party, Opinion 15/2011 on the definition of consent.

The average teen in a recent U.S. survey owns 3.5 gadgets out of these five: cell phones, mp3 players, computers, game consoles, and portable gaming devices.[7] So the technologies impacting children have evolved beyond the typical devices such as PCs using web browsers to access informational and e-commerce sites to a plethora of new electronic devices, software applications, websites, controls, and other capabilities, such as:

- Social networks
- Virtual worlds/Augmented reality
- Online gaming
- Chat rooms
- Instant messaging
- Blogging/Micro-blogging
- Texting/Email
- Online learning systems
- Children activity websites
- Mobile devices
- Digital cameras/webcams
- E-cash/debit cards
- Location services/GPS tracking
- Child monitoring software
- Age verification systems
- Single sign-on

Children's use of these varying technologies also is indicative of some of the risks that they will face (discussed in Chapter 2). Whether the technologies are more or less socially oriented can determine what types of relationships children will develop through it. Social networking sites are set up for the very purpose of sharing with friends, through photos, videos, and text messages. Many of these technologies are used by like-minded and similarly aged children communicating with each other. Children using a social network are "more likely to interact with friends or friends-of-friends than complete strangers" while in online gaming communities, it is more typical "for youth to interact with people they do not know."[8]

---

7. Pew Research Center, *Social Media & Mobile Internet Use Among Teens and Young Adults* (2010).

8. U.S. INTERNET SAFETY TECHNICAL TASKFORCE, ENHANCING CHILD SAFETY & ONLINE TECHNOLOGIES (2008).

The particular uses of these technologies will be further explored later in this chapter, but there may be differing experiences and risks for children based on which technology they are utilizing. In numerous studies on these various technologies regarding the risks to children online, children using differing technologies may encounter different kinds of risks.[9] For example, *chatrooms and online messaging* play a leading role in the online solicitation of children by predators and are a leading source of cyberharassment, due in large part to their bi-directional nature and rapid communication. Those children involved in *blogging* have also experienced more cyberharassment and cyberbullying. *Social networking sites* do not seem to offer an increased risk for online solicitation of youth, but children who used these were more at risk for cyberharassment and cyberbullying. Contrarily, a factor in these results may be related to the type of children who uses the technology, their individual circumstances and personal proclivity to risk-taking behavior, and the types of technology that they choose rather than any indication about the technology itself.

D.   *Differences among Children*

The risks for children in using the Internet may be different for different groups of children, including those of different ages, genders, socioeconomic groups, and countries. Although they all may start out similarly by sitting at a PC or on a mobile phone, what they experience both in their response to what they find on the Internet and how others interact with them can vary based on who they are, their family situation, and the culture that surrounds them. Numerous studies have been done to survey these experiences.

For example, based on many studies, only a few of which are listed here,[10] girls tend to be more at risk for online solicitation, mostly at ages 14–17,[11] and also for online harassment,[12] while boys

---

9. *Id.*

10. *Id.*; *see* App. C. for a complete listing of studies.

11. Janis Wolak, Kimberly Mitchell & David Finkelhor, *Online Victimization of Youth: Five Years Later.* National Center for Missing and Exploited Children, #07-06-025 (1960).

12. Patricia W. Agatston, Robin Kowalski & Susan Limber, *Students' Perspectives on Cyber Bullying*, JOURNAL OF ADOLESCENT HEALTH 41:S59–S60 (2007).

tend to actively seek out and view more pornography online.[13] Girls have a tendency to share passwords with friends (47 percent of online girls ages 14-17 versus 27 percent for boys the same age) and find social networking experiences less positive than boys, especially when younger.[14] As children get older, their online activities increase, and their physical and mental maturity develops, they become more at risk online for being solicited or cybergroomed (explained in Chapter 2).[15] Older children are also more likely to search out pornographic material online.[16] Exposure to harmful, unwanted materials and conduct also occurs more with older children.[17] Online harassment appears less frequently among younger children,[18, 19] while peaking among children aged 13–14.[20] The following section of this chapter contains additional information about online activities and age differences.

Children in different socioeconomic conditions or countries may not be able to experience the Internet in exactly the same manner. Those sitting behind a "great firewall" or with other country-imposed limitations on or political control of what is allowed in and out will have a different experience from those who are allowed to see and feel as much as their parents or teachers allow. Those who do not have constant access to the Internet, have slower access, have to share

---

13. Kenzie A. Cameron et al., *Adolescents' experience with sex on the web: results from online focus groups*, JOURNAL OF ADOLESCENCE 28(4):535–40 (2005).

14. Pew Research Center, *Teens, Kindness and Cruelty on Social Network Sites* (2011).

15. Timothy J. Beebe et al., *Heightened Vulnerability and Increased Risk-Taking Among Adolescent Chat Room Users: Results From a Statewide School Survey*, JOURNAL OF ADOLESCENT HEALTH 35:116–23 (2004).

16. Jochen Peter & Patti M. Valkenburg, *Adolescents' Exposure to Sexually Explicit Material on the Internet*, COMMUNICATION RESEARCH 33(2):178–204 (2006).

17. Howard N. Snyder & Melissa Sickmund, *Juvenile Offenders and Victims: 2006 National Report*, U.S. Dep't of Justice, March 2006.

18. Amanda Lenhart & Mary Madden, *Teens, Privacy, & Online Social Networks*. Pew Internet and American Life Project, April 18, 2007.

19. Samuel C. McQuade & Neel M. Sampat, Survey of Internet and At-risk Behaviors, Undertaken by School Districts of Monroe County, N.Y. (2008).

20. Robin M. Kowalski & Susan P. Limber, *Electronic Bullying Among Middle School Students*, JOURNAL OF ADOLESCENT HEALTH 41:S22–S30 (2007).

their access devices, or have access only through the smaller screens of mobile phones may have a different experience from those who are always wired and can afford the latest access devices with content flowing across high-speed networks.

While there are clearly different experiences among different categories of children who use the Internet, this book looks at the risks to all children. The implementation of techniques to address the risks to children online may differentiate certain groups, such as the use of more rigorous safeguards to protect younger children (see the best-practices discussion in Chapter 6). The solutions to socioeconomic differences are outside the scope of this discussion, but there are many international and national efforts to bridge and narrow those gaps for children's access (of which the One Laptop Per Child project has been notable). The differences across the various countries speak to both the types of online activities that children engage in (as discussed in the next section) and therefore the risks they will be exposed to and the legal protections available, all of which will be covered in succeeding chapters.

E.   *The Mandate*

The risks that are discussed in the next chapter should spell out a clear mandate for parents, educators, and legislators to do something to address the dangers online for children. Children and parents have a certain set of rights online, including those to maintain their reputations, their property, and their privacy; to participate openly or be anonymous; to be physically safe and mentally at peace; to purchase (and sell) online; to maintain the integrity of their identity and trust the integrity of others; and (for parents) to be able to monitor and, as appropriate, control the activities of their children online. These rights must be safeguarded, through laws, policies, technologies, and awareness, by all of the stakeholders in this effort: parents, guardians, educators, lawyers, law enforcement, and the children themselves.

To accomplish this will require efforts far beyond business as usual. For example, parents must probably learn more technology and get more involved in their child's school events and activities than they might be comfortable with or feel that they have time for. Schools must proactively challenge their current safeguards and risk assessments and reach out further to keep parents informed of online risks and safeguards. Organizations have to reach far above minimum levels of standards and statutes to truly safeguard children online and to discard general platitudes about privacy protection ("we are committed to keeping your child safe"). Lawyers must learn new technologies and techniques and try to get involved in children's safety in a proactive manner before harm occurs. And children themselves must give up a little of their cherished privacy to be safer online.

1.2   The Online Experiences of Children

Children in general are able to enter new worlds when they use the Internet. They get to experience interactions with their current friends but in new environments, and to make new friends from many places. They get to leave the real world for the fantasy world in realistic games, flashy videos, and virtual lives. They get to learn about topics and cultures with which they had no previous knowledge or expand what they already knew. They get to experience the touch and feel of places they have never been to and may never physically visit. And they get to do this all from the comfort of their own home or school.

The children's experiences of using differing technologies on the Internet are varied but the following provides a generalized overview of those that are having a significant impact. As it is the use of these technologies that may predict certain outcomes and will need to be risk assessed and managed, it is appropriate to have a basic understanding of each. Some of the technologies will assist parents and others in risk management, while most will help facilitate the services provided on and access to the Internet. Familiar access devices such as desktop and laptop computers are not described here, while some services that are used by both adults and children are. Although some of these technologies are now rising in end-user popularity while others may be decreasing, that may be a local and not global phenomenon. These child-related technologies, referenced by the case studies cited later, all started out as distinct products, services, or standards, but increasingly are starting to converge and overlap, offered by most providers, blurring their distinctiveness.

A.   Online Services

1.   Social Networks

These are interactive websites for friends to gather and chat, post various items for sharing, make recommendations, ask advice, and generally hang out. People "friend" one another by adding them to their "friends" list. Posted items can be shared with only those on one's friends list or publicly. Two of the most popular social networking sites in the United States and globally (they appear in the applicable local language) are MySpace and Facebook. Some other popular social networking sites globally include Orkut, Qzone, Renren, Habbo, Badoo, and Bebo. When children go to the MySpace website, they can find music, videos, games, and can browse people based on their ages, genders, and locations. On Facebook they can upload pictures, send messages, view profiles, "like" something, use virtual currency, and invite "friends" who can view their "wall" or they can choose to make their postings public. There are other social networking sites dedicated to children, especially those under the age of 13, which monitor uploaded items, do not allow children to add friends outside their age group or restrict friends to those approved by parents, restrict or eliminate outside links, allow deletion of profiles by parents, require photos of the children and credit card verifications from the parents, limit formats for messages, and have codes of conduct. There are various lists of safe social networking sites for children.[21]

2.   Virtual Worlds

In virtual worlds, realistic fantasy scenarios are portrayed, with the player as an active participant in the fantasy world. Whole new existences can come alive in stunning, graphical 3D imagery that approaches the capabilities of the imagination. Players can be someone either like themselves, at least in basic characteristics, or totally different, with special powers. The most popular virtual world has been Second Life, which allows participants to use their avatar to live for them as part of both fantasy and real-world experiences. Players can

---

21. *See, e.g.*, NPR, "Ten Safe Social Networking Sites for Kids" (July 11, 2011).

chat and buy items that are both make-believe and actual purchases, look like whoever they want, and have whatever capabilities they wish. Some children's websites offer their own virtual worlds as part of their sites' service offerings. Between virtual reality and physical reality is augmented reality. Whereas virtual reality replaces the real world with a virtual one, augmented reality modifies a live view of the real physical world with various other computer inputs, such as feeds for video, audio, location data, and graphics.

3.   Online Gaming

These are video games that are available online as part of Internet gaming websites, through gaming consoles, or on mobile phone networks. These games may be free or paid and may be a front-end for marketing of other products or purely related to entertainment. Some are given away free, operating at a basic level on a local device that becomes much more sophisticated online or after purchasing an advanced version. There may be significant numbers of other players involved in some of the online games, such as in massively multiplayer online games, many if not most of whom are strangers to the children. Although there are far too many popular game sites to mention, there are several that are dedicated to safe playing for children and include links to videos, games, and other websites that have all been prescreened and that provide parents with reports on their child's activities at the site.

4.   Chat Rooms

These are forums on websites where children, as members, can join their friends in typing comments to be read by other chatroom users and then read the replies. Some chat rooms have audio and visual capabilities as well. This has a high level of interactivity among the participants, including the possible exchanging of personal information to those who may not be the intended audience. A number of social networking and online gaming sites have added the ability to chat, so there has been a decrease in popularity of pure chat-room sites, but the technology continues to be used.

5.   Instant Messaging (IM)

Instant-messaging capabilities allow users in the various other technologies to send brief messages to their friends. This is typically a one-to-one communication but may also be one-to-many with a known set of listeners. For example, personal computer users may have the ability to send an IM through a common application and protocol that they share with other computer users. This may come from a website (e.g., Yahoo or AOL) or peer to peer, but there are security issues with IM such that personal information should not be entered. It is commonly used on all of the major mobile phones now. One of its biggest users is Skype, a service that allows for low- and no-cost telephony between members and also non-members, both local and international. In addition to IM, it provides for live video and audio of the other participants in the conference telephone call using webcams.

6.   Blogging/Micro-blogging

Blogging allows children to write and post their own messages and for others to visit these blogs and comment on the post. As opposed to email messages that are typically one to one, blogging can be a one-to-many experience, which can be shared with only the members of the blog or with the public. Twitter is a micro-blogging site that allows for the posting of a limited number of text characters and to have any number of "followers" who receive the posts. When tweets are received, they can be responded to by further tweets. There are websites dedicated, for example, to providing safe blogging capabilities for students through their teachers or parents.

7.   Texting/Email

Texting is the use of an email-like capability from mobile devices such as mobile phones, while email uses a more structured system whose client software may reside on a PC or be online through a browser and allows for the use of attachments, encryption, calendaring, and many other related functions to be tied together. Short Message Service (SMS), probably the most typical texting format, is what texting is commonly called in much of the world. Historically, texting acted more like email, being sent to a phone number, while the increasingly similar-featured IM (although different architecturally) was sent to a handle and required synchronous communications. Although there may also be financial differences (SMS is treated as a voice call, while IM is part of the data traffic), in essence they can be considered to perform the same function of quick communications not requiring the formalities of creating an email.

8. Online Learning Systems

Children utilize specialized educational software online to learn how to read, write, do math, understand science, etc. Specialized vendors may have expanded their offline products online, but many have started online. These systems may be provided in conjunction with in-school learning but may also serve home-schooled children. These applications can provide many capabilities in a manner far superior to what is available offline, such as the ability to interact directly with children; to teach children a topic, then test them on it in fun and graphical ways and help them discover what areas they did not learn well the first time; to increase the challenges on the fly based on how the child reacts; to mix the learning experience with play so that the child does not lose interest; and to monitor progress, both in reports and measurement graphics presented to the child (with appropriate encouragements added) and more detailed reports for the adults.

9. Children's Activity Websites

These websites may provide games, fun activities, and learning experiences all on one site. Very well-known brand names (e.g., Disney) that have a market for children's products have these sites, as do organizations that provide experiences to adults as well (e.g., National Geographic). While not connected directly with academic learning, these sites provide exposure to topics ranging from many science disciplines to tie-ins to well-known children's characters, toys, and games. Sometimes the line between advertising/selling and fun can blur. These sites often take many of the single-site capabilities like blogging, social networks, and virtual worlds and offer them as a feature under the umbrella of their children's or family website.

B.   Online Access Devices

1.   Mobile Devices

There are many types of mobile devices, including mobile phones (smart and otherwise), PDAs, thumb drives, music players (e.g., iPods), tablets (e.g., iPads), etc. All can be involved in issues related to privacy of personal information, while only certain types can be involved in two-way communications with other participants on the Internet. Mobile phones allow for voice communications, browsing of the Internet, and the downloading of applications (apps), including a variety of games, and are the typical device of choice far away from home. These come with capabilities such as global positioning systems (GPS), described below. Closer to home, tablet devices allow for both mobility and intuitive Internet access in ways the desktop computer never fully reached. Given their mobility and ease of use, the ability to safeguard these devices is not yet at the maturity level of the legacy desktop computers, so greater attention to their evolving capabilities is required.

2.   Digital Cameras/Webcams

Digital cameras, which are typically now part of mobile phones but also available as separate still and video cameras, allow photos and video to be taken and uploaded to the Internet. While a great benefit in facilitating of much of the content on photo-/video-sharing sites and between friends, it can also be used inappropriately, as described in the discussions in Chapter 2 on child abuse images and "sexting." Webcams are connected right to the computer or tablet and allow real-time video capture and simultaneous or later transfers among participants. It is used beneficially to capture faces in videoconferences or calls between friends but again has a downside when it is used to share child abuse imagery and conduct.

C.   Other Capabilities

1.   E-cash/Debit Cards

E-cash is a method of being able to use a device, such as a mobile phone that is charged up with a certain amount of cash credit, for purchases. Debit cards perform the same function but are not precharged; instead, they are charged against the users' bank account when purchases are made. These, along with credit cards, when in the possession or control of children, can be used for excessive or inappropriate purchases, financial fraud (when the numbers are acquired), or identity fraud, which enables children to access websites that are age-inappropriate but use possession of a credit card to check for adult verification. These financial payment options are important for children to shop online—especially older children, as they purchase downloaded music or tickets to their favorite events. These can also be used for real-world purchases of virtual-world currencies.

2.   Location Services/GPS Tracking

Location services allow end-user devices such as mobile phones to specify where the user is at that time, using the tracking towers of the cellular phone network. GPS tracking uses the GPS satellites and provides more precise locations for mobile phones and tablets, and is even more precise than tracking by mobile phone cell. Tracking by IP address is also possible but less precise. These capabilities provide parents with the ability to know where their children are at any time (especially critical for working parents), but also provide children the ability to be found—both when they wish it and when they may not.

3.   Child-Monitoring Software

To keep control of their child's access to the Internet, parents will want to be able to restrict the websites that their children visit, be able to keep track of their uploading and downloading activity including apps and files, and know who their online friends and contacts are. They will also want to be aware of any personal information that is requested of their children and then actually provided. This software is used in addition to more traditional networked computer-protection software, such as antivirus, antispyware, content filers, and junk-mail filters. This software may be loaded onto the end-user device or monitoring device, or it may be available as a feature on child-specific websites.

4.   Age Verification Mechanisms

To keep children away from inappropriate content, such as violent video games or adult pornography, statutory requirements in many countries (discussed in later chapters) specify that websites displaying these types of content must block children's access. As explained further later, besides appropriate warning labels on the site itself, techniques include requiring a credit card (which children are not expected to possess), verifying the user's data to a public database of ages, or independent third-party verification. There is no single mechanism that works in all cases or for websites in countries that do not have statutory restrictions.

5.   Single Sign-on

Internet users can sign into their favored online site and gain access to resources on other websites without having to expressly sign-in (authenticate) for each new website and can link the results of some of their current activities across sites. Long a goal of organizations to have a viable federated identity management capability, popular Internet sites such as Facebook, Google, Twitter, and LinkedIn allow uses to sign in just one time to their site and gain access to other sites/services. Properly done, this should both enrich and safeguard the child's online experience. Any authentication system has three components: verifying the registrant's identity and providing log-in credentials (e.g. user ID and password); authenticating those login credentials during log-in; and granting access to those credentials for certain resources on the website. When resources on other websites are requested, the two websites exchange credentials about the user and the user is then authenticated for resources at the second website.

D.   *Usage Around the World*

A child's use of the Internet, especially older children, may involve the use of all of these technologies. According to one global survey covering 12 countries,[22] children use the Internet for school projects

---

22. Symantec, *Norton Online Living Report 09* [2,614 children ages 8 to 17 from 12 countries: Australia, Brazil, Canada, China, France, Germany, India, Italy, Japan, Sweden, United Kingdom, United States] (2009).

(94%), entertainment (62%), games (96%), and shopping (49%). About 92 percent of kids socialize with family and friends online for approximately five hours a week, and 55 percent of kids have made friends online. Of their use of specific technologies, 86 percent send text messages, 73 percent email from their phones, and 23 percent are using a Twitter-like service and spend three hours per week texting. Fifty-five percent of kids have made friends online, up from 45 percent of kids in countries surveyed the previous year, and have an average of 37 online friends.

One year prior, this report had detailed that 76 percent of children in the United States aged 13–17 used social networking sites constantly, frequently, or sometimes (46 percent for all U.S. children), while in China 85 percent of children did so.[23] Thirty-five percent of U.S. children were confident about shopping online, while 69 percent in China were. Ninety-six percent of U.S. children played online games, and 99 percent did so in China. Ninety-eight percent of children in China downloaded music, while 89 percent in Brazil did so. And more than 90 percent of the children in the United States, China, France, and Germany used the Internet for research. Two years later, children from 14 countries surveyed were online for 1.6 hours per day, an increase of 10 percent.[24] Online the children were playing games (83%), surfing the Internet (73%), doing schoolwork (71%), and talking to friends (67%). Most recently, 33 percent of children from 24 countries surveyed are now shopping online for items such as music, video games or software, and movie tickets.[25]

---

23. Symantec, *Norton Online Living Report* [2,717 children ages 8 to 17 from 8 countries: Australia, Brazil, China, France, Germany, Japan, United Kingdom, United States] (2008).

24. Symantec, *Norton Online Family Report* [2,805 children ages 8 to 17 from 14 counties: Australia, Brazil, Canada, China, France, Germany, India, Italy, Japan, New Zealand, Spain, Sweden, United Kingdom, United States] (2010).

25. Symantec, *Norton Online Family Report* [4,553 children ages 8 to 17 from 24 counties: Australia, Belgium, Brazil, Canada, China, Denmark, France, Germany, Holland, Hong Kong, India, Italy, Japan, Mexico, New Zealand, Poland, South Africa, Singapore, Spain, Sweden, Switzerland, UAE, United Kingdom, United States] (2011).

There were also differences in the activities of children in various countries. For example, in the United States children text 10 hours per week, while kids in Japan and Germany text one hour per week. Children in the United States have the most online friends at 82, and kids in Japan have the fewest at 13. Sixty percent of Brazilian children include their parents as social networking friends, but only one-third do in Canada, and only 6 percent of French parents friend their children. Eighty-eight percent of children in China felt that reading online was as valuable as reading an offline book, as opposed to 66 percent globally. Thirty-eight percent of German kids agree that that online texting, emailing, instant messaging, and posting information on social networks may interfere with learning to write well, while 53 percent of children in the United Kingdom (UK), 73 percent in Brazil, and 50 percent globally feel so. Fifty-nine percent of Indian children say it is easier to communicate with their families on touchy subjects online instead of in person or on the phone, while 33 percent do globally. Children globally socialize online for five hours per week, while children do so in Sweden for nine hours and Brazil for 13 hours per week. Eighty-six percent of parents in Australia feel the Internet makes learning easier for children; 90 percent of Australian children feel that way.

Another set of studies looked at the use by children of mobile phones. With the increasing capabilities of smart phones, including Internet access, these devices are increasingly the access device of choice for children. The most recent study found that nearly 70 percent of children use mobile phones, with younger children tending to use voice calls; but as children get older, they send more text messages.[26] They also text each other but call their parents, and most access the Internet on their mobile devices at least daily—more if they have smart phones. Seventy-two percent of children by age of 12 who had Internet access on their mobile phones were using it to access social networking sites, compared with 85

---

26. GSMA & NTT Docomo, *Children's use of mobile phones—An international comparison* [survey of 3,528 children in four countries: Japan, India, Paraguay, Egypt. Previous years' studies had included children in China, South Korea, Mexico, India and Japan.] (2011).

percent of those with smart phones. The biggest uses of features were for cameras, music listening, and movie viewing, with new features like mobile money and GPS still in single digits. Downloading games, music, and movies and using the Internet to get news and information were both done by about half the children, while playing Internet games, texting messages, doing school research, and downloading or using applications were done by one in four or five children in the surveyed countries. The majority of these children's parents feel much safer with the child having a mobile phone, especially in an emergency, but are concerned about overuse by their children, the costs of operating the devices, and privacy issues.

Clearly the online experiences of children around the world are not monolithic, and the risk-response measures discussed in Chapter 6 must be localized as appropriate. The online experience and the risk is based somewhat on what is allowed in the country where the child resides, and on factors as varied as the Internet filtering done and the applications that are allowed to operate there. While each child's use of these various online technologies will vary by country, age, and gender, at the core their online experience will likely include at least accessing local and global entertainment sources like music and video, contacting friends and family through some messaging service, and using learning resources from the Internet.

As the child grows up, this will result in an increasingly adept ability to interact with others in social networks and through messaging tools, using both fixed-location and mobile devices. It will mean obtaining access to more sophisticated learning and real-world resources, including e-commerce sites, virtual worlds, and whatever new technologies and services the Internet offers. And it will entail an emerging sense of privacy as the child matures into an adult (again, likely shaded by local norms). To allow that personal maturation to run its normal course, parents and caregivers must first understand and be aware of the risks involved with their child being online, as described in the next chapter.

Chapter 2

Risks to Children and the Internet

Along with the benefits of the Internet for children are substantial risks. These risks manifest themselves in many forms, as does the way they can impact a child. As safe as a child seems sitting at an electronic device surrounded by family in her own home, the dangers that lurk at the other end of those network connections are very real. The damage to children can occur in the form of physical, emotional, social, or intellectual harms, or any combination thereof. Children can be exposed to graphic images of a sexual nature or to violent words and images. They can be recruited by sexual predators for a variety of reasons, including sexual contact or for utilization in sexual abuse images, including videos and photos. They can become the victim of child prostitution by clients who are recruited online, including those who travel overseas to pursue victims as part of child sex tours.

The perpetrators may instead be peers who engage in online forms of harassment or bullying. Children can be recruited online by others in need, as in the group suicides that often originate from online contacts. Or they may merely be subject to harmful or illicit online content. Children may also be coaxed into entering personal information, which may be used to steal their identities or invade their privacy, or it may be taken without their knowledge. Personal information may be used to steal financial assets or to encourage, possibly legally, the commercial offering of products to children. Children can also be abducted with the help of the Internet, either to work as forced labor for products that themselves may be sold over the Internet or be taken overseas as part of family disputes.

The dangers not only are very real, they are multifaceted and may come with a smile. What looks so innocent, perhaps starting out just as a school-related activity, suddenly leads to contact from a predator through the Internet. Because there are many sources, parents, teachers, and others responsible for the care of children must be constantly vigilant. In Chapter 6, a program to assess the online risks to children in their particular situations is presented. This chapter will describe those risks, what they are, how they may arise, and where they can lead.

POINTS FOR PARENTS

o   There are many risks to children online that often appear quite innocent at first.
o   These risks may lead to physical, financial, reputational, or emotional harm for a child.
o   One type of risk manifesting itself may lead to another type of risk arising.
o   Parents are also at risk online from the actions of their children and potentially others.

2.1   Child Abuse Images (Child Pornography)

The Internet has served as a mechanism for an explosion in the creation and distribution of what is commonly termed "child pornography" but more accurately called "child abuse images." Not only does the Internet's open network architecture allow for fast and voluminous movement of these images, it also allows for anonymity of the criminal actors. And the scale of the problem is increasing, in the volume and violent nature of the content trafficked through the Internet, the number of offenders, and the number and decreasing age of the victims.[1] The perpetrators have become bet-

---

1. NATIONAL DRUG INTELLIGENCE CENTER, NATIONAL CHILD EXPLOITATION THREAT ASSESSMENT 2010.

ter at hiding their tracks through increasingly sophisticated uses of technology,[2] including shifting the dissemination of the newest and worst child abuse images from worldwide websites to peer-to-peer networks used among predators.[3]

Child abuse images include photos, videos, and any other graphic images that depict children involved in real or simulated sexual acts or "any representation of the sexual parts of a child for primarily sexual purposes."[4] The risk of child abuse images includes not only the creation and distribution of these images but the possession of such images. In a disturbing trend, professionals in the field "universally report connections between child pornography offenses and sexual contact offenses against children."[5] And the Internet has allowed the child sexual abuse image offenders to work together to trade, possess, and discuss the images among themselves rather than just downloading the images, in effect creating a mutually reinforcing support group among these offenders, who were previously more isolated.

The fight against child abuse images must by definition be global (to preclude predators from hiding behind the laws of the weakest country), and international forums recognize that. The G-8 ministers made the following points in a joint statement:[6]

> Child pornography grievously harms all children: it harms the child who is sexually assaulted in the making of the image; the same child is re-victimized every time that image is viewed; and it harms all children because it portrays them as a class of objects for sexual exploitation. We categorically denounce those who sexually exploit children by producing images of their sexual abuse and by distributing or collecting such images. Because no child should be victimized in this horrific way, today we pledge to redouble

2. *Id.*

3. Council of Europe Octopus Conference, Developments at EU level regarding the fight against child abuse images (Nov. 2011).

4. G-8 Justice and Home Affairs Ministers, *Ministers' Declaration: Reinforcing the International Fight Against Child Pornography* (May 2007).

5. NATIONAL CHILD EXPLOITATION THREAT ASSESSMENT 2010.

6. *Ministers' Declaration: Reinforcing the International Fight Against Child Pornography.*

our efforts to enforce the international fight against child pornography.

The lifecycle of child sexual abuse images can be viewed as one of production, sale, distribution, possession, and use. But this lifecycle has quite a number of other connections. First, to create the image, there must be a victim. By the definition in Chapter 1, children cannot legally consent to participation in such exploitation activities. So their participation is involuntary and based on one or more crimes to ensure their participation, including kidnapping, sexual crimes, etc. Possession and use of such abuse images leads the offender to try to obtain more images, which in many of the peer networks requires him to also produce more images, and so to also seek out more victims.[7] There is also a growing belief that the use of these images leads to offline contact offenses, as discussed below.

In a related area, children are creating their own pornographic images, either at the behest of those involved in soliciting their participation in offline sexual exploitation or in more voluntary peer activities like "sexting," where "20 percent of the teens had sent or posted nude or seminude pictures or video of themselves."[8] A cautionary note comes from the following statistics on the victims of child pornography, where almost all child-professional respondents to interview questions stated that "children suffer from knowing that their images exist in perpetuity . . . other[s are] . . . out there viewing their images, offenders that the victims may run into in social settings."[9]

A recent paper outlined how some of the new technologies, including payment systems, are facilitating the spread of child abuse images.[10] Alternative payments systems, some based in countries with minimal regulatory oversight, make it difficult for law enforce-

---

7. U.S. Dept. of Justice, Report to Congress, *The National Strategy for Child Exploitation Prevention and Interdiction* (2010).

8. National Campaign to Prevent Teen and Unplanned Pregnancy (2008).

9. NATIONAL CHILD EXPLOITATION THREAT ASSESSMENT 2010.

10. Financial Coalition Against Child Pornography, *Report on Trends in Online Crime and Their Potential Implications in the Fight Against Commercial Child Pornography* (2011).

ment to shut them down. The uses of digital currency in virtual worlds, prepaid cards, and mobile payment systems all give rise to more anonymity and less oversight and so are ideal for the fraudster to use to facilitate or launder funds from the sale of child abuse images. Identity theft is also used to facilitate the purchase of child abuse images. Social networks provide anonymous contacts between consumers and sellers, while URL shorteners mask the seller's true URL for spam posts sent to microblogs. Technologies such as malware and botnets are used to compromise user sites, which then act as unknowing hosts to child abuse images, with the cybercriminals using the rapid shifting of devices and IP addresses to mask the sending location.

2.2   Online Contact and Cybergrooming

Sexual (and other) predators often target children through the Internet, using disturbing techniques to solicit or "groom" them for sexual conquest. One study of children aged 9 to 16 in Europe showed that a third had received sexual comments online, while almost 40 percent had been invited to meet in person (and a quarter agreed to do so).[11] Other studies in the United States and globally have shown lower percentages of children who receive online sexual solicitations, at one in six or seven children on the Internet (and that many of these are coming from other children or young adults 18–21 years old), but one in six do make online contacts that lead to offline meetings.[12, 13] Many of the "aggressive" and "distressing" contacts were aimed at the older children.[14]

   The type of techniques used to make contact include going online to where children are, such as gaming and music sites. Grooming online is the process of using the psychological weaknesses of the vulnerable child to turn him or her into a victim of sexual exploitation. "Predators often act in a patient and manipulative manner, lis-

---

11. National Centre for Technology in Education, *SAFT Children's Study—Investigating online behavior* (2003).

12. U.S. Internet Safety Technical Taskforce, *Enhancing Child Safety & Online Technologies,* App. C (2008).

13. International Youth Advisory Council Annual Surveys.

14. *SAFT Children's Study—Investigating online behavior.*

tening to children's problems and becoming indispensable with advice. . . . Predators . . . alienate children from others in their lives, assume the parental role, and then declare their love, creating emotional dependence and infatuation simultaneously. . . . At some point, the children provide compromising information about or images of themselves. . . . Predators then threaten exposure of the victims to friends and family and may even threaten lives. Ultimately, many predators coerce victims into sexual abuse."[15]

Contacts online are made through all the available media, such as social networks, email, chat rooms, and instant messaging. The grooming process may go on for a number of months, with increasing requests for personal information, some of which (such as mobile phone numbers that have GPS location-tracking capabilities) make it easier for the predator to identify where the child is. For children being groomed for sexual exploitation, the use of child pornography is often sent by the perpetrator to normalize this conduct. The combination of the anonymity of the Internet plus knowledge of the pop culture of children often allows the offenders to masquerade as someone much younger than they are. In one case in the United Kingdom, the perpetrator groomed 22 female victims between the ages of 12 and 15 by claiming to be a modeling agency's talent scout, hiding behind 23 fake profiles.[16]

One study has delineated the stages in the grooming process, which may have differing durations, as: friendship-forming stage, relationship-forming stage, risk assessment stage, exclusivity stage, and sexual stage.[17] Online sites list a number of examples that demonstrate how the grooming process may work.[18] An abbreviated version of one such example follows:[19]

---

15. *The National Strategy for Child Exploitation Prevention and Interdiction.*

16. *Nursery worker admits raping child,* THE GUARDIAN (June 7, 2011).

17. R. O'CONNELL, A TYPOLOGY OF CHILD CYBERSEXPLOITATION AND ONLINE GROOMING PRACTICES (2003).

18. *See, e.g.,* http://www.youtube.com/watch?gl=US&v=Q2kU3gXF8f4; http://www.netsmartz.org/RealLifeStories/AmysChoice.

19. Edited example from www.wiredkids.org/parents.

Child: I hate my mom! I know it's her fault that my parents are getting divorced

Predator: I know. My parents are getting divorced, too.

Child: We never have any money anymore. Every time I need something, she says we can't afford it.

Predator: Me too. I hate that!

Child: I waited for six months for the new computer game to come out. My mom promised to buy it for me but we don't have enough money! I hate my mom!

Predator: I'm so sorry! I got it! I have this really kewl uncle who buys me things all the time.

Child: You're sooooo lucky. I wish I had a rich and kewl uncle.

Predator: Hey! I got an idea! I'll ask my uncle if he'll buy you one too.

Child: Really!? Thanks!!

Predator: BRB [cybertalk for "be right back"] . . . I'll go and call him.

. . .

Predator: Guess what? He said okay. He's gonna buy you the game!

Child: Wow, really? Thanks. I can't believe it!!!

Predator: Where do you live?

Child: I live in NJ. What about you?

Predator: I live in New York. So does my uncle. New Jersey isn't far.

Child: Great!

Predator: Is there a mall near you? We can meet there.

Child: Okay. I live near the GSP Mall.

Predator: I've heard of that. No prob. What about Saturday?

Child: Kewl.

Predator: We can go to McDonald's too if you want. We'll meet you there at noon.

Child: Okay. Where?

Predator: In front of the computer game store. My uncle's name is George. He's really kewl.

Child: Great . . . thanks, I really appreciate it. You're so lucky to have a rich and kewl uncle.

The ability to groom depends on predators being able to locate vulnerable individuals with sufficient information to befriend them. To find that kind of information, a number of high-technology tools are available. Here is one (edited) description:[20]

> The attacker collects data concerning the activity of his target group (children) in cyberspace by browsing profiles, posts and other digital traces left by the target's activities (e.g., avatars, blogs) and by seeding the areas the target uses with data that may encourage contact (e.g., spoofed information), as well as by collating data with other attacker groups to enable better victim profiling. They could use advanced versions of meta-search engines to discover children participating in a website. Additional information can be retrieved via tools that provide information on the whereabouts of a specific social group (in this case children), based on their musical preferences and other personal information, by integrating information from their friends. A lot of information about an individual can be inferred from his/her friends, even though his/her profile may be locked. Other tools analyse behavioural data of specific users; such data represent a totally different class of data from those explicitly posted by the user. They concern communication patterns of the current user; for example, they might indicate location, the time, date, and recipient of chatting, instant and e-mail messages. They could acquire information from the mobile devices of their potential victims, by remotely installing malicious software on the victim's smart phone.

In Europe, the European Online Grooming Project identified three types of online groomers: distorted attachment groomer (believed contact was a "relationship" but did not have abuse image collections or contact with other offenders), adaptable online groomer (see victim as mature and capable but not a "relationship" and minimal abuse images or contact with similar offenders), and hyper-sexualized groomer (no "relationships" and extensive abuse

---

20. ENISA, *Cyber-Bullying and Online Grooming: helping to protect against the risks* (2011).

image collections and contact with other similar offenders).[21] The third group tends to have prior criminal convictions and the first group tends to want to meet offline in each instance, while other two groups only want to meet offline sometimes.[22]

Perhaps the most discouraging statistic regarding online grooming is from U.S. national studies that show that only a small number of the online solicitations that were made (5% in Youth Internet Safety Survey (YISS)-2 and 9% in YISS-1) were actually reported by children or their parents to law enforcement, ISPs, or other authorities who are able to fully address the actions of these predators.[23]

2.3   Offline Contact and Harmful Conduct

It is after the child agrees to meet the online predator in person offline, either "voluntarily"' or by coercion, that harmful conduct can occur. This conduct can range from various types of physical and sexual abuse to murder. In addition to adult predators, this type of conduct can also originate from other children. Beyond the sexual predator, the Internet can introduce children to harmful websites encouraging "anorexia, self-harm or suicide, as well as sources of political influence espousing violence, hate and political extremism."[24] A multiyear review by the International Association of Internet Hotlines (INHOPE, discussed in Chapter 3) showed that reports of websites espousing "racism or xenophobia," while not a large percentage of the total, were increasing at a rate of 24 percent a year.[25]

Some studies indicate that children do not always have the proper amount of trepidation about meeting others offline whom they have met online, such as where "one in four children say they have met people offline whom they had previously only become acquainted

---

21. *A Dark Side of Computing and Information Sciences: Characteristics of Online Groomers,* JOURNAL OF EMERGING TRENDS IN COMPUTING AND INFORMATION SCIENCES (2011).

22. *Id.*

23. WOLAK ET AL., ONLINE VICTIMIZATION OF YOUTH: FIVE YEARS LATER (2006).

24. ENACSO, A DIGITAL MANIFESTO – AN AGENDA FOR CHANGE (2009).

25. INHOPE, *2007 Global Internet Trend Report.*

with online."[26] A recent survey of children from European countries showed that about one child in 10 had actually met offline a contact whom they had met online in the past year,[27] while in Australia the figures are about half that rate.[28] The risks for children from offline meetings with those they meet online can bring them face-to-face with criminals who prey on children.[29]

While children may not see the many risks inherent in meeting offline strangers they have met online, their parents and leaders do. For example, the G8 Ministers of Justice and Home Affairs produced a declaration concerning the links between children's pornography viewing and subsequent contact offenses.[30] The report stated that "there is sufficient evidence of a relationship between possession of child pornography and the commission of contact offenses against children" and that "a significant portion of those who possess child pornography [and have been convicted thereof] have committed a contact sexual offense against a child."[31]

Other studies have described this risk. "In many instances, when law enforcement officers execute search warrants for a computer and premises of an offender who appears only to be possessing images, evidence of molestation is uncovered."[32] Seventy eight percent of those arrested for child exploitation contact offenses were found to possess child pornography.[33] Then there are the headline incidents that are feared by every parent, such as the case of 33-year-old Peter Chapman of the UK who solicited a 17-year-old col-

---

26. CEOP, Strategic Overview 2006–2007 (based on a sample of 6,000 children aged between 11 and 16).

27. European Commission, *EU Kids Online* survey of 9–16-year-olds and their parents in 25 countries (2011).

28. *AU Kids Online* survey of 9–16-year-olds and their parents (2011).

29. *See, e.g.,* http://www.netsmartz.org/RealLifeStories/AmysChoice.

30. G-8 Justice and Home Affairs Ministers, *Ministers' Declaration: The Risk to Children Posed by Child Pornography Offenders* (May 2009).

31. G-8 Experts Working Group LEPSG, *Global Symposium for Examining the Relationship Between Online and Offline Offenses and Preventing the Sexual Exploitation of Children,* Final Report (2009).

32. DOJ CEOS, USPIS, FBI & ICE, Operation Joint Hammer (started 2007).

33. NATIONAL CHILD EXPLOITATION THREAT ASSESSMENT 2010, Analysis of Overnight Case Summaries (2005–2009).

lege student online to meet him, pretending to be a teenager, and then proceeded to kidnap, rape, and murder her.[34] He had almost 3,000 "friends" on this social networking site, but was not "friends" with any of his victim's friends.[35]

Since its inception in 1998, the agents of the ICAC Task Force (discussed in Chapter 3) have dealt with almost a quarter of a million complaints of alleged child sexual victimization and have made approximately 25,000 arrests.[36] Between the fiscal years 2004 and 2008, they dealt with over 20,000 online enticement complaints, and about 8,000 were of "aggressive and dangerous online child predators who travel to the location of a child for the purpose of establishing [illegal sexual] physical contact."[37] There have been significant increases in reported online enticement to the NCMEC CyberTipline (707 to 8,787 in 10 years) and the number of documented enticement complaints processed by ICAC Task Force agents (3,573 to 8,313 in five years).[38]

Another possible consequence of online enticement is abduction. As required by law,[39] studies were done (National Incidence Studies on Missing, Abducted, Runaway and Throwaway Children) that showed that the primary motive in non-family abductions is sexual (family abductions are discussed below), with 64 percent of non-family abductions resulting in the child being sexually victimized and 36 percent of the victims of non-family abductions being murdered by their abductor.[40] The subsequent study showed that nearly half of non-family abductions resulted in sexual victimization, and the murder rate for non-family abductions fitting the pattern of stereotypical kidnappings was 40 percent.[41]

---

34. *'One mistake' cost teenager her life*, THE TELEGRAPH (Mar. 8, 2010).

35. *Peter Chapman targeted thousands of young girls,* THE TELEGRAPH (Mar. 8, 2010).

36. *See* www.ojclp.gov/programs.

37. *The National Strategy for Child Exploitation Prevention and Interdiction*.

38. *Id.*

39. Missing Children's Assistance Act, Pub. L. 98-473 (1984).

40. National Incidence Studies on Missing, Abducted, Runaway and Throwaway Children (NISMART), Study 1 (1990).

41. NISMART Study 2 (1999).

Other harmful offline contacts can be based not on any online contacts but on using the Internet to gain information about potential victims and then stalking them offline. As one part of the crime of "cyberstalking," this type of conduct can be more difficult to identify and avoid, due to the lack of communications between the parties. It is an extension of offline stalking, with the online aspect merely to identify potential victims. Many definitions of cyberstalking also include some of other risks described later in this chapter. One recent study broke cyberstalking into three categories: email stalking (communicating with the victim), Internet stalking (information gathering and possibly harassment online), and computer stalking (taking over the PC of the victim remotely without authorization), and identified Internet stalking as the one "the most likely to spill over into physical space."[42]

2.4   Harmful Content/Violent Video Games

It is not merely child abuse images that are considered harmful to children. There are videos, movies, and video games with violent or sexual or other adult content that is also not appropriate for children. There is a whole sector of content that is per se not illegal, such as adult pornography or images of extreme violence or cruelty. But their legality does not make the content appropriate for the impressionable and still-developing minds of children. Children's games are sometimes also used inappropriately as a front for the advertising of commercial products.

Adult pornography is one content category harmful to children. One study found that almost half of the children were exposed to pornography, although sometimes intentional, exposure was mostly accidental and resulted from spam emails and mistyped URLs or unexpected search engine results.[43] Another study showed that the "rates of unwanted exposure were higher among youth who were older, reported being harassed or solicited online, victimized offline, and were depressed." In somewhat of a mixed

---

42. *Cyberstalking: Crime and Challenge at the Cyberspace,* INT'L JOURNAL OF COMPUTING AND BUS. RESEARCH, Vol. 2 issue 1 (2011).

43. *Enhancing Child Safety & Online Technologies, supra* note 12.

result, while a majority of older children reported having viewed pornography, very few of those under the age of 12 reported having been exposed to it.[44]

Children get exposed to violent and extreme images from videos and games on the Internet. Over half of children have reported in surveys to having taken part in online games that were not rated for children.[45] The games available on the Internet run the gamut from very simple "Pong"-like games to multiplayer complex gaming and virtual worlds with avatars representing a distinct gaming-only persona of a child. Although many children play video games through one of the big three video game consoles, a substantial number also play them online either directly on the Internet or on mobile phones or other handheld devices, such as iPads. Fortunately, only a relatively small percent of the games (5 percent) are rated for ages 18+,[46] while many are considered safe for even young children.

The research on the impact of violence in video games has not yielded a definitive answer, with one set of researchers believing that the evidence shows violence in video games increases (at least in the short term) children's "aggressive and antisocial behaviour," while another group believe it depends on the social/cultural context instead of only the game's content.[47] This begs the question of whether children become more aggressive after playing such violent video games or more aggressive children play the more violent games. Online games are seen as having the "same issues of content, contact and conduct" as use of the Internet in general.[48] Problematic content includes that uploaded from other players, contact leading to disclosing personal information, and conduct involving harassment by other players. There are also the issues of providing age-appropriate content and verification of players' ages.

Although voluntary rating systems (as described in Chapter 3) are being used today, mandatory restrictions on violent video games may not possible in countries like the United States, where the Su-

---

44. *Id.*
45. *Id.*
46. *Safer Children in a Digital World,* BYRON REVIEW (2008).
47. *Id.*
48. *Id.*

preme Court recently ruled that such statutory limits violate the First Amendment.[49] This in spite of the fact that the scientific amicus curiae brief supporting this decision did not have the expertise behind it[50] that the other scientific amicus curiae brief did, which stated the following:[51]

> Both the American Psychological Association (APA, 2005) and the American Academy of Pediatrics (AAP, 2009) have issued formal statements stating that scientific research on violent video games clearly shows that such games are causally related to later aggressive behavior in children and adolescents. . . . Overall, the research data conclude that exposure to violent video games causes an increase in the likelihood of aggressive behavior. . . . [V]iolent video games have also been found to increase aggressive thinking, aggressive feelings, physiological desensitization to violence, and to decrease pro-social behavior.

2.5   Cyberharassment/Cyberbullying

Cyberbullying and cyberharassment are often used interchangeably to mean the intentional use of the online environment to inflict harm on another. For purposes of this book, cyberbullying can be considered a more intense and repeated form of cyberharassment. Cyberbullying most typically occurs in the context of the learning environment. One set of definitions defines these two terms, plus cyberstalking, as follows:

> Cyberharassment differs from cyberstalking in that it is generally defined as not involving a credible threat. Cyberharassment usually pertains to threatening or harass-

---

49. Brown v. Entertainment Merchants Assn., 130 S. Ct. 2398 (2011).

50. *Do Violent Video Games Harm Children? Comparing The Scientific Amicus Curiae "Experts" in* Brown v. Entertainment Merchants Ass'n, Nw. U. L. REV., vol. 106 (2011).

51. Brief of Amicus Curiae of Cal. State Sen. Leland Y. Yee, Cal. Chapter of the American Academy of Pediatrics and the Cal. Psychological Ass'n in Support of Petitioners, Brown v. Entm't Merchs. Ass'n, 130 S. Ct. 2398 (2010) (No. 08-1448).

ing email messages, instant messages, or to blog entries or websites dedicated solely to tormenting an individual. Cyberbullying and cyberharassment are sometimes used interchangeably, but . . . cyberbullying is used for electronic harassment or bullying among minors within a school context.[52]

In addition to its detrimental impact on areas such as academic performance,[53] the immediacy of the problem with bullying was stated by the President of the United States: "We've got to dispel the myth that bullying is just a normal rite of passage—that it's some inevitable part of growing up. It's not."[54] Bullying is an increasingly common threat that children face online, with, according to one study, "one in five children saying they have experienced it."[55] Other studies show that up to half of children have experienced incidents that would be categorized as cyberbullying.[56] Studies also show that over half the children are negatively affected in some manner, which can lead to the same symptoms as offline bullying, such as "self-destructive behaviors, interpersonal violence, and various forms of delinquency."[57]

Cyberbullying methods include using all of the various online technologies to harass the victim, such as: using instant messaging in chat rooms or text messages with inappropriate language, sending offensive images or viruses, locking a person out of his/her own account by stealing their password, revealing personal information on a blog or pretending to be his/her victim, broadcast emailing degrading photos of the victim, directing junk email to his/her email inbox, or creating a hostile-content (e.g., racist or sex-

---

52. National Conference of State Legislatures, State Cyberstalking, Cyberharassment and Cyberbullying Laws (2011).

53. Lacey, et al., *The Impact of Bullying Climate on Schoolwide Academic Performance* (2011).

54. President Obama, White House Conference on Bullying Prevention (Mar. 10, 2011).

55. A Digital Manifesto—An Agenda for Change.

56. *Enhancing Child Safety & Online Technologies, supra* note 12.

57. *Id.*

ist) website and then listing the victim's name, address, and phone number as a supporter.[58]

Typically, school anti-bullying policies will include cyber bullying or cyberharassment as prohibited activities among students as the school. However, some have also extended sanctions to include cyberbullying and cyberharassment that originates off-campus but concerns students or educators at the school, under the belief that this off-campus-initiated conduct and speech can have a strongly disruptive effect on the school environment. In countries like the United States, where restrictions on free speech are permissible in only limited circumstances, it may not be possible for schools to punish students for off-campus Internet speech activities without a current or prospective substantial disruption impacting a public school environment or a significant threat against another, as highlighted by a recent series of judicial decisions.[59-63]

Cyberbullying seems to be committed primarily by children on other children, often in the same grade. Girls seem to be the target more than boys in cyberbullying incidents, at least in Australia and

---

58. C. Spyropoulous, *Victimization of children by cyber-bullies and online groomers: minor netizens facing the Web's reality* (2011).

59. D.J.M. v. Hannibal Pub. Sch. Dist., Case No. 10-1428 (8th Cir. 2011) [holding that off-campus IM messages do not violate the First Amendment if they represent "true threats" or cause a "material and substantial" disruption at school].

60. Kowalski v. Berkeley Country Schools, Case No. 10-1098 (4th Cir. 2011) [holding that the creation off-campus of MySpace page targeting a student for harassment and inviting other students to join was not protected speech].

61. T.V. and M.K. v. Smith-Green Community School Corp. et al., Case No. 1:09-CV-290 (N.D. Ind. 2011) [holding that off-campus risqué photos of students self-published on the Internet cannot be used as a basis for school discipline].

62. J.S. v. Blue Mountain School Dist. et al., Case No. 08-4138 (3d Cir. 2011) [holding that off-campus speech on a MySpace profile degrading to the school principal was protected because it caused no current or prospective substantial disruption at school].

63. Layshock v. Hermitage School Dist. et al., Case No. 07-4465 (3d Cir. 2010) [holding that off-campus speech on a MySpace profile degrading to the school principal was protected for the same reasons of not causing a substantial disruption at the school].

Europe.[65] There seems to be a significant degree of overlap among those who are cyberbullied to those who are bullied at school.[65] Online harassment is somewhat common, as "almost 30 percent of youth [ages 10–17] had harassed others online during the previous year."[66] In a recent U.S. study, 88 percent of teens reported that they have seen someone be mean or cruel to another person on a social networking site.[67] And those who are the victims of cyberbullying have been shown to be more likely to be involved in offline behavioral problems, such as alcohol and drug use, cheating at school, truancy, assaulting others, damaging property, and carrying a weapon.[68]

2.6   Child Prostitution/Child Sex Tourism

The Internet allows for more efficient (and anonymous) sale of the services of child prostitutes and the rise of sex tourism. With this global open network, it is much more cost-effective and less risky to post advertisements publicly online or in closed networks of subscribers than in the normal business manner where identities can be exposed. It is also much more efficient for the consumers of child sex tourism to use the Internet to find the optimal locations to travel to to engage in this unlawful conduct. Statistics have shown that historically the most common locations for child sex tourism are economically developing countries, such as Mexico, the Philippines, Thailand, Cambodia, and Costa Rica.[69]

Child prostitution involves use of the Internet through the posting of advertisements on websites with sections for escorts. To avoid detection, these ads "don't obviously state that sex with children is being sold, . . . but customers who want children know to look for

---

64. *AU Kids Online* survey of 9–16-year-olds and their parents (2011).

65. *Id.*

66. Ybarra et al., Prevalence and Frequency of Internet Harassment Instigation (2008).

67. Pew Research Center, *Teens, Kindness and Cruelty on Social Network Sites* (2011).

68. U.S. Internet Safety Technical Taskforce, *Enhancing Child Safety & Online Technologies,* App. C (2008).

69. *The National Strategy for Child Exploitation Prevention and Interdiction.*

words like "fresh," "candy" and "new to the game." The underage victims are often runaways and victims of sexual abuse.[70] Once the arrangements are made, a location is required to fulfill this illicit arrangement and many high-end hotels are used. This has led to efforts to get these hotels around the world to ban the use of their facilities for such purposes by following a code of conduct.[71]

Commercial sex traffickers "manipulate children into a life of prostitution and then use physical and emotional abuse to keep their victims trapped in that way of life."[72] The victims are children with already low self-esteem who likely do not have strong family bonds and may already be the victims of prior physical and sexual abuse. As with online solicitation, these vulnerable children are often bound into this relationship with their abuser when they are looking for those emotional relationships and stability missing from their lives, which leads to sexual exploitation.

Since 2004, the number of child sex tourism incidents reported to the NCMEC CyberTipline has increased significantly overall.[73] Child sex tourists also gain information about local children through Internet chat rooms, message boards, and online forums, which can provide locations of child brothels, prices, accounts of child sexual abuse by other tourists, and sites for trading child pornography. Sex tourists are increasingly creating child pornography by recording their acts of child sexual abuse to bring home as souvenirs. After returning home, child sex tourists may share or sell their images and videos with other child predators over the Internet. Of the child professionals interviewed for the Threat Assessment, 79 percent reported that child sex tourists "commit contact offenses abroad and engage in physical, sexual, emotional, and psychological abuse abroad" of children, and 43 percent also did so in the U.S.[74]

---

70. *Fighting sex trafficking in hotels, one room at a time*, CNN (Feb. 29, 2012).

71. ECPAT, *The Tourism Child-Protection Code of Conduct* (1998).

72. *The National Strategy for Child Exploitation Prevention and Interdiction*.

73. *Id.*

2.7   Loss of Physical Freedom

The loss of physical freedom can involve the abduction of children in marital disputes, kidnapping for sexual exploitation (which was discussed above), or forcing them into child labor or servitude. This can include cross-border trafficking of children for purposes of exploitation, which involves getting them into a vulnerable situation outside the support of their families or, in the case of marital dispute abductions, taken outside the support of their habitual environment and one parent's care by the other parent and likely back to the country of that parent's origin. According to U.N. statistics, over one million children are trafficked each year, with victims from 127 countries trafficked to be exploited in 137 countries.[75]

The Internet can facilitate the crimes of exploitation on both the demand side and the supply side and the crime of family child abduction by allowing the abducting parent to gain access to a variety of details to facilitate the crime, including communication by the noncustodial parent with the child outside the knowledge of the custodial parent. The demand for child labor/servitude is facilitated by products sold through the Internet, such as the recent example of a famous brand that thought it was acquiring Fair Trade–certified organic fibers used in its products, which were sold around the world through the Internet.[76]

According to the U.S. government,[77] child and forced labor is a practice that goes on in 71 countries and involves 119 products, with agriculture (cotton, sugarcane, tobacco, coffee, and cattle), manufactured goods (bricks, garments, carpets, and footwear), and mining (gold, diamonds, and coal) being the largest categories. Child labor is defined as children in employment who are under the minimum legal age for work or older than that age and subject to work

74. *National Child Exploitation Threat Assessment 2010.*

75. United Nations Global Initiative for Fighting Human Trafficking, *Human Trafficking: The Facts* (2008).

76. *Victoria's Secret Revealed in Child Picking Burkina Faso Cotton,* BLOOMBERG MARKETS (Feb. 2012).

77. U.S. Dept. of Labor, *List of Goods Produced by Child Labor or Forced Labor* (2011).

that is either forced or a threat to their health, safety, or morals.[78] Further, as of 2008, 215 million children around the world were believed to be working as child laborers (153 million are between the ages of 5 and 14), and 115 million of those children labor (53 million between the ages of 5 and 14) under hazardous conditions in producing items such as tobacco, bricks, sugarcane, mined goods, and leather.[79]

The cross-border trafficking of children occurs for many reasons, including sexual exploitation and their use in various kinds of forced labor. The Palermo Protocol (discussed in Chapter 3) defines trafficking in children to mean "the recruitment, transportation, transfer, harbouring or receipt of a child for the purpose of exploitation . . . which include, at a minimum, the exploitation or the prostitution of others or other forms of sexual exploitation, forced labour or services, slavery or practices similar to slavery, servitude or the removal of organs."[80] Some of the supply-side factors in child trafficking include "poverty, power and violence," while some of the demand side factors include "sexual exploitation, other forms of economic exploitation, traditional practices, adoption and post-conflict scenarios."[81]

For family abductions, children may be taken from their countries of habitual residence or may simply be taken into hiding by one of the biological parents or a guardian in their country of habitual residence. For international child abductions, one divorced parent may take a child contrary to custodial rights specified under court orders or post-marital agreements, or the parents may still be legally married. This area is often greatly confused by the feelings of the children, the disagreements between parents, the views of disparate cultures, and differing legal regimes. According to international law, ratifying countries are supposed to return "wrongfully removed or retained" children to their countries of habitual resi-

---

78. Int'l Labour Office, *Accelerating Action Against Child Labour* (2010).

79. *Id.*

80. Protocol to Prevent, Suppress and Punish Trafficking in Persons, Especially Women and Children, Supplementing the United Nations Convention Against Transnational Organized Crime (U.N. GA res. 53/383 (2000)).

81. UNICEF, *Trafficking in Human Beings, Especially Women and Children, in Africa* (2003).

dence.[82] But some major countries (e.g., Japan) have not ratified the principal international law convention in this area (despite ratifying related international conventions), and so incidents continue to occur where children are taken by one parent to their country, which will not extradite the offending parent, and they grow up never having contact with their other biological parent.[83]

2.8 Invasion of Privacy

When children are online, they may be prompted to or may inadvertently disclose information of a personal nature about themselves or their families. Online websites may require the information as part of commercial transactions, as part of joining the community at the site, or as something that a predator or criminal posing as a friend may request. Children obviously may want the ability to talk openly with their friends online but may not recognize that they are disclosing personal information, especially when not doing so expressly, by the sheer act of operating their online access device. Location information, browsing preferences, friends contacted, duration of calls or sessions, files or images uploaded or downloaded, and much more data are all recorded and available at least to those who operate the services being used. And the content is both transmitted across the open networks and stored somewhere online.

Once the information is available, it may be used by any number of those who have access to it. It can be used by the other party to the commercial transaction, for example, for additional direct-marketing activities to the child or family members. Websites may sell their subscriber data to data miners or third-party marketers who may engage (or sell to others to engage) in behavioral advertising. Website browsing information may be collected from across a number of websites to identify online activities (for example, by using various types of cookies or other tracking techniques), which again can then be sold or used by bad actors. Mobile-phone data can be utilized to location-track children and reveal their primary

---

82. Hague Conference on Int'l Private Law, Hague Convention on the Civil Aspects of International Child Abduction (1980).

physical area of activity. And personal information can be used to harass or intimidate, as was discussed in the sections above.

Of the information that is freely given by children, some of it may be in response to queries related to online games, puzzles, personality tests, or friendly avatars, while at other times content and advertising may be seamlessly integrated. While there are statutes and codes of conduct to discourage such activities and require parental consent, the violations of these prohibitions continue. The Federal Trade Commission (FTC) in the United States regulates unfair or deceptive trade practices and has recently settled actions against several children-focused organizations for such practices.

In one case, the FTC charged that the defendant violated the COPPA statute (see Chapter 4), affecting hundreds of thousands of children over many years. Contrary to its stated privacy policy, parents were not adequately notified, children's information was collected and publicly disclosed, verifiable consent from parents was not properly obtained, and, to circumvent COPPA, certain website operations were transferred overseas.[84] In another case, the FTC reached a settlement with a mobile app (for mobile devices) developer over alleged COPPA violations. The complaint alleged that the defendant's apps collected information from children under the age of 13 without notice or their parents' prior consent, including their email addresses or any link to their privacy practices. By collecting and sending information over the Internet, these apps qualify as an online service.[85]

Most recently the FTC was asked to investigate the digital market practices of some well-known companies for disguising their marketing with data collection practices targeted at adolescents.[86]

---

83. *See, e.g.,* Joint Press Statement by the Ambassadors and Representatives of Australia, Canada, Colombia, The European Union, France, Hungary, Italy, New Zealand, Spain, the United Kingdom and the United States of America (Feb. 9, 2011).

84. USA v. Playdom, Inc., Case No. 11-cv-00724 (C.D. Cal. 2011).

85. United States v. W3 Innovations, LLC and Justin Maples, Case No. 11-cv-03958 (N.D. Cal. 2011).

86. *In the Matter of Complaint and Request for Investigation of _____ Deceptive Practices in Marketing _____ to Adolescents* (2011).

Another organization has asked the FTC to investigate a popular website, targeted at children aged six to thirteen, for violating COPPA by using unfair and deceptive acts to collect information usable to contact a child, using cookies and web beacons to track children and serve up targeted ads, and not allowing parents to opt out of the viewing of third-party ads.[87] The regulators in other countries are also enforcing privacy standards on the operators of children's websites.[88] Further cases are described in Chapter 4.

Children also can inadvertently give up personal information in much the same way as adults can, through getting "phished" or by other various hoaxes that are perpetrated on sometimes even the most discerning adults. With the access to computers both at home and at school and to mobile phones, there are several access points with which bad actors can reach children. PCs and mobile phones are made up of so many different layers and types of software that malware could easily make its way into that mix, allowing various types of eavesdropping capabilities to be installed. Even legitimate service providers do this through use of cookies.

Children will be maneuvered into providing information by attractive and interesting sites with sparkling graphics that allow a small amount of interaction or playing but then return a message saying that the most recently clicked application requires registration. Registration of course is fast, easy, and free, and comes with some other incentive, like membership point awards, but it also requires providing some personal information (not to mention a long list of terms in some degree of legalese). Like most adults, the children will breeze through this to get to the "good stuff."

The personal information may be used to help solicit the child and others in the family. The following is an extract about what occurred on the well-known Barbie brand website:

> The Barbie site provides girls with an opportunity to design and dress their own Barbies, do a Barbie make-over, sing

---

87. *In the Matter of Complaint and Request for Investigation of* ____ *Deceptive Practices in Connection with* ____ ____*, a Children's Website* (Dec. 13, 2011).

88. Canada, Office of the Privacy Commissioner, *Social networking site for youth breached Canadian privacy law* (Mar. 1, 2012).

along with Barbie as she sings "Friends like we are" to the child, or "Make Happy Family Memories" with Barbie's "friends" Alan, Midge, their son Ryan, Midge's parents, and Midge's new baby (whom the child gets to name when she fills out the Birth Certificate). The site actively encourages girls to buy Barbie products. For example, each child can record their purchasing preferences in their "Wish list," and email it to their parents. . . .

Barbie.com also uses the information they collect from girls to market directly to parents. In their February issue of *For Parents*, they used quotes collected from girls about what makes them anxious, and then told parents that creative play relieves children's anxieties. The article concluded with a list of Barbie products that can help their children feel less anxious.[89]

Finally, there is the question of whether it should be considered an invasion of privacy when parents monitor the online activities of their own children. Parents obviously will want to monitor their children's Internet use out of a desire to safeguard their experiences there, but children, especially as they get older, will likely see that as an invasion of their privacy, with their desire to draw a line between their world and the adult world.

2.9   Identity Theft

Offenses related to identity are the most common form of consumer fraud.[90] Once personal information has been has been acquired, it can be used to steal the identity of children for the ultimate purpose of illicit gain. The gain is not directed against the financial assets of the identity that is stolen but against some third party, such as financial institutions or government agencies. "Phishing" is a common method used to get this information directly. Some of these email invitations appear preposterous ("The uncle of Mr. XXX just passed

---

89. V. Steeves, *It's Not Child's Play: The Online Invasion of Children's Privacy*, U. OTTAWA L. & TECH. J. (2006).

90. UNODC, *The Globalization of Crime—A Transnational Organized Crime Threat Assessment* (2010).

away and I need your help to transfer $20 million. Please provide your personal details."), but there are the more realistic ones ("The IRS is hereby notifying you that you will not be audited. Please confirm your personal details."), or a "fake courier will send an email saying there is a package waiting for the victim and ask for personal information in order to retrieve it."[91] While these ploys can be difficult to evaluate even for adults, for children, knowing the difference may just not possible at their stage of development. The result of one attack may be combined with others to give enough information to impersonate the stolen identity and thereby acquire credit cards, bank loans, or government benefits.

The unauthorized access and theft of personal data may be obtained from a number of different sources. For example, keylogger systems, spyware, or other malware installed on computers can be used to intercept data in transit or access stored data. Data breaches of organizations responsible for the custodial care of their customers' data has been responsible for allowing unauthorized access to the personal data of millions of records (e.g., the Sony PlayStation Network provided access to upwards of 100 million records by itself[92] while another breach at a game developer could affect millions[93]). There are various ways using mobile apps can access information such as address lists and the location data from photos and videos from popular mobile phones.[94] And a new study from Europe has shown that it is not that difficult to intercept calls made by mobile phones using easily accessible Internet tools.[95]

Theft of children's identities is a target for criminals because children's financial and other history is basically nonexistent, so it can be filled in however the criminal intends. And because they are

---

91. *Holiday Phishing and Online Cyber-scams,* Nat'l Cybersecurity & Commc'ns Center Bull. (2011).

92. Thomas Shaw, *2011 (2H) Information Law Updates—Cases, Statutes and Standards,* INFORMATION SECURITY AND PRIVACY NEWS (newsltr. of the ABA Sec. Science & Technology Law), Vol. 3 Issue 1 (Winter 2012).

93. *Hackers breach servers of Japan's Square Enix,* AFP (Dec. 14, 2011).

94. *Apple Loophole Gives Developers Access to Photos,* N.Y. TIMES (Feb. 29, 2012).

95. *Hacker Finds Weak Mobile Security in Europe,* N.Y. TIMES (Dec. 25, 2011).

not financially active, their credit score is not likely to be checked for many years, so the crime can go undetected. This crime can impact the financial activities a child wants to carry out when he or she comes of age, including obtaining student loans, buying a car, or opening a bank account, or later to rent an apartment or get hired for a job.

One study of the financial activity of children's identities found that over 10 percent of Social Security numbers (SSNs) of children were being used by someone else for things like obtaining credit cards, opening accounts, buying cars and homes, obtaining work, and getting driver's licenses.[96] This is at a rate 50 times higher than for adults. Examples include children's SSNs being used by many different individuals to get home and car loans, home utilities, and credit cards, most of which end in foreclosure or collection, thereby ruining the credit of the child.[97] According to a government report, in 2010 the identities of almost 9 million U.S. residents were stolen.[98] To make this even worse, the manner in which numbers are assigned by the Social Security Administration has made it easier for criminals to guess the SSNs of children born after 1971[99] (although new randomization techniques have been announced to address this).[100]

2.10 Financial Crimes

The personal information acquired from children may also be used to perpetrate a number of different types of financial crimes. This may take the form of directly trying to steal money online by accessing the financial assets of children or family members, or indirectly by the e-commerce sales of products that are age-inappropriate

---

96. Carnegie Mellon CyLab, *Child Identity Theft—New Evidence Indicates Identity Thieves Are Targeting Children for Unused Social Security Numbers* (2011).

97. *Id.*

98. U.S. Bureau of Justice Statistics, *Identity Theft Reported by Households Rose 33 Percent from 2005 to 2010* (Nov. 30, 2011).

99. A. Acquisti & R. Gross, PNAS, *Predicting Social Security numbers from public data* (July 2009).

100. Social Security Online, *Social Security Number Randomization* (June 13, 2011).

to children. But children may also become involved in illegal financial crimes, such as being recruited to be part of a scam against others to steal their money online[101] or joining illegal file-sharing sites (e.g., of music or videos) that violate the intellectual property or ownership rights of others.

The use of online systems to sell goods and for financial transactions continues to increase, such that the number of people now doing their banking online has reached 75 percent in the United States. The online sales during the most recent holiday season had the highest amounts ever spent, up double-digit percentages from the year before, in spite of lingering economic difficulties.[102] While the number of people participating in online financial transactions continues to increase, so have the online attempts at theft of financial assets.[103] While children might not have financial assets, they can easily be convinced to click on links from pop-up windows, in email attachments, or behind attractive interfaces that lead to attempts to gather information or to the loading of malware that steals financial information.[104]

When personal information from children is acquired in any of the ways previously described, it may be used to try to access the bank accounts of the children or their parents. The following is a typical example of using stolen personal data for financial crimes, this one concerning older children. Fraudsters targeted students who were applying for government loans by using a phishing scheme that asked for the student's bank account information in conjunction with the loan program, and then used that information to subsequently withdraw funds from those accounts.[105]

The sale of age-inappropriate products to children is another type of financial crime. Children now have the ability to buy prod-

---

101. *Gone phishing . . . gangs using Aussie kids to steal millions,* SYDNEY MORNING HERALD (June 4, 2006).

102. Press Release, U.S. Online Holiday Spending Approaches $25 Billion for the Season, Up 15 Percent vs. Year Ago (Dec. 12, 2011).

103. Internet Crime Complaint Center, *2010 Internet Crime Report* (2011).

104. *Children's Online Games Hides Bank Account Stealing Malware,* BITDEFENDER (Oct. 3, 2011).

105. *Arrests of £1m student loan phishing scam,* THE GUARDIAN (Dec. 9, 2011).

ucts online that they could not purchase face-to-face in a physical store. While some of this may be beyond the control of the online vendors due to weak age-verification systems or untrue entries by the children, targeting children with products marketed above their age is discouraged by the codes of conduct for online vendors.[106] Beyond voluntary industry codes, it may not be possible, at least in the United States, to hold online retailers accountable when they are selling legal products that do not violate limits on free speech, such as obscenity, as a recent U.S. Supreme Court decision shows.[107]

A recent study examined the various "advergames" that are made available to children by product advertisers.[108] The study was focused on the concern that computer games on the websites of food companies allow these firms to "engage children for unlimited lengths of time to promote calorie-dense nutrient-poor foods." The study found that children who play games on these sites promoting primarily promote candy, high-sugar cereals, and fast food tended to consume more nutrient-poor snack foods and fewer fruits and vegetables.

2.11   The Risks for Parents

Parents themselves are subject to a set of risks involving their children's use of the Internet, including the following:[109]

- New threats will arise that parents are not aware of.
- Parents will not have the knowledge and software to properly secure their child's online activities.
- Parents will not have tools that allow for proper monitoring of their child's online activities.

---

106. *See, e.g.,* Internet & Mobile Marketing Ass'n of the Philippines, *Code of Ethics for Online and Mobile Advertisement Material,* B. Advertising Directed to Children (2008).

107. Brown v. Entertainment Merchants Ass'n, 131 S. Ct. 2729 (2011).

108. Harris, et al., *US Food Company Branded Advergames on the Internet: Children's exposure and effects on snack consumption,* JOURNAL OF CHILDREN AND MEDIA (Vol. 6 Issue 1, 2012).

109. Some of these are from ENISA, *Cyber-Bullying and Online Grooming: helping to protect against the risks* (2011).

- Children will develop certain online or offline behaviors that parents are not aware of.
- Children will gain the knowledge and ability to escape online monitoring.
- Children will come under the influence of pernicious outside influences online at vulnerable periods in their lives.
- Children will take advantage of new technologies before parents are aware of the technology or certain capabilities of known technologies.
- Children will not properly defend themselves online, either inadvertently or intentionally.
- Other caretakers of children, including teachers, will not carry out the same duties to control and monitor their online environment.
- Activities of children online will materially impact the lives, reputations and assets of other members of the family.

Beyond this, other online risks may arise from what would normally be considered the safe part of the Internet. This requires that parents understand more deeply the activities, ethics, and standards of the caretakers of their children. For example, it seems that teachers are now frequently using the social networks available on the Internet to communicate with students, some even "friending" their students. A teacher in the UK was disciplined for talking about her drinking and partying, even though she had friended quite a number of her former students, many of them teenagers.[110] This has led to situations where schools have created new or revised social media policies and where law enforcement has had to intervene to stop inappropriate private conversations between teachers and students on these social networking sites or mobile phones, as exemplified by the following:[111]

- Facebook and text messages helped fuel a relationship between an eighth-grade English teacher and her 14-year-old

---

110. *Facebook drinking posts teacher Elizabeth Scarlett reprimanded*, BBC (Feb. 7, 2012).

111. *Rules to Stop Pupil and Teacher From Getting Too Social Online,* N.Y. TIMES (Dec. 17, 2011).

male pupil. The teacher was arrested on charges of aggravated child molestation and statutory rape.

- A 56-year-old former language-arts teacher was found guilty of sexual abuse and assault charges involving a 17-year-old female student with whom he had exchanged more than 700 text messages.
- A 37-year-old high school band director pleaded guilty to sexual misconduct stemming from his relationship with a 16-year-old female student; her Facebook page had more than 1,200 private messages from him, some about massages.
- A 39-year-old male high school athletic director pleaded guilty to charges of attempted corruption of a minor; he was arrested after offering a former male student gifts in exchange for sex.
- A Bronx principal's Facebook page included a risqué picture that was then posted in the hallways of her school.

This is not to say that all teachers who use social media to communicate with students are now suspect; rather, this is an additional type of Internet usage risk that must be assessed and addressed. Many, if not most, educators will not "friend" current students and will communicate only on non-private media. A recent survey showed that only 34 percent of teachers will friend students on social networking sites, while 67 percent believe it exposes them to risks.[112] The benefits of using the new technologies for instruction are quite significant, and parents should expect and want their educators to fully embrace all such tools that can help their children's learning experience.

Beyond educators, some of the very software and service organizations that are supposed to be helping parents with their duties in overseeing their children's Internet activities now must themselves be assessed. For example, in a recent case, the FTC filed a complaint and eventually reached settlement with a children's online monitoring software company that was engaged in deceptive busi-

---

112. Symantec, *Norton Online Family Report* (2011).

ness practices.[113] In this case, the company was alleged to have taken information collected by the monitoring software about children's activities and used it for marketing purposes without the families' express consent.

Parents may also be putting themselves and their children into a delicate situation by vouching for their age as being older than they are. To gain access to certain social websites who refuse to admit register children under the age of 13 (primarily to avoid COPPA obligations explained in Chapter 4) "many parents knowingly allow their children to lie about their age—in fact, often help them to do so—in order to gain access to age–restricted sites."[114] While some number of parents clearly are obeying the terms of service on these sites, as 46 percent of 12 year olds in a recent U.S. study used social network sites versus 62 percent of 13 year olds,[115] it is questionable whether all of these 12 year-olds belong to SNS that actually give the parent a choice to collect the child's personal data.

One final set of risks that parents have is that they themselves may become a victim, in that they have to contend with their child being the aggressor against others on the Internet. As discussed above, children are the most likely to be the cyberbulliers of other children. Children may send other children sexting messages, photos, or videos, which may ultimately make them the victims of various kinds of sexual exploitation. "Cyberbaiting" is when children "irritate or 'bait' a teacher until the teacher gets so frustrated they yell or have a breakdown. Students are ready for the teacher to crack and they film the incident on cell phones so they can later post the footage online, causing further shame or trouble for the teacher or school." This is a practice that 21 percent of teachers globally report to be an issue within their experience.[116] And children may violate the intellectual property rights of others by the illegal downloading of content such as movies, music, apps, and other copyrighted materials and so become a defendant in civil or

---

113. FTC v. EchoMetrix, Inc., Case No. 10-cv-05516 (E.D.N.Y. 2010).

114. *Why parents help their children to lie to Facebook about age*, First Monday Vol.16, No. 11 (Nov. 7, 2011).

115. Pew Research Center, *Social Media & Mobile Internet Use Among Teens and Young Adults* (2010).

116. *Id.*

criminal proceedings.[117] Twenty percent of children were found to be illegally downloading music files in a study in the UK.[118] Under certain conditions, it is possible that parents may be held liable under U.S. state or other countries' national or local parental responsibility laws for such acts of their children.[119]

---

117. *See, e.g., 50,000 BitTorrent users sued for alleged illegal downloads*, CNN Money (June 10, 2011).

118. *11 Year-Olds Regularly Downloading Illegal Music*, HuffPost Tech UK (Nov. 9, 2011), *quoting* a study by Childnet International.

119. *See, e.g.*, Cal. Civ. Code § 1714.1; Ontario Canada, Parental Responsibility Act (2000); U.K., Anti-Social Behaviour Act (2003); Western Australia, Parental Support and Responsibility Act (2008).

Chapter 3

International Agreements Protecting Children and the Internet

International agreements provide the foundation layer in the wall of legal protections safeguarding children in their relationship with the Internet. Of these, some agreements are binding upon the member countries (states), while others are merely guidelines or inspirational. The first of these agreements involve the basic rights of children as defined by United Nations and Hague Conventions. On top of that base structure is the work of various governments, nongovernmental organizations, and other groups in carrying out the spirit of these agreements. These global efforts provide the underpinnings to the regional and national laws that serve to protect children involved with the Internet, as discussed in Chapters 4 and 5. Because of the global nature of the Internet, multiple countries may often be involved in resolving a matter that occurred online, which requires that the proper jurisdiction over the defendants and subject matter be determined. This chapter first discusses the international agreements concerning children, then the various activities undertaken globally to protect children online by governments and public-private partnerships, and concludes by discussing the difficult issues of multicountry jurisdiction on the Internet.

POINTS FOR PARENTS

o The rights of children are established in international agreements among most countries.

o Public-private partnerships provide a strong platform for implementation of these rights.

o Among their activities are help lines, awareness training, and cybersafety programs.

o The global nature of the Internet raises questions as to which nations have jurisdiction.

3.1 UN, Hague, and other Conventions

A. UN Convention and Optional Protocols

The United Nations (UN) Convention on the Rights of the Child[1] (Convention) is a foundational document addressing specifically the needs of children globally. The Convention itself comes from the Universal Declaration of Human Rights,[2] which proclaimed that its listed rights applied to everyone. It also stated that childhood is "entitled to special care and assistance."[3] The Convention is also based on previous documents, such as the Geneva Declaration of the Rights of the Child (1924)[4] and the U.N.'s Declaration of the Rights of the Child (1959).[5] The latter document stated that "the child, by reason of his physical and mental immaturity, needs special safeguards and care, including appropriate legal protection."[6]

The Universal Declaration of Human Rights is one of three documents making up the International Bill of Human Rights. The other two are the International Covenant on Economic, Social, and Cul-

---

1. United Nations, Convention on the Rights of the Child, UN GA res. 44/25 (1989).

2. United Nations, Universal Declaration of Human Rights, UN GA res. 217A (III) (1948).

3. *Id.* art. 25(2).

4. League of Nations, Geneva Declaration of the Rights of the Child (1924).

5. United Nations, Declaration of the Rights of the Child, UN GA res. 1386 (XIV) (1959).

6. *Id.* Preamble.

tural Rights (with its optional protocol)[7] and the International Covenant on Civil and Political Rights (with its two optional protocols).[8] For purposes of children, the former addresses the right to education and the latter the right to privacy. While the Declaration is not technically binding, its provisions appear in many national statutes and treaties and also the latter two documents, which are binding on the signatories and came into force in 1976.

The Convention starts by declaring that the age of childhood goes until the age of 18, unless otherwise prescribed by statute.[9] It requires each member state to "respect and ensure" the rights listed in the Convention for each child within their respective jurisdiction without discrimination[10] and undertake appropriate legislation to support them.[11] In the actions of the states involving children, the "best interests of the child" are to be the primary consideration and to ensure that children receive "such protection and care as is necessary for his or her well-being."[12]

Among the many rights and freedoms listed in the Convention are the following that could have some impact on children as they participate online:

- Right to preserve their identity[13]
- Right to avoid the illegal overseas transfer and non-return[14]
- Right to express their views freely[15]
- Right to freedom of expression, restricted only to avoid harming the rights of other or for national security[16]

---

7. United Nations, International Covenant on Economic, Social & Cultural Rights, UN GA res. 2200A (XXI) (1976).

8. United Nations, International Covenant on Civil and Political Rights, UN GA res. 2200A (XXI) (1976).

9. Convention on the Rights of the Child, art. 1.

10. *Id.* art. 2.

11. *Id.* art. 4.

12. *Id.* art. 3.

13. *Id.* art. 8.

14. *Id.* art. 11.

15. *Id.* art. 12.

16. *Id.* art. 13.

- Right of association and peaceful assembly, restricted only by the impacts on public safety, order, health or morals or the rights of others[17]
- Right to not be subject to interference with their privacy[18]
- Right of access to information from mass media and children's books[19]
- Right to protection from "all forms of physical or mental violence, injury or abuse, neglect or negligent treatment, maltreatment or exploitation"[20]
- Right to an education, including appropriate school discipline[21] and to developing the child's abilities "to their fullest potential"[22]

Certain articles also deal with rights regarding the sale of children, child prostitution, and child pornography. As a foundation, there are provisions in the Convention that protect the child from economic exploitation or work that is harmful to the child's development[23] or from "all forms of sexual exploitation," including prostitution and pornography.[24] Others address prevention of child abduction or trafficking[25] or protection from exploitation that affects the child's welfare.[26] Building on that, there is the Optional Protocol requiring separate ratification that focuses specifically on prohibiting the sale of children, child pornography, and child prostitution; and related acts, such as attempt and complicity, improperly inducing consent, and sex tourism; and on protecting the rights and interests of the child victims.[27]

---

17. *Id.* art. 15.
18. *Id.* art. 16.
19. *Id.* art. 17.
20. *Id.* art. 19.
21. *Id.* art. 28.
22. *Id.* art. 29.
23. *Id.* art. 32.
24. *Id.* art. 34.
25. *Id.* art. 35.
26. *Id.* art. 36.
27. United Nations, Optional Protocol to the Convention on the Rights of the Child on the Sale of Children, Child Prostitution and Child Pornography, UN GA res. 54/263 (XXI) (2000).

These rights and freedoms are applicable to all member states which have acceded to the Convention. It entered into force in 1990, and, as of early 2012, 193 states had done so (Somalia and the United States are the only nations where it has not come into force), plus 151 have acceded to the Optional Protocol regarding child pornography, prostitution, and the sale of children, which came into force in 2002. These states are required to report on measures they have taken "which give effect to the rights,"[28] although any state may implement statutes "more conducive" to realizing these rights.[29] In addition, a committee is established to monitor the progress on achieving the obligations established under the Convention.[30] States are also required to educate parents and children about these rights.[31]

B.   *Hague Conventions*

The Hague Conference on Private International Law is a permanent organization that works to harmonize the differences in private international law ("progressive unification of the rules") and has almost 40 conventions across a wide variety of areas, including commercial and financial law, legal cooperation and litigation, property/succession, and the family. It has at least three conventions that directly impact children. The first involves children and intercountry adoption,[32] the second involves children and transborder abduction,[33] and the third is a broader set of civil protections for children.[34] The relevant parts of each will be discussed in turn.

---

28. Convention on the Rights of the Child, art. 44.
29. *Id.* art. 41.
30. *Id.* art. 43.
31. *Id.* art. 42.
32. Hague Conference on Private Int'l Law, *Hague Convention on the Protection of Children and Co-operation in Respect of Intercountry Adoption* (1993).
33. Hague Conference on Private Int'l Law, *Hague Convention on the Civil Aspects of International Child Abduction* (1980).
34. Hague Conference on Private Int'l Law, *Hague Convention on Jurisdiction, Applicable Law, Recognition, Enforcement and Cooperation in Respect of Parental Responsibility and Measures for the Protection of Children* (1996).

1. Convention on Adoptions

The purpose of this convention is to establish minimum standards and increase cooperation among states to thereby "prevent the abduction, the sale of, or traffic in children." This requires states to ensure that improper financial gain is not involved in the adoption process. There is to be an accreditation process for regulating agencies and individuals involved in the adoption process. There are steps that both the state of origin and the receiving state must take to ensure that the adoptive parents and children in need are both qualified, including seeking consent of the child where appropriate. Data gathered during this process should be preserved confidentially and only used appropriately. Reservations to the convention are not allowed.

2. Convention on Abductions

The purpose of this convention is "to secure the prompt return of children wrongfully removed to or retained in any Contracting State; and to ensure that rights of custody and of access under the law" of one state are respected in the other states. What it does not do is determine the custodial rights, which are to be determined in the appropriate court under its law. The convention addresses the interruption of the rights of custody and access of children up to the age of 15 in the country of habitual residence. Central authorities in each of the contracting states are charged with working with other central authorities to find, keep from harm, and return the removed or retained child. The central authority in the requested state need not comply if there was consent to the removal, the child objects, or there is a grave risk of "physical or psychological harm" to the child. Reservations to the convention are allowed.

3. Convention on Civil Protections

This purpose of this convention is to establish the jurisdiction, governing law, enforcement, and cooperation between states in matters related to these civil protections of children. It starts with determining which of the states should have jurisdiction, moves to the appropriate governing law, and then ensures that any decisions are then enforceable in all of the contracting states. The topics covered include the person or property of children, parental responsibility and care, parental disputes over custody and access, and legal representation of the child. There are limited reservations allowed to states when acceding.

C. Other Agreements

In addition to the UN and Hague agreements, there have been a number of other joint activities undertaken in support of the rights of children. While by no means a complete list, the following illustrates some of the actions that have been undertaken and may be ongoing to support the above-listed laws, in many cases further defining and expanding the legal obligations of member states.

1. Programme of Action for the Prevention of the Sale of Children, Child Prostitution, and Child Pornography[35]

This program arose from the Optional Protocol discussed above. It defines the sale of children, child prostitution, and child pornography as modern forms of slavery, unjustifiable by traditional practices or poverty, and requiring effective legislation and law enforcement measures. It covers the categories of information, education, legal measures, law enforcement, social measures, development assistance, rehabilitation, reintegration, and international coordination. There are also specific measures in the areas of trafficking and sale of children (e.g., laws prohibiting the abduction and sale of children for "whatever purposes"); child prostitution (e.g., preventing "new forms of technology from being used for soliciting for child prostitution"); and child pornography (e.g., preventing "new technology being used to produce pornography, including video films and pornographic computer games" and "to protect children from exposure to adult pornography, especially through new forms of technology").

---

35. U.N. Commission on Human Rights, Programme of Action for the Prevention of the Sale of Children, Child Prostitution and Child Pornography, UN CHR res. 1992/74.

2.   Elimination of the Worst Forms of Child Labour[36]

The objectives of this convention under the International Labour Organization, a UN agency, are to eliminate what is considered the worst forms of child labor, defined as the following:

(a) All forms of slavery or practices similar to slavery, such as the sale and trafficking of children, debt bondage and serfdom, and forced or compulsory labour, including forced or compulsory recruitment of children for use in armed conflict.

(b) The use, procuring, or offering of a child for prostitution, for the production of pornography, or for pornographic performances.

(c) The use, procuring, or offering of a child for illicit activities, in particular for the production and trafficking of drugs as defined in the relevant international treaties.

(d) Work which, by its nature or the circumstances in which it is carried out, is likely to harm the health, safety, or morals of children.

This convention is binding only upon the states that are members of the International Labour Organization and that have ratified or acceded to it. As of early 2012, 174 nations have ratified this convention.

3.   Palermo Trafficking Protocol[37]

This protocol has as its objectives to prevent human trafficking, especially of women and children; to protect and assist such victims; and to promote cooperation among states. It deals with subjects such as criminalization of such conduct, protecting and repatriating victims, trafficking prevention, border controls, legiti-

---

36. Int'l Labour Organization, Convention No. 182 on the Prohibition and Immediate Action for the Elimination of the Worst Forms of Child Labour (1999).

37. United Nations, Protocol to Prevent, Suppress and Punish Trafficking in Persons, Especially Women and Children, Supplementing the United Nations Convention Against Transnational Organized Crime, UN GA res. 53/383 (2000).

macy and control of documents, and how the contracting states can work together. This protocol entered into force in 2003.

4.   Stockholm Declaration[38]

This program comes from the Convention on the Rights of the Child discussed above, with the goal of ending the commercial sexual exploitation of children everywhere. Its action plan includes passing laws, providing education, fostering networks, and creating services and programs, consolidated into the following five areas:

- Coordination and Cooperation (at national, regional, and international levels)
- Prevention
- Protection
- Recovery and Reintegration
- Child Participation

5.   Matters Involving Child Victims and Witnesses of Crime[39]

These guidelines, while not having the effect of a legal obligation, nevertheless provide rules for member states to follow. This document is targeted toward government and professionals and those caring for children. It is based on the principles of: dignity, nondiscrimination, best interests of the child, and right to participation. This leads to the described rights to: be treated with dignity and compassion, be protected from discrimination, be informed, be heard and express views and concerns, effective assistance, privacy, be protected from hardship during the justice process, safety, repatriation, and special preventive measures (for recurring victimization). The program concludes with a description of training and the roles for professionals involved, including cooperation. A Model Law for this area has been developed.[40]

---

38. First World Congress against Commercial Sexual Exploitation of Children, *The Stockholm Declaration and Agenda for Action* (1996).

39. United Nations Economic and Social Council, Guidelines on Justice Involving Child Victims and Witnesses of Crime, UN E res. 2005/20.

40. U.N. Office on Drugs and Crime, *Justice in Matters Involving Child Victims and Witnesses of Crime Model Law and Related Commentary* (2009).

6.   Protecting Children against Sexual Exploitation and Sexual Abuse[41]

The Council of Europe passed this resolution, which goes further than the Optional Protocol in criminalizing additional specific conduct and in the obligations it places on states. These include the requirements of prevention, protection, assistance, and intervention. The objectives are to prevent and combat sexual exploitation and sexual abuse of children; protect the rights of child victims of sexual exploitation and sexual abuse; and promote national and international cooperation against sexual exploitation and sexual abuse of children. This agreement does not impact the "rights and obligations" of other international agreements in this subject area.

Examples of specific substantive criminal law provisions include those for sexual abuse (including coercion or threats), child prostitution, child pornography (producing, distributing, or possessing), pornographic performances, corrupting a child, solicitation, and aiding, abetting, and attempting such. It addresses procedural rules so as to minimize the burden on the child victim and to ensure national databases of convicted offenders, including DNA information. It also addresses obtaining jurisdiction over incidents occurring in its territory, on ships flying its flag, on aircraft registered there, by one of its nationals, by one who has habitual residence there, or against one of its nationals or one who has habitual residence there, or where it has not extradited an alleged offender within its territory.

7.   A World Fit for Children[42]

To make a world fit for children, this UN resolution describes in some detail a list of actions needed, based on the following 10 principles and objectives:

- Put children first.
- Eradicate poverty: invest in children.
- Leave no child behind.

---

41. Council of Europe, Convention on the Protection of Children against Sexual Exploitation and Sexual Abuse, CETS No. 201 (2007).

42. United Nations, A World Fit for Children, UN GA res. S-27/2 (2002).

- Care for every child.
- Educate every child.
- Protect children from harm and exploitation.
- Protect children from war.
- Combat HIV/AIDS.
- Listen to children and ensure their participation.
- Protect the Earth for children.

3.2   Public and Public-Private Partnership Activities

Expanding beyond these agreements addressing the comprehensive rights of children are efforts coming out of regional or national governments that deal more specifically with children and the Internet and public-private or public-public partnerships that go beyond the agreements into the actual implementations of these initiatives. Long-standing organizations like UNICEF and the Children's Rights Information Network and many newer nongovernmental organizations (NGOs), such as ECPAT (End Child Prostitution, Child Pornography and Trafficking of Children for Sexual Purposes), and professional organizations such as the Financial Coalition Against Child Pornography are joining with governmental agencies in the effort to make the Internet safer for children. Because there are so many of these efforts under way, the following is merely representative of the activities undertaken globally.

A.   *Combating Child Pornography on the Internet*[43]

Sponsored by the U.S. and Austrian governments, the recommendations that came out of this conference included the following:

- Zero tolerance against child pornography on the Internet
- The need for a global partnership among all actors and stakeholders
- Worldwide criminalization of child pornography
- Strengthening law enforcement at the national level and improving international cooperation among law enforcement agencies

---

43. Int'l Conference on Combating Child Pornography on the Internet (Vienna, 1999).

- Closer cooperation and partnership between governments and the Internet industry
- The critical role of hotlines or tiplines
- Training and capacity building
- Raising awareness and empowerment of users

B.   *Protecting Children in a Digital World*[44]

The European Commission has created this report, following on two previous reports with sets of recommendations issued in 1998[45] and 2006.[46] The 1998 recommendations include a set of guidelines involving self-regulation of the online audiovisual and information services industry at the national level with these four components:[47]

- Consultation and representativeness of the parties concerned
- Code(s) of conduct
- National bodies facilitating cooperation at European Community level
- National self-regulation framework

The code of conduct should include the ability to warn of risks of the content to children and any available safeguards, such as warning pages or age verifications, offering of parental controls, and handling of complaints through hotlines when those safeguards are not met.

---

44.   EU COMMISSION, PROTECTING CHILDREN IN THE DIGITAL WORLD (2011).

45.   EU, Council Recommendation of 24 September 1998 on the development of the competitiveness of the European audiovisual and information services industry by promoting national frameworks aimed at achieving a comparable and effective level of protection of minors and human dignity.

46.   EU, Recommendation 2006/952/EC of 20 December 2006 on the protection of minors and human dignity and on the right of reply in relation to the competitiveness of the European audiovisual and on-line information services industry.

47.   EU, Council Recommendation of 24 September 1998 Annex, *Indicative Guidelines for the Implementation, at the National Level, of a Self-Regulation Framework for the Protection of Minors and Human Dignity in On-Line Audiovisual and Information Services.*

The 2006 recommendations dealt with several issues, including the right of reply to contested information found online. For minors, the recommendations include a focus on media literacy, to "enable minors to make responsible use of audiovisual and online information services," increasing awareness of parents and teachers of new Internet services and how they can be made safe for children, and identifying quality and services appropriate for minors. It also looks to industry to make the Internet safer for children by using service provider "quality labels," reporting illicit content, and content filtering and labeling systems.

The new report starts off by acknowledging that because regulation cannot keep pace with technology, the prior two sets of recommendations emphasized a self-regulatory model. It also notes the rapid change in the availability of new on-demand services to children. The report looks to the effectiveness of the implementations of the recommendations from those prior two reports and provides new recommendations. For example, while the self-regulation of online content using codes of conduct does seem to have proliferated, the levels of implementation of these safeguards are not sufficient to discontinue monitoring of the content made available to children.

Additional areas reported on include:

- *Hotlines*: Many member states are following the INHOPE Code of Practice for their hotlines and notice/takedowns of illicit content, but there is not sufficient convergence among the members.
- *ISPs*: Although not responsible for content under the E-Privacy Directive,[48] ISPs and their associations should become more involved in the protection of children.
- *Social Networking Sites*: Although a wonderful opportunity, the risks from SNS for children include: "illegal content, age-inappropriate content, inappropriate contact, and inappropriate conduct." To counter these risks, SNSs should adopt comprehensive guidelines and implementation monitoring and "Privacy by Default" settings for children.

---

48. *See* discussion on Europe in Chapter 5.

- *Access Restrictions to Content*: Age rating and content classification systems need to become more standardized while the technical systems, such as those for filtering, age verification, and parental controls, need to increase their usefulness and reliability.
- *Video Games*: A number of member states use existing age-rating systems.[49] Media literacy and awareness raising and codes of conduct from retailers are needed.
- *Right of Reply*: There needs to be a standardized right of reply to an assertion of facts in online media.

C.   European Union

The European Union NGO Alliance for Child Safety Online (eNACSO)[50] is a network of 22 NGOs focusing on children's rights in the EU, trying to establish a safer online environment for children and promote their rights on the Internet and other new technologies. Its Digital Manifesto,[51] which is presented to governments, industry, and other stakeholders on how to create a safer online environment for children and young people, has the following key recommendations:

- Government must set and follow through on the policies to keep children safe, including international harmonization laws.
- Online child abuse/child abuse images require harmonized laws, better detection, faster removal, misuse of peer-to-peer networks, and encryption technology.
- Advertising, e-commerce, privacy, and data protection should require better commercial practices to not expose children to age-inappropriate advertising or commercial practice, and a minimum age should be set below which parental approval is required for online activity.

---

49. *See, e.g.*, Pan-European Games Information System (PEGI) Online, http://www.pegionline.eu/en/.
50. *See* www.iwf.org.uk.
51. eNACSO, A DIGITAL MANIFESTO—AN AGENDA FOR CHANGE (2009).

- Mobile Internet users should have child features and reduced features by default and allow adult activities only behind an adult bar.
- Location services need stronger safeguards.
- Social networking sites need to better monitor their sites for inappropriate content and have an easy ability to report abuse.
- ISP liability should follow for non-removal if there is actual knowledge.
- Self-regulation needs to show improvements in child safety to maintain public confidence.

eNACSO gets some of its funding from the European Commission's Safer Internet Programme, which brings together a network of NGOs, researchers, and law enforcement. The Safer Internet Programme has as its objectives to raise awareness and to fight against illegal and harmful content and conduct on the Internet.[52] It also provides the Safer Internet Centres in 30 European countries,[53] which include awareness centres and helplines, both of which belong to the INSAFE network,[54] and hotlines, which belong the INHOPE network.[55] It funds a number of activities besides eNACSO, such as: Interpol to fight child pornography (child sexual abuse materials); ICOP in developing forensic software to find these abuse materials on peer-to-peer networks; the EU Kids Online program, which studies the actions and attitudes toward online safety among children and their parents; and development and assessments of parental control,[56] labeling, and filtering tools.

The European Commission is also involved in sponsoring two self-regulation initiatives for safer mobile use by young people[57]

---

52. *See* http://ec.europa.eu/information_society/activities/sip/policy/programme/index_en.htm.

53. *See* http://ec.europa.eu/information_society/activities/sip/projects/centres/index_en.htm.

54. *See* http://www.saferinternet.org/.

55. *See* www.inhope.org.

56. Safer Internet Programme, *Benchmarking of parental control tools for the online protection of children* (2011).

57. *European Framework for Safer Mobile Use by Younger Teenagers and Children* (2007).

and safer social networking use[58] and assessments thereof.[59] In addition, the Coalition to Make the Internet a Better Place for Kids was recently launched. The founding documents[60] state that the direction of this organization is to work with existing "successful endeavors" (those mentioned above plus two others[61]) and to find pragmatic solutions to real problems, such as the following:

- Simple and robust reporting tools for users;
- Age-appropriate privacy settings;
- Wider use of content classification;
- Wider availability and use of parental control; and
- Effective takedown of child abuse material.

D.   United Kingdom

One of the leading organizations for online child safety in the United Kingdom is the Children's Charities' Coalition on Internet Safety (CHIS).[62] CHIS is an umbrella group for 11 charities and promotes safe and equal access to the Internet and related digital technologies for all children. CHIS was instrumental in the creation of both the UK Council for Child Internet Safety (UKCCIS)[63] and the Child Exploitation and Online Protection Centre (CEOP).[64] UKCCIS, bringing together over 140 organizations and individuals, sponsored the first Internet safety strategy for children.[65] The UKCCIS itself is the outgrowth a report by a UK professor in 2008.[66] This report recommended, among many other items, three objectives for safeguard-

---

58. European Commission, *Safer Social Networking Principles for the EU* (2009).

59. European Commission, *Assessment of the Implementation of the Safer Social Networking Principles for the EU* (2011).

60. Coalition to make the Internet a better place for kids, *Statement of Purpose* (2011).

61. GSMA's *Mobile Alliance against Child Sexual Abuse Content* (started 2008) and Digital Agenda's *Principles for a Safer Use of Connected Devices and Online Services* (2011).

62. *See* www.chis.org.uk.

63. *See* www.ukccis.gov.uk.

64. *See* www.ceop.gov.uk.

65. UKCCIS, *Click Clever, Click Safe* (2009).

66. *Safer Children in a Digital World,* Byron Review (2008).

ing the child's online environment: reducing availability, restricting access, and increasing resilience to harmful and inappropriate material online. UKCCIS has been involved in a number of safety projects, including anti-cyberbullying campaigns and promoting the KiteMark,™[67] created by the British Standards Institution for parental control software.

CEOP has the responsibility for handling child sexual exploitation in the UK, including online, but not other issues like cyberbullying. It sends illegal content that its finds online to the Internet Watch Foundation. It has been involved with the ThinkUKnow education program[68] and the CEOP/Virtual Global Taskforce (VGT) "Report Abuse" Mechanism.[69] VGT is an international alliance of law enforcement agencies dealing with child sexual exploitation whose objectives are to make the Internet a safer place; to identify, locate, and protect children at risk; and to hold perpetrators appropriately to account.

CEOP sponsored the International Youth Advisory Congress[70] in 2008, focusing on online safety and security. This Congress led to the Children and Young Persons' Global Online Charter,[71] which is what young people "feel they need and want from relevant agencies and corporations to keep them secure and safe from harm when using the Internet and mobile technologies." This is a list of 10 recommendations directed at five groups: education, government, industry, law enforcement, and the media, which in turn received pledges from CEOP and VGT.

E. United States

In the United States, there are many state and federal efforts involved in keeping children safe online. Federal efforts include what is being done by the Internet Crimes Against Children (ICAC) Task Force Program and by many of the agencies in the Department of

---

67. *See* www.bsigroup.com/en/ProductServices/Child-Safety-Online-Software.
68. *See* www.thinkuknow.co.uk.
69. *See* ceop.police.uk/Safer-By-Design/safety-centre.
70. *See* www.iyac.net.
71. IYAC, *Children and Young Persons' Global Online Charter* (2008).

Justice. For example, the FBI produces a guide to help parents understand the risks from online predators and signs of at-risk behaviors,[72] and also a list of safety rules for children on the Internet.[73] Other efforts come from NGOs, universities, and professional organizations. For example, i-SAFE is a nonprofit organization that is dedicated to showing children how to "safely and responsibly take control of their Internet experiences."[74]

The U.S. federal government's Department of Justice (DOJ) is responsible for coordinating national activities and reporting on their strategy to prevent child exploitation,[75] as required by the PRO-TECT Our Children Act[76] (discussed in Chapter 4). The strategy focuses on the following types of exploitation: child pornography (child sexual abuse images), online enticement of children for sexual purposes, commercial sexual exploitation of children, and child sex tourism. Under the guiding principle of reducing the incidence of the sexual exploitation of children through "efficiently leveraging assets across the federal government in a coordinated manner," the following are the federal government's high-level objectives:

- Continue to partner closely with state, local, tribal, and non-governmental entities, as well as other federal agencies and the private sector, to implement the National Strategy in a coordinated fashion.
- Build on the success of the Project Safe Childhood initiative.
- Increase its commitment to a leadership role in finding a global solution to the transnational problem of the sexual exploitation of children.
- Work toward improving the quality, effectiveness, and timeliness of computer forensic investigations and analysis.

---

72. FBI, A PARENT'S GUIDE TO INTERNET SAFETY (1999).

73. FBI, KIDS—SAFETY TIPS, *available at* www.fbi.gov/fun-games/kids/kids-safety.

74. *See* www.isafe.org.

75. U.S. Dept. of Justice, Report to Congress, *The National Strategy for Child Exploitation Prevention and Interdiction* (2010).

76. Providing Resources, Officers & Technology to Eradicate Cyber Threats to Our Children Act of 2008, Pub. L. 110-401.

- Increase its commitment to effective and sophisticated training for prosecutors and investigators.
- Continue to partner with industry to develop objectives to reduce the exchange of child pornography.
- Explore opportunities to increase the education and awareness of federal, state, local, and tribal judges of the difficult issues involved in child sexual exploitation.

The ICAC Task Force Program is a vast enterprise representing over 2,000 law enforcement agencies and prosecutor offices across the country handling Internet-related crimes involving children. Since 1998, it has been providing technical assistance to these agencies and information to the community. The ICAC Task Force Program is statutorily provided for in the PROTECT Act[77] to do the following:

- Increase the investigative capabilities of state and local law enforcement officers in the detection, investigation, and apprehension of Internet crimes against children offenses or offenders, including technology-facilitated child exploitation offenses.
- Conduct proactive and reactive Internet crimes against children investigations.
- Provide training and technical assistance to ICAC Task Forces and other federal, state, and local law enforcement agencies in the areas of investigations, forensics, prosecution, community outreach, and capacity-building, using recognized experts to assist in the development and delivery of training programs.
- Increase the number of Internet crimes against children offenses being investigated and prosecuted in both federal and state courts.
- Create a multiagency task force response to Internet crimes against children offenses within each state.
- Participate in the Department's Project Safe Childhood initiative, the purpose of which is to combat technology-facilitated sexual exploitation crimes against children.

---

77. *Id.* at § 103.

- Enhance nationwide responses to Internet crimes against children offenses, including assisting other ICAC Task Forces as well as other federal, state, and local agencies with Internet crimes against children investigations and prosecutions.
- Develop and deliver Internet crimes against children public awareness and prevention programs.
- Participate in such other activities, both proactive and reactive, that will enhance investigations and prosecutions of Internet crimes against children.

The FBI is involved in a number of different initiatives. One is the Innocent Images National Initiative, which is tasked with attempting to locate online predators who try to hide behind various technical defenses, such as remote proxy servers and encryption, including forensic analysis of digital evidence. The Innocence Lost National Initiative helps to recover children involved in domestic sex trafficking in the United States and prosecute the offenders. The Child Sex Tourism Initiative is responsible for tracking U.S. citizens and residents who travel abroad "to procure children in other countries for sexual purposes." It works with target-country governments and NGOs to interdict and prosecute such offenders.

The Justice Department's Child Exploitation and Obscenity Section (CEOS) handles the worst child exploitation cases; it suggests policy direction and helps to guide others in the department. For example, it will provide expertise in forensic evidence, rules of evidence, and specialized statutes to prosecutors help convict offenders. The department has also worked with states and localities in developing their AMBER Alert programs to respond to missing children before something bad occurs.

Project Safe Childhood Conference is a national project that started in 2006 under local federal district attorneys to prevent and interdict technology-facilitated child exploitation. It coordinates with all of the other federal and states agencies and select NGOs in investigations and prosecutions and offers training and awareness programs. On the international level, the State Department has the Children's Passport Issuance Alert Program to help prevent international parental child abduction. It provides parents with advance warning of possible plans for international travel of their child when a child's passport is applied for.

A number of other federal government departments are involved in protecting against child exploitation, including the departments of Homeland Security, Health and Human Services, Postal Inspectors, Defense, Immigration and Customs Enforcement, and others. The U.S. office of INTERPOL works with many of these government agencies on international efforts, including the creation of a database that compares newly seized child abuse images to those in the database to try to identify and rescue exploitation victims.

A leading example on NGOs, of which there are far too many to even begin to enumerate, is the National Center for Missing and Exploited Children (NCMEC). Created in the 1980s and with access to missing-child alerts, it has a high return rate for missing children. Although it is a private NGO, it also has a set of 20 statutory mandates.[78] The statutory requirements for its services include the following:

- Operate the clearinghouse of information about missing and exploited children.
- Operate a toll-free 24-hour hotline for reporting the location of missing children.
- Operate a Cyber Tipline that the public may use to report Internet-related child sexual exploitation, in these areas:
  - o possession, manufacture, and distribution of child pornography;
  - o online enticement of children for sexual acts;
  - o child prostitution;
  - o sex tourism involving children;
  - o extrafamilial child sexual molestation;
  - o unsolicited obscene material sent to a child;
  - o misleading domain names; and
  - o misleading words or digital images on the Internet.
- Provide forensic technical assistance to individuals and law enforcement agencies in the prevention, investigation, prosecution, and treatment of cases.

---

78. 42 U.S.C. § 5771 *et seq.* (first 19 mandates); 42 U.S.C. § 5119a.

- Assist the State Department in cases of international child abduction in accordance with the Hague Convention on the Civil Aspects of International Child Abduction.[79]
- Offer training programs to law enforcement and social-service professionals.
- Distribute photographs and descriptions of missing children worldwide.
- Coordinate child-protection efforts with the private sector.
- Network with NGOs and state clearinghouses about missing-persons cases.
- Provide information about effective state legislation.
- Under the Child Victim Identification Program (CVIP), help to prove a real child is depicted in a child abuse image (as required by the Supreme Court's holding[80] on the Child Pornography Prevention Act[81]) and assist in locating unidentified victims.

There are also the many efforts under way to address cyberbullying and identity theft. For example, the StopBullying website[82] contains information from various governmental agencies on how to address this conduct, addressing each of the three age groups of "kids, teens and young adults." The Anti-Bullying Alliance[83] brings together over 100 organizations to develop a consensus on stopping bullying and then disseminates best practices. The FTC provides the Identity Theft Data Clearinghouse, which allows for searches of a database[84] of other victims and their offenders to look for patterns.

The Federal Trade Commission (FTC) is responsible for setting and enforcing the Children's Online Privacy Protection Rule (see Chapter 4). As part of its efforts to assist children in protecting their privacy, the FTC has created the OnGuard Online website to help parents

---

79. NCMEC, LITIGATING INTERNATIONAL CHILD ABDUCTION CASES UNDER THE HAGUE CONVENTION (2007).

80. Ashcroft v. Free Speech Coalition, 535 U.S. 234 (2002).

81. Child Pornography Prevention Act of 1996, 18 U.S.C. § 2251 *et seq.*

82. *See* www.stopbullying.gov.

83. *See* www.antibullyingalliance.org.

84. *See* www.ftc.gov/idtheft.

help their children to stop and think before they connect online, avoid scams, secure kids' computers, and understand parental controls.[85] The FTC also sponsors the *Net Cetera* publication, which explains in more detail to parents how to deal with children of different ages, social networks, online communications, and the impact of mobile devices, and provides a number of other resources for parents.[86]

To understand more deeply the issues raised by virtual worlds, the FTC analyzed and developed a report on the content available in virtual worlds (as opposed to the Internet generally) and the restrictions on children's access to that content.[87] The report found that the vast majority of explicit content in child-oriented virtual worlds was available only to those registered as older children (i.e., teenagers) or adults instead of children and that it was typically in a text format, such as "chat rooms, message boards, and discussion forums." More explicit content was in virtual worlds targeted at teenagers, with about half the content in graphic form. The FTC made a number of recommendations, including better age-screening and age-segregation techniques, stronger language filters, and better-trained live moderators.

The FTC has also recently released a report on the privacy disclosures for mobile apps targeted at children.[88] This report starts by informing that there are almost one million mobile apps available from the apps stores of just two vendors (Apple and Google), which have been downloaded close to 30 billion times to date. Concerned that mobile apps can automatically collect and share information from the device, including "user's precise geolocation, phone number, list of contacts, call logs, unique device identifiers" and personal information without parents' knowledge, the commission surveyed available apps in the stores of these two vendors. It looked at those apps targeted at children, their types, the children's age ranges, the types of data collection and sharing disclosures provided, links to social networking sites and other interactive features, "in-app" advertising, ratings, and parental controls.

---

85. *See* www.onguardonline.gov.

86. FTC, Net Cetera – Chatting with Kids About Being Online (2009).

87. FTC, Virtual Worlds and Kids: Mapping the Risks (2009).

88. FTC, *Mobile Apps for Kids: Current Privacy Disclosures are Disappointing* (2012).

The FTC found that there was very little information on either the app store promotion pages or developer's landing pages regarding the collection or sharing of data by the mobile apps, the majority of which were available at no cost. These apps were either intended for or also targeted at children, so the FTC is recommending that the industry police itself in providing parents the necessary information to make decisions about downloading such apps. This has to be done considering both plain language and the small screen sizes of mobile devices. It also recommends that the app stores provide a standardized method for app developers to provide this information and to better enforce this requirement.

F.   International Telecommunication Union

The International Telecommunication Union (ITU), a specialized UN agency in the field of telecommunications, information, and communication technologies, promulgated the Child Online Protection (COP) initiative in late 2008 as part of its Global Cybersecurity Agenda (GSA).[89] GSA has as its five pillars/work areas: legal measures, technical and procedural measures, organizational structures, capacity building, and international cooperation. COP is based on its charge coming out of the Geneva Declaration[90] and on the Rio Declaration.[91] The objectives of the initiative are to:

- Identify the key risks and vulnerabilities to children and young people in cyberspace.
- Create awareness of the risks and issues through multiple channels.
- Develop practical tools to help governments, organizations, and educators minimize risk.
- Share knowledge and experience while facilitating international strategic partnerships to define and implement.

---

89. ITU, GLOBAL CYBERSECURITY AGENDA BROCHURE (2007).

90. World Summit on the Information Society Outcomes, Doc. 5 (2003).

91. World Congress III against Sexual Exploitation of Children and Adolescents, *Rio de Janeiro Declaration and Call for Action to Prevent and Stop Sexual Exploitation of Children and Adolescents* (2008).

The ITU Guidelines for parents and educators[92] are broken into the following categories: security of the PC; usage rules; education of parents, teachers and guardians; review of features of the Internet sites; education of children; review of the child's use of a site; and communication with the child. The ITU has also teamed up with the European Commission on the Safer Internet Day, part of the Safe Internet Programme discussed above, with more than 500 events in more than 50 countries.[93] The ITU held the Strategic Dialogue on Safer Internet Environment in Japan and agreed to these three objectives: to develop a basic framework for achieving safety, promoting voluntary initiatives in the private sector, and promoting user education initiatives.[94] The ITU's Council Working Group on Child Online Protection has also produced a report categorizing the online threats to children.[95] The ITU's Telecommunications Standardizations Sector (ITU-T) also has recommendations on cybersecurity.[96]

G. UN Office on Drugs and Crime

The United Nations also has sub-organizations focused on crime and, more specially, cybercrime. The General Assembly has passed resolutions on international organized crime,[97] cybersecurity,[98] and cybercrime,[99] and has called on the private sector to "promote and support efforts to prevent child sexual abuse and exploitation through the Internet."[100] The UN Office on Drugs and Crime

---

92. U.S. Dept. of Justice Report to Congress, *The National Strategy for Child Exploitation Prevention and Interdiction* (2010).

93. UN Press Release, Nov. 2, 2009.

94. MIT/ITU, Tokyo Communique on Safer Internet Environment for Children (2009).

95. ITU, The Source of Online Threats to Youth and Children (2010).

96. ITU-T, Recommendation ITU-T X.1205, *Overview of Cybersecurity* (2008).

97. United Nations, UN Convention Against Transnational Organized Crime, UN GA res. 55/25 (2000).

98. United Nations, Creation of a Global Culture of Cybersecurity, UN GA res. 64/211 (2010).

99. United Nations, Twelfth United Nations Congress on Crime Prevention and Criminal Justice, UN GA res. 65/230 art. 41 (2010).

100. *Id.* art. 40.

(UNODC) sees a "clear connection" between organized crime and Internet crime such as child pornography and identity theft.[101] The UN Economic and Social Council has adopted a resolution calling on member states to address the misuse of new technologies in the abuse and exploitation of children.[102] UNODC is teaming with the ITU to assess, build capacity, facilitate legislation, and provide technical assistance in the developing world to fight cybercrime.[103] UNODC, UNICEF, and the ITU sponsored the recent Framework for International Cooperation on Child Online Protection workshop.[104] In its role working with developing countries, it is specifically focusing on "the misuse of ICTs for child sexual abuse and exploitation in developing countries."[105] The UNODC has also published a handbook on identity crime.[106]

H.   OECD

The Organisation for Economic Co-Operation and Development (OECD) "promotes policies that will improve the economic and social well-being of people around the world." At its meeting of ministers in Seoul in 2008, a declaration[107] was issued stating that the collective states would "[e]nsure a trusted Internet-based environment which offers protection to individuals, especially minors and other vulnerable groups," and "[e]ncourage collaboration between governments, the private sector, civil society and the Internet technical community in building an understanding of the impact of the Internet on minors in order to enhance their protection and support when using the Internet." As follow-up to those points of the declaration, the OECD Working Party on Information Security and Privacy initiated a symposium in conjunction with APEC (described

---

101. UNODC, LINKS BETWEEN CYBERCRIME AND ORGANIZED CRIME (2011).

102. UN Economic and Social Council, Prevention, protection and international cooperation against the use of new information technologies to abuse and/or exploit children, UN E res. 2011/33 (2011).

103. UNODC/ITU, Memorandum of Understanding (2011).

104. Sixth Internet Governance Forum, Nairobi, Kenya (Sept. 2011).

105. UNODC, *Proposed Program on Cybercrime* (2011).

106. UNODC, HANDBOOK ON IDENTITY-RELATED CRIMES (2011).

107. OECD Ministerial Meeting, *The Seoul Declaration for the Future of the Internet Economy* (2008).

below) and authored a paper on the issues involved with protecting children online, including various policy, legal, and cooperatives approaches to addressing the risks faced by children using the Internet.[108] The OECD has addressed child protection issues in both its e-commerce guidelines[109] and its guidance on mobile commerce,[110] and in follow-on conferences.[111] It has also addressed the area of identity theft.[112]

I. *APEC*

The Asia-Pacific Economic Co-operation (APEC) seeks to promote free trade and economic cooperation throughout this region. Its declaration for promoting a "safe and trusted" networking environment recognized that "[a]n environment that offers protection for users, especially for minors and other vulnerable groups . . . is essential for promoting and maintaining the trust and confidence."[113] In its 2009 symposium held with the OECD, the member states exchanged best practices, including the need for close cooperation between the government and private sector; a comprehensive approach that considers legal, educational, and technical developments; promotion of awareness of children, parents, and teachers; and the strengthening of international cooperation to address the flow across borders of illegal and harmful content on the Internet.[114] APEC has also initiated a project on preventing child sexual exploitation via the Internet through the Telecommunications and Information Working Group (TELWG) that will inventory current efforts in the re-

---

108. OECD, THE PROTECTION OF CHILDREN ONLINE: RISKS FACED BY CHILDREN ONLINE AND POLICIES TO PROTECT THEM (2011).

109. OECD, GUIDELINES FOR CONSUMER PROTECTION IN THE CONTEXT OF ELECTRONIC COMMERCE (1999).

110. OECD, *Policy Guidance for Addressing Emerging Consumer Protection and Empowerment Issues in Mobile Commerce* (2008).

111. OECD, Conference on *Empowering E-Consumers: Strengthening Consumer Protection in the Internet Economy* (2010).

112. OECD, SCOPING PAPER ON ONLINE IDENTITY THEFT (2007).

113. APEC, *Bangkok Declaration - Digital Prosperity: Turning Challenges into Achievement* (2009).

114. Joint APEC-OECD Symposium on Initiatives among Member Economies Promoting Safer Internet Environment for Children, Singapore (Apr. 15, 2009).

gion, look at areas of cybersecurity that can be strengthened, and then to provide training to members.[115] TELWG continues to make protection of children from online threats a top priority.[116]

J.   Canada

Canada was one of the first countries to document a national strategy for protecting children online. This cyberwise strategy addressed awareness raising and public-private partnerships in safe Internet use.[117] The new national strategy, announced in 2004, consisted of five-year funding for the RCMP's National Child Exploitation Coordination Centre, developing online educational resources, and funding for Cybertip.ca (explained below).[118] This was subsequently renewed in 2009.[119] Along with its domestic and international legal efforts, the Department of Justice is involved with the Policy Centre for Victim Issues and produces information about safety on the Internet.[120]

Cybertip.ca is Canada's national 24/7 tipline for reporting the online sexual exploitation of children and is operated by the Canadian Centre for Child Protection (CCCP).[121] The tipline receives and analyzes tips from the public and is involved in national awareness campaigns and online safety strategies. The CCCP is a charitable organization dedicated to the personal safety of all children and has published a study on child abuse images.[122] The CCCP has been a long-time partner of the national government in the national strategy on child exploitation on the Internet. It partnered with the national government on "The Door That's Not Locked" portal, which

---

115. APEC, CAPACITY BUILDING WITHIN THE ASIA-PACIFIC REGION IN THE PREVENTION OF CHILD SEXUAL EXPLOITATION FACILITATED THROUGH THE INTERNET (2009).

116. APEC TELWG, *Proposed Workplan for 2011*.

117. Government of Canada, THE CANADIAN STRATEGY TO PROMOTE SAFE, WISE AND RESPONSIBLE INTERNET USE (2000).

118. Public Safety Canada, NATIONAL STRATEGY TO COMBAT CHILD EXPLOITATION ON THE INTERNET (2004).

119. Public Safety Canada Press Release, Government of Canada signals commitment to fight internet child exploitation (Feb. 10, 2009).

120. *See, e.g.*, Dept. of Justice Canada, *Safety on the Internet- how an abuser/ offender can obtain your internet activity history* (Dec. 01, 2011).

121. *See* www.cybertip.ca.

122. CCCP, CHILD SEXUAL ABUSE IMAGES (2009).

provides a single place where parents and teachers can go to find out whatever they need to keep children safe online.[123] It also is involved in personal safety education, missing children's services, and training organizations on preventing child sexual abuse.

K. *Australia*

The Australian national government started its four-year Cyber Safety Plan in 2008 to address a number of areas, including education, a help line, international cooperation activities, cybersecurity research, law enforcement investigations and prosecutions, and content filtering.[124] The national Cyber Security Strategy[125] sets three objectives, the first of which is that all Australians be aware of cyber risks, secure their computers, and take steps to protect their identities, privacy, and finances online. The national cybersecurity policy must be coordinated with "its approach to cyber safety, which is focused on protecting individuals, especially children, from exposure to illegal and offensive content, cyber-bullying, and grooming online for the purposes of sexual exploitation." The Cyber Safety Plan also includes education and awareness outreach by ACMA (discussed next) and advice from the Youth Advisory Group and its Consultative Working Group on Cybersafety. The government's Department on Broadband, Communications and the Digital Economy is responsible for the Cyber Safety Plan and also supports the "Stay Smart Online" website.[126]

The Australian Communications and Media Authority (ACMA) is a statutory authority within the federal government portfolio of Broadband, Communications and the Digital Economy, responsible for the regulation of broadcasting, the Internet, radiocommunications, and telecommunications. Starting in 2008, it issued the first of three annual reports regarding online risks. The first report analyzed the filtering technologies in use and also how other countries were addressing the issue of online risk to children.[127] The second report

123. *See* www.thedoorthatsnotlocked.ca.
124. Australian Government, Cyber Safety Plan (2008).
125. Australian Government, Cyber Security Strategy (2009).
126. *See* www.staysmartonline.gov.au.
127. ACMA, *Developments in Internet Filtering Technologies and Other Measures for Promoting Online Safety,* first annual report (2008).

analyzes in more detail some of the online behavioral risks, new technologies such as social media as they impact available safety measures, and looking at safety from an online content and services supply chain perspective.[128] The third report looks at trends such as the use of mobile devices and other trends and programs used to address those, and how risks are encountered differently by adults and children using those new technologies.[129]

Australia has used a co-regulatory model for online content, meaning ISPs are asked and expected to volunteer to filter certain content, similar to Canada, the UK, and certain European countries, but has recently started the process to require ISPs to filter content in a certain category to avoid inadvertent disclosure. Based on the National Classification Scheme run by ACMA, "Refused Content" material that must be filtered includes the following categories: child sexual abuse imagery, bestiality, sexual violence, detailed instruction in crime, violence or drug use, and/or material that advocates performing a terrorist act.

The Australian Federal Police Child Protection Operations team works on both national and international levels addressing online exploitation, illicit online content, and child sex tourism,[130] and partners on the ThinkUKnow Australia website.[131] It is involved in training others in the region on combating child sex tourism as part of the Bali Process co-chaired by Australia that arose out of the 2002 ministerial conference on smuggling and trafficking.[132]

L. *Japan*

In Japan a statute has been passed that specially targets the safe use of the Internet by children and encourages the use of content filters, the Internet education of children, and private-sector efforts at safeguards for children.[133] The Ministry of Internal Affairs and Com-

---

128. *Id.*, second annual report (2009).

129. ACMA, *Online Risk and Safety in the Digital Economy,* third annual report (2010).

130. *See* www.afp.gov.au/policing/child-protection-operations.

131. *See* www.thinkuknow.au.

132. Regional Ministerial Conference on People Smuggling, Trafficking in Persons, and Related Transnational Crime (2002).

133. Japan, Act on Development of an Environment that Provides Safe and Secure Internet Use for Young People (2009).

munications launched the Japan Safer Internet Program in 2008 with three parts: (1) for parents and children to gain the necessary Internet safety skills, including parental monitoring; (2) for the private sector to provide education and develop safety measures such as filtering of harmful and illicit content and content ratings; (3) and the appropriate legal framework of national and local laws and international cooperation.[134]

Japan has had 3G mobile phones for longer and with higher penetration rates than almost any other country. Japanese children are big users of mobile phones (as discussed in Chapter 1) and often tend to prefer to use them instead of in-person communications. Eighty-three percent of these children access the Internet on their mobile devices at least daily, with a majority doing so for at least 30 minutes.[135] Use of social networking sites tends to be lower among Japanese children—42 percent—versus almost 80 percent or more for children in other countries, and the number of contacts is smaller (15 versus 95).[136] Unlike in other countries, Japanese children tend to contact their parents via messaging instead of voice.[137] Studies have indicated that Japanese children tend to feel anxious if they do not receive immediate answers to their text messages, that many children use their mobile phone's email features more than voice calls due to its lower cost, that children email each other more often when they do not like spending time with their families, and that they value their mobile phones more than anything except their lives.[138]

Given the difficulties of parental monitoring for devices used outside the home, and that almost all high school students in the country have such a mobile phone to access the Internet, programs

---

134. JAPAN MINISTRY OF INTERNAL AFFAIRS AND COMMUNICATIONS, ICT POLICY TOWARD UBIQUITOUS NET SOCIETY (2009).

135. GSMA & NTT Docomo, *Children's use of mobile phones – An international comparison* (2011) [survey of 3,528 children in four countries: Japan, India, Paraguay, Egypt].

136. *Id.*

137. *Id.*

138. CELL PHONE USERS IN JAPAN: CHILDREN, TEENAGERS, SCHOOLS, HEALTH, BULLYING AND DEPENDENCE (2011).

targeting schools for safe mobile phone use were implemented.[139] But by statute, all mobile phones for children must include parental controls that block content at a minimum.[140] In addition to these minimum controls, time of day, sender, and other controls are possible, and many phones for younger children have a one-button call feature and GPS-tracking capabilities. Given that these mobile phones can be used as digital cash (*"osaifu keitai"*), to charge credit cards, for public transportation, or for opening physical doors, their security features are critical, including a standard security protocol (FeliCa) and remote information gathering and disabling capabilities. Other industry initiatives for mobile phones include network-level content filters and age-verification details sent to websites.[141]

3.3 Multicountry Jurisdiction

A. Jurisdiction in General

Determining which government should be protecting children online with enforcement of its laws is somewhat complex in a globally connected world. Perpetrators can commit crimes in their own nation of citizenship, within countries where they reside, or while located in other countries to which they have no citizenship or residential connection. The victims likewise can be citizens of the country where the act or acts are committed, residents there, or neither. So the question is, in which case can a country prosecute the offender or assist the victim, and what happens when more than a single country claims jurisdiction?

This issue is addressed in a number of the conventions covered above, such as the Convention on the Protection of Children against Sexual Exploitation and Sexual Abuse's lengthy provisions on jurisdiction.[142] This provision looks to states taking jurisdiction over

---

139. Japan Ministry of Education, Culture, Sports, Science and Technology, *Survey on the use of mobile phones by children* (2009).

140. Japan, Act on Development of an Environment that Provides Safe and Secure Internet Use for Young People, art. 17.

141. KDDI CSR Report, *Creating a Safe and Secure Information and Communication Environment for Each Child* (2011).

142. Council of Europe, Convention on the Protection of Children against Sexual Exploitation and Sexual Abuse, CETS No. 201, art. 25 (2007).

relevant offenses that are committed in the state's territory, on a ship that flies its flag, on an aircraft registered under the state's laws, or by one of its nationals or a habitual resident of the state. This would make a state responsible for prosecuting not only acts that happen on its territory but those by people who reside there but commit offenses in another country. In addition, states are supposed to obtain jurisdiction where their nationals or residents are the victims of one of these offenses. When more than one state claims jurisdiction, the states shall "consult with a view to determining the most appropriate jurisdiction for prosecution."

The Optional Protocol, discussed above, has similar provisions regarding jurisdiction over offenses including the sale of children, child prostitution, and child pornography that occur on its territory, by its citizens and residents, or of which the victim is a citizen.[143] If a state requests extradition of a receiving state's citizens because the crime took place on its territory and the receiving state refuses to extradite its citizen, the receiving state must have jurisdiction to prosecute the offender in its own courts[144] and must take "suitable measures to submit the case to its competent authorities for the purpose of prosecution."[145] Bilateral extradition treaties between the states are not required, as the Protocol itself establishes a sufficient basis. To extradite nationals of one state who committed the crime in a second state and then moved to a third state, the Protocol requires the third state to consider extradition requests from the first state as if they happened in the first state.[146]

B. *Jurisdiction and the Internet*

The Internet in practice immediately introduces each participant to the global community. Thus a crime or civil infraction committed by a perpetrator in country A to a victim situated in country B begs

---

143. United Nations, Optional Protocol to the Convention on the Rights of the Child on the Sale of Children, Child Prostitution and Child Pornography, art. 4, UN GA res. 54/263 (XXI) (2000).

144. UNICEF, HANDBOOK ON THE OPTIONAL PROTOCOL ON THE SALE OF CHILDREN, CHILD PROSTITUTION AND CHILD PORNOGRAPHY (2009).

145. Optional Protocol to the Convention on the Rights of the Child on the Sale of Children, Child Prostitution and Child Pornography, art. 5.

146. *Id.*

the question first of where the crime or civil infraction was perpetrated—country A or country B? But more so for prosecution purposes, can country B's courts reach the defendant in country A to prosecute the crime or civil infraction? In other words, can the country B courts exercise jurisdiction over a defendant not its own national or resident for a crime or civil infraction committed in cyberspace against one of its own citizens?

Jurisdiction over entities who are not citizens is an area that has long played out in the United States. Under well-known cases such as *International Shoe*[147] (civil cases, requiring minimum contacts of the defendant with the forum state and "fair play and substantial justice") and *Strassheim*[148] (criminal cases, requiring an act done outside the state that is intended to produce and does cause detrimental effects within the state), the ability to reach foreign defendants has been set forth. Those defendants in foreign countries are treated essentially the same as those in foreign (other) U.S. states.

When the Internet is involved in the complained-of conduct in a civil context in the United States, beyond the minimum contacts test, there are two cases and standards that are typically involved, the *Calder* effects test[149] and the *Zippo* sliding-scale test.[150] The effects test looks to see whether there were effects directed at the jurisdiction, following the Supreme Court's purposeful availment standard in *Burger King*.[151] It requires that the defendant intended to target the forum state, knowing its effects would be felt there. The sliding-scale test looks at interactivity of the respective websites, whether they are active, passive, or somewhere in between. Those websites that are more passive and less commercial are less likely to be subject to personal jurisdiction of courts outside their forum states. Other countries have reached results essentially similar to the effects test.[152]

---

147. Int'l Shoe Co. v. Washington, 326 U.S. 310 (1945).

148. Strassheim v. Daily, 221 U.S. 280 (1911).

149. Calder v. Jones, 465 U.S. 783 (1984).

150. Zippo Mfg. Co. v. Zippo Dot Com, Inc., 952 F. Supp. 1119 (W.D. Pa. 1997).

151. Burger King v. Rudzewicz, 471 U.S. (1985).

152. Australia, Dow Jones & Co. Inc. v Gutnick [2002] HCA 56; France, *La Ligue Contre le Racisme et l'Antisémitisme (LICRA) and l'Union des Etudiants Juifs de France (UEJF)* v. *Yahoo Inc! and Yahoo France*, Trib. de 1re Instance, Paris (2000).

C.   *Other Approaches*

Beyond a state being able to obtain legal jurisdiction over the remote perpetrator, other approaches are possible. For example, countries can harmonize their laws so that what is an offense in one country is an offense in another, and the need to gain jurisdiction over remote defendants diminishes due to remote prosecution of remote offenders or the ability to extradite. The UN made the point that "[s]tates should ensure that their laws and practice eliminate safe havens for those who criminally misuse information technologies."[153] But due to differing cultures and values, some laws may never be harmonized (e.g., European laws on certain types of hate speech versus U.S. free speech protections), and some countries may not belong to the applicable extradition treaties or have not updated their list of extraditable crimes to include the current offenses.[154] To avoid potential safe havens for areas of prohibited conduct or nations not under international treaties, states can instead consider punishing that which they can reach, as the prohibited conduct will have at least two sides to the transaction. If the seller is outside the jurisdiction, they can punish the buyer who is inside the jurisdiction or punish the seller if the buyer is outside the jurisdiction, or they may criminalize the conduct of both parties to an Internet-based multinational cybercrime. Another option is the creation of an international court that has jurisdiction over defendants globally in matters related to significant cybercrimes.[155] The optimal solution may, of course, be an international cybercrime convention that all member states can ratify, which "should be given careful and favourable consideration."[156]

---

153. United Nations, Combating the criminal misuse of information technologies, art. 4, UN GA res. 55/63 1(a) (2000).

154. ITU, *Global Strategic Report* (2010).

155. THE EASTWEST INSTITUTE CYBERCRIME LEGAL WORKING GROUP, AN INTERNATIONAL CRIMINAL COURT OR TRIBUNAL FOR CYBERSPACE (2011).

156. United Nations, Twelfth United Nations Congress on Crime Prevention and Criminal Justice, art. 46 (2010).

Chapter 4

U.S. Laws Protecting Children and the Internet

The legal protections for children on the Internet in the United States come from a variety of sources. Besides the rights provided in the Constitution, there are state and federal laws and regulations protecting children on the Internet directly and indirectly—directly when the purpose of the law targets children and indirectly when the law deals with a topic like computer crime or data protection that impacts all Internet users. There are also a number of laws that deal with offline behavior that may have started online, as discussed in the previous chapters. Because of the number of relevant statutes at the state level, this chapter will look first to the applicable federal statutes and then at an example of the type of state laws that are available. The state and federal laws may, but do not necessarily, cover the same areas, and in certain cases the federal law will preempt certain aspects of the state law. This chapter groups the statutes into two broad areas: general cybercrime and data protection statutes that impact all users online and those laws and cyberstatutues that are specific to the protection of children. Many general laws that impact organizations rather than children are not covered or are covered only briefly here, but are described in detail in another book from the author.[1]

---

1. THOMAS J. SHAW, ESQ., INFORMATION SECURITY AND PRIVACY – A PRACTICAL GUIDE FOR GLOBAL EXECUTIVES, LAWYERS AND TECHNOLOGISTS (2011) [hereafter *Information Security and Privacy*].

While this chapter looks only at statutes, the starting point for certain protections is judicial interpretations of the U.S. Constitution. In two such examples, the First Amendment rights to freedom of expression have been tested for both obscenity and child pornography. Two well-known cases, *Miller v. California*[2] (which addressed whether obscenity is protected under the First Amendment) and *New York v. Ferber*[3] (which addressed whether child pornography is protected under the First Amendment), clarified the legal protections against those who are involved in creating, distributing, or possessing child sexual abuse images. Additional cases will be used in this chapter as applicable to further describe statutes passed to protect children.

POINTS FOR PARENTS

o   U.S. state and federal laws address cybercrimes against computers and people.

o   U.S. state and federal laws regulate consumer privacy protections offline and online.

o   Child-specific U.S. laws address the protections of children both online and offline.

o   Legal protections for children online depend partly on the locations of those involved.

4.1   General Cybercrime and Data Protection Statutes— Federal

This category of U.S. federal statutes protect various privacy and property rights and either directly or indirectly are connected to conduct on the Internet. Some were passed before the Internet came into widespread use, and so have had to be amended and/or reinterpreted by the courts to be able to fit the advancing state of technology. Some punish violations with criminal liability, others with civil liability, and some with both. Due to the general nature of the statutes, their age, and the rapidly changing nature of technology, there have been quite a number of court cases interpreting different aspects of the statutes, including addressing new types of technology enhancements (of which only a few will be mentioned to provide

---

2. 413 U.S. 15 (1973).
3. 458 U.S. 747 (1982).

illustrations). Those statutes that focus on privacy protection apply equally to Internet-stored or -transmitted information and to offline data. The provisions that are not related to protections potentially available to children will generally not be discussed.

One further clarification is the term "cybercrime." Although it could be understood as any computer-based offense involving a network, perhaps it is easiest to utilize the four categories from the European Convention on Cybercrime[4] (discussed in Chapter 5), which are:

- Offences against the confidentiality, integrity and availability of computer data and systems;
- Computer-related offences;
- Content-related offences; and
- Offences related to infringements of copyright and related rights

A.   Computer Fraud and Abuse Act (CFAA)[5]

The CFAA is a statute that protects against unauthorized access to computers. The statute is violated if a person accesses a protected computer (one used by the U.S. government, a financial institution, or in interstate or foreign commerce or communication) without authorization or in excess of his or her authorized access and obtains information, or knowingly does so with the intent to defraud and obtain anything of value (unless the only thing obtained is use of the computer for less than the threshold amount), or with intent to extort or to traffic in passwords, or intentionally causes damage to a computer (including the transmission of malware), with a threshold for civil suits of U.S. $5,000 in damages in one year (or physical injury, impairment of medical equipment, threats to public health or safety, or damage affecting 10 more computers in one year).

The issue of the types of damages that can be included to meet the $5,000 damage threshold has been repeatedly litigated, with at least the following potentially included as recoverable: "damages, defined as 'any impairment to the integrity or availability of

---

4. Council of Europe Convention on Cybercrime (CETS No. 185).
5. Pub. L. 99-474 (1998).

data, a program, a system, or information' or loss of 'any reasonable cost to any victim, including the cost of responding to an offense, conducting a damage assessment, and restoring the data, program, system, or information to its condition prior to the offense, and any revenue lost, cost incurred, or other consequential damages incurred because of interruption of service."[6] The CFAA is also used not only against hackers from the outside but also against insiders who steal electronic information, such as departing employees who exceed their computer system authorization when acting contrary to well-known organizational policies.[7] It is also commonly asserted in Internet tracking cases, such as the flash cookies lawsuits.[8] It was also used to convict a woman involved with the cyberbullying through a social networking site of a child who later committed suicide.[9]

B.   Controlling the Assault on Non-Solicited Pornography and Marketing (CAN-SPAM)[10]

This statute targets bulk unsolicited commercial emails, so-called junk mail, including that which is "vulgar or pornographic in nature." This statute prohibits, in interstate or foreign commerce, the unauthorized use of a protected computer to send multiple commercial emails relaying such messages with the intent to deceive as to their origin, or materially falsifying email header information or subject lines, or falsely registering email user IDs or IP addresses before sending such emails. Such senders must use a valid return email address where the recipient can opt out of receiving such

---

6. Bose et al, v. InterClick, Inc., et al., Case No. 10-cv-9183 (S.D.N.Y. 2011); see Thomas Shaw, *2011 (2H) Information Law Updates – Cases, Statutes and Standards*, INFORMATION SECURITY AND PRIVACY NEWS (newsltr. of the ABA Sec. Science & Technology Law), Vol. 3 Issue 1 (Winter 2012).

7. United States v. Nosal, 2011 WL 1585600 (9th Cir. Apr. 28, 2011); see Thomas Shaw, *2011 (1H) Information Law Updates – Cases, Statutes and Standards*, INFORMATION SECURITY AND PRIVACY NEWS (newsltr. of the ABA Sec. Science & Technology Law), Vol. 2 Issue 4 (Autumn 2011).

8. *See, e.g.*, Aguirre v. Clearspring Technologies, Inc., et al., Case No. 2:10-cv-05948 (C.D. Cal. 2010).

9. United States v. Lori Drew, Case No. 2:08-cr-00582 (C.D. Cal. 2008). The initial conviction under the CFAA was eventually overturned.

10. Pub. L. 108-187 (2003).

future emails, which the sender must then honor. Recipient email addresses cannot be sold or transferred after the opt-out request. Such messages need to use appropriate wording to identify themselves, a "clear and conspicuous identification that the message is an advertisement or solicitation." Sexually oriented materials must have an appropriate warning label in the subject line of the email (e.g., "Sexually Explicit").

C.   Digital Millennium Copyright Act (DMCA)[11]

This statute's primary purpose is to protect the copyrights of digital technologies. It prohibits circumventing or tampering with the technological controls used to protect the digital rights of copyrighted works from unauthorized use. For children, the primary provision is an exception that permits a court to exempt programs that circumvent controls that have "the sole purpose to prevent the access of minors to material on the Internet." While such a program could be exempt from the DMCA prohibitions, if used on the same control that was performing other, more valid purposes, it would no longer be exempt from the DMCA.

D.   Family Educational Rights and Privacy Act (FERPA)[12]

This statute protects the privacy of student education records for any school that receives funds from the federal government. It grants three types of rights: to inspect the student's education records, to challenge the content therein, and to consent in writing to the disclosure of these records (with limited exceptions for school officials, financial aid, law enforcement, health and safety emergencies, etc.). These rights are granted to the parent until a child attains 18 years of age or is attending post-secondary education. The holder of the rights needs to be informed by the school of these rights. The parent or child is to be given an opportunity to correct or delete any "inaccurate, misleading, or otherwise inappropriate data contained therein" and to also insert into the records a written explanation to the parents regarding the contents.

---

11. Pub. L. 105-304 (1998).
12. Pub. L. 93-380 (1974).

Also, if any of this type of information (the student's name, address, telephone listing, date and place of birth, major field of study, participation in officially recognized activities and sports, weight and height of members of athletic teams, dates of attendance, degrees and awards received, and the most recent previous educational agency or institution attended by the student) is to be released by the school in a public directory, the parents or child should be given advance notice of the categories that will be used and given a reasonable period of time to opt out. Schools also need to maintain a record of those who have requested or obtained access to the student's educational records and the legitimate interest they have in doing so. Recent revisions to the FERPA regulations have gone into effect to further protect the privacy of student's personally identifiable information.[13]

E.   *HIPAA*[14]*/HITECH*[15]

The purpose of these two related statutes is to protect the personal health information of patients, including that of children and their parents. Under the Privacy Rule, covered health-care entities and their business associates are required to safeguard confidentiality, integrity, and accessibility of patients' protected health information (PHI), to give patients notice of their privacy practices, have procedures for allowing patient access to and update of their PHI, account for access to PHI, and get approval for disclosures thereof, and then release only the minimum amount necessary. The privacy of the PHI of children is the same as that of parents, with the added provision that parents generally can see the PHI of their children, except when contrary to state law or professional standards, in cases of abuse or neglect, or when a child becomes emancipated. The Security Rule requires appropriate risk assessments and security programs to address threats to the PHI in electronic form, including any that is outsourced. There is also a requirement for breach notification in case of a data breach.

---

13. Dept. of Ed., *Family Educational Rights and Privacy*, 76 Fed. Reg. 232, 75604 (Dec. 2, 2011).
   14. Pub. L. 104-191 (1996).
   15. Pub. L. 111-5 (2009).

F.   *Gramm-Leach-Bliley Act (GLBA)*[16]

The purpose of this statute is to require financial institutions to protect the personal information of consumers, including that of children and their parents. To do so, under the Privacy Rule, financial institutions must provide notices to their customers describing their privacy practices, including how information is collected, used, protected, and disclosed. They must also allow the customers the opportunity to opt out of sharing information with the financial institution's affiliates. Under the Safeguards Rule, the financial institutions are required to have a written information security and risk management program and appropriate safeguards that protect the confidentiality and security of their customers' non-public information. There is also a requirement for notification in case of a data breach.

G.   *FCRA*[17]*/FACTA*[18]

The purpose of these statutes is to protect the financial credit information of consumers, including that of (older) children and their parents. Credit-reporting agencies are required to implement "reasonable procedures" to safeguard the "confidentiality, accuracy, relevancy and proper utilization" in the collection, use, and disclosure of consumer credit, personnel, and insurance information that will be used to determine a consumer's eligibility for credit, employment, or insurance. Consumers need to be able to review and dispute the accuracy of information in their credit history file and have inaccurate information corrected. Consumer-reporting agencies need to look for "red flags" that indicate signs of identity theft (e.g., address changes) and take appropriate steps (e.g., fraud alerts) to prevent such theft when notified by consumers, and block any credit information resulting from identity theft.

---

16. Pub. L. 106-102 (1999).
17. Pub. L. 91-508 (1970).
18. Pub. L. 108-159 (2003).

H.   Identity Theft and Deterrence Act[19]

This statute is violated when a person "knowingly transfers or uses, without lawful authority, a means of identification of another person with the intent to commit, or to aid or abet, any unlawful activity" and this activity gains at least $1,000 during one year. It prohibits the use in interstate or foreign commerce or through the postal mail of the production, transfer, possession, or use of a false identification document or trafficking in false or actual authentication features for use in false identification documents. The statute is violated when the identity information is acquired.

I.   Federal Trade Commission (FTC) Act[20]

The FTC Act under section 5 provides the FTC the ability to pursue unfair or deceptive acts or practices in interstate or foreign commerce. Unfair acts are those that either cause or are likely to cause substantial injury to consumers that they cannot reasonably avoid, and are not outweighed by countervailing benefits. Deceptive acts are those material representations, omissions, or practices that either mislead or are likely to mislead consumers using an interpretation considered reasonable under the circumstances. The enforcement actions of the FTC are referred throughout this and preceding chapters, including actions under COPPA.

J.   Electronic Communications Privacy Act (ECPA)[21]

The ECPA protects the communications and storage of data on networks. A very complex statute that is made up of three distinct acts, including the Wiretap Act,[22] which generally protects messages as they transit through communication networks, and the Stored Communications Act,[23] which generally protects the messages when they are in storage. Passed in 1986 before many of the modern uses of communications technology were in widespread use, it has been

---

19. Pub. L. 105-318 (1998).
20. Pub. L. 63-203 (1914).
21. Pub. L. 99-508 (1986).
22. 18 U.S.C. § 2510 *et seq.*
23. 18 U.S.C. § 2701 *et seq.*

repeatedly interpreted to deal with the realities of technological improvements. The various U.S. appellate courts have interpreted its provisions differently.[24] Although widely considered to be outdated, it does provide legal privacy protections for the data in messages sent over networks, transiting through electronic communications service (ECS) providers and stored with remote-computing storage (RCS) providers.

K.   *Social Security Number Protection Act*[25]

This statute is a very short one, prohibiting any federal, state, or local government agency from displaying a Social Security account number of an individual on any check issued by any government agency. Previously, the Privacy Act[26] had prohibited any federal, state, or local government agency from denying an individual "any right, benefit, or privilege provided by law because of such individual's refusal to disclose his social security account number" and mandated that a government agency requesting a Social Security number had to tell the person if the request was mandatory or voluntary and the uses that would be made of it. Amendments to the Social Security Act prohibit government agencies from disclosing SSNs under subsequent statutes.[27]

L.   *Economic Espionage Act*[28]

This statute was targeted at the theft of commercial trade secrets for foreign governments. But it is also a criminal offense under this statute for a person who knowingly and without authorization "copies, duplicates, sketches, draws, photographs, downloads, uploads, alters, destroys, photocopies, replicates, transmits, delivers, sends, mails, communicates, or conveys a trade secret." This can be applied to any theft of computer data qualifying as a trade secret.

---

24. *See Information Security and Privacy,* Ch. 3.5.B
25. Pub. L. 111-318 (2010).
26. Pub. L. 93 -579 (1974).
27. Pub. L. 101-508 (1990).
28. Pub. L. 104-294 (1996).

M.   Wire Fraud Statute[29]

This law deals with fraud committed over the Internet (as well as by wire, radio, or television). It criminalizes the creation of a scheme to defraud or obtain money using false pretenses and then transmitting in interstate or foreign commerce using one of those media "any writings, signs, signals, pictures, or sounds" intending to execute that scheme. There are added penalties for doing so if related to a declared disaster or emergency or if affecting a financial institution.

4.2   General Cybercrime and Data Protection Statutes— States

Most U.S. states have some combination of constitutional provisions, statutes, and common law addressing a general right to privacy, such as common-law torts for invasion of privacy (the right to be left alone), being cast in a false light, the appropriation of a famous person's name or likeness, and the public disclosure of private true facts.[30] Beyond personal privacy, states have laws protecting information that is stored, used, or transmitted in digital format and the myriad cybersecurity issues that burgeoning uses of technology require. For example, the following is a list of these types of state consumer data protection and cyberstatutes:

- Hacking and unauthorized access
- Malware
- Junk mail
- Phishing
- Social Security numbers
- Spyware
- Identity theft
- Online tracking
- Online privacy
- Data privacy
- Consumer credit

---

29. Pub. L. 82-554 (1952).
30. *See, e.g.,* CAL. CONST. art 1; CAL. CIV. CODE 3344; and Lugosi v. Universal Pictures, 603 P.2d 425, 428 (Cal. 1979).

- Secure data disposal
- Data breach notification
- Encryption
- Information security

To illustrate these types of statutes, the laws in California, a state often at the forefront of cybercrime and privacy legislation and litigation, will be used (and other states when they provide a better or more comprehensive example). These laws are not meant to be exhaustive or complete, as there are additional applicable provisions in both civil and criminal state law, but are used here merely to illustrate the breadth both of the Internet-related risks that U.S. states are addressing in their statutes and the different types of protections that are available.

A. *Hacking and Unauthorized Access*

Similar to the CFAA, the vast majority of states have passed laws to protect computers from cybercriminals and hackers. To protect computers, computer systems, and the data thereon, and to address the "proliferation of computer crime," this law was added to California's criminal code.[31] All of the following acts that are done knowingly and without permission are prohibited:

- Alters, damages, deletes, destroys, or otherwise uses any data, computer, computer system, or computer network in order to either (A) devise or execute any scheme or artifice to defraud, deceive, or extort, or (B) wrongfully control or obtain money, property, or data
- Takes, copies, or makes use of any data from a computer, computer system, or computer network, or takes or copies any supporting documentation, whether existing or residing internal or external to a computer, computer system, or computer network
- Uses or causes to be used computer services
- Adds, alters, damages, deletes, or destroys any data, computer software, or computer programs which reside or exist

---

31. CAL. PENAL CODE § 502.

internal or external to a computer, computer system, or computer network

- Disrupts or causes the disruption of computer services or denies or causes the denial of computer services to an authorized user of a computer, computer system, or computer network
- Provides or assists in providing a means of accessing a computer, computer system, or computer network in violation of this section
- Accesses or causes to be accessed any computer, computer system, or computer network
- Uses the Internet domain name of another individual, corporation, or entity in connection with the sending of one or more electronic mail messages, and thereby damages or causes damage to a computer, computer system, or computer network

B.   *Malware*

Sending a computer virus, Trojan, worm, or other malware has been made illegal in more than half the states. Under California's criminal code, adding malware to a system is prohibited: "Knowingly introduces any computer contaminant into any computer, computer system, or computer network."[32] Under Colorado law, it is a crime to transmit "a computer program, software, information, code, data, or command with the intent to cause damage to or cause the interruption or impairment of the proper functioning of any computer, computer network, or computer system.""[33]

C.   *Junk Mail*

The large majority of states have laws restricting the sending of unsolicited commercial email messages. California prohibits[34] the sending of these messages from California or to a California email address and to collect email addresses from the Internet or by automated means. Such messages cannot be sent using unauthorized

---

32. Cal. Penal Code § 502(c)(8).
33. Colo. Rev. Stat. § 18-5.5-102(f).
34. Cal. Bus & Prof. Code § 17529.

domain names, with fraudulent header information, or with misleading subject lines or to mobile phones. The federal CAN-SPAM
statute described above preempts state laws that regulate commercial email except for prohibitions on "falsity or deception in any
portion of a commercial electronic mail message or information
attached thereto."[35]

D. Phishing

Anti-phishing laws prohibit the various methods of using email or
similar techniques to get users to provide confidential information.
Under the Anti-Phishing Act of 2005,[36] California has made it illegal to use a web page, an email message, or other Internet technique to solicit another person to provide identifying information
(e.g., SSN, driver's license number, bank account number, credit/
debit card number, PIN, electronic signature, biometric data, account password) by falsely pretending to be a (legitimate) business.

E. Social Security Numbers

With the status of a unique, unchanging identifier, Social Security
Numbers (SSNs) are a prime target for identity thieves, and states
are passing laws to curb the disclosure of SSNs. Under California
law, SSNs may not be publicly displayed, including use over an
unsecure Internet connection.[37] There are also a number of California provisions that require the truncating of the SSN to the final
four digits when used in court records, local government records,
higher education, and on pay stubs. In Colorado, in addition to
similar provisions as in California, merchants cannot record an SSN
to verify a check (although they may ask to see it),[38] and government agencies cannot request an SSN over the Internet unless required by federal law or essential.[39]

---

35. CAN-SPAM Act § 8(b)(1).
36. CAL. BUS & PROF. CODE § 22948.
37. CAL. CIV. CODE § 1798.85.
38. COLO. REV. STAT. § 4-3-506.
39. COLO. REV. STAT. § 24-72.3-102.

F.   *Spyware*

Spyware allows the capture of keyboard inputs by software secretly installed on a computer. Under the Consumer Protection Against Computer Spyware Act in California,[40] it is illegal for an unauthorized user to copy software onto the computer of a consumer using "intentionally deceptive means":

- Modifies the home page, the default ISP or the Internet browser bookmarks.
- Collects personally identifiable information by keystroke logging, on websites visited, extracts data from an authorized user's hard drive.
- Prevents reasonable efforts to block the installation of or to disable software, by causing software that was properly removed or disabled to automatically reinstall or reactivate.
- Misrepresents that software will be uninstalled or disabled, with knowledge that the software will not be so uninstalled or disabled.
- Removes, disables, or renders inoperative security, antispyware, or antivirus software installed on the computer.

G.   *Identity Theft*

All states have some form of identity theft laws, including measures to recover from the theft. Under California's criminal code,[41] the false impersonation of another to convert money or property is prohibited. Also, it is unlawful for a person who obtains the personal identifying information of another to use that information without consent for any unlawful purpose (e.g. obtaining credit, goods, services, real property, or medical information) or who, with the intent to defraud, acquires, transfers, or retains possession of the personal identifying information of another.

Personal identifying information is defined quite broadly to include: any name, address, telephone number, health insurance number, taxpayer identification number, school identification number, state or federal driver's license or identification number, So-

---

40. CAL. BUS & PROF. CODE § 22947.
41. CAL. PENAL CODE § 530.

cial Security number, place of employment, employee identification number, professional or occupational number, mother's maiden name, demand deposit account number, savings account number, checking account number, PIN (personal identification number) or password, alien registration number, government passport number, date of birth, unique biometric data (including fingerprint, facial scan identifiers, voiceprint, retina or iris image, or other unique physical representation), unique electronic data (including information identification number assigned to the person, address or routing code, telecommunication identifying information or access device), information contained in a birth or death certificate, or credit card number of an individual person, or an equivalent form of identification.

H. Online Tracking

Although there does not seem to be any state that currently has an enacted statute covering online tracking, California has introduced such legislation in 2011. Given that this may not pass and will certainly have revisions, it is useful to understand the intended scope of this bill.[42] It states that it will apply to a person or entity doing business in California that collects, uses, or stores online data containing covered information from a consumer in California, who must be provided with a method to opt out of the collection, use, and storage of such information. The bill would require that a covered entity disclose to a consumer certain information relating to its information collection, use, and storage practices and prohibit a covered entity from selling, sharing, or transferring a consumer's covered information.

The term "covered information" includes, if transmitted online, the following:

- The online activity of the individual, including, but not limited to, the Internet websites and content from Internet websites accessed; the date and hour of online access; the computer and geolocation from which online information was accessed; and the means by which online information

---

42. Cal. S.B. 761 (2011).

was accessed, such as, but not limited to, a device, browser, or application.

• Any unique or substantially unique identifier, such as a customer number or Internet Protocol (IP) address.

• Personal information including, but not limited to, a name; a postal address or other location; an e-mail address or other user name; a telephone or fax number; a government-issued identification number, such as a tax identification number, a passport number, or a driver's license number; or a financial account number or credit card or debit card number; or any required security code, access code, or password that is necessary to permit access to an individual's financial account.

I.   Online Privacy

Some states require that website operators have privacy policies. In California, under the Online Privacy Protection Act,[43] a commercial website or online service provider (ISP) who collects personally identifiable information from California residents is required to implement, post on its site, and comply with a privacy policy, including data collection and sharing practices. A few states require ISPs to keep personal information of customers confidential. Minnesota prohibits ISPs from disclosing a Minnesota consumer's personally identifiable information absent consent or court order and requires that they maintain the privacy and security of this information.[44]

J.   Data Privacy

In addition to the types of privacy laws discussed so far, states also have other laws that deal with data privacy based both on the data source and on the various devices used. Under California law, driver's license information must remain confidential.[45] California law also requires that a medical patient's health information must

---

43. CAL. BUS. & PROF. CODE § 22575.
44. MINN. STAT. § 325M.
45. CAL. VEH. CODE § 1808.

remain confidential,[46] personally identifiable information held by financial institutions must not be sold, privacy notices are required, and there are opt-out rules on sharing of this information.[47]

Also, it is prohibited to skim radio frequency identification (RFID) information (driver's licenses; identification cards; health insurance or benefit cards; government-supported aid program benefit cards; licenses, certificates, registration, or other means to engage in a business or profession; or public library cards, or to steal related encryption keys.[48]

K.   Consumer Credit

To protect against identity theft, almost all states have passed consumer credit laws of several kinds. One type deals with regulating the information contained in consumer credit reports. Another type allows users to freeze the use of their credit when they believe it has been compromised. Under California law, consumer credit-reporting agencies must allow consumers to inspect their credit information, including request for it,[49] and must be allowed to put security alerts and security freezes on consumer credit reports, depending on the severity of the situation.[50]

L.   Secure Data Disposal

The illicit use of personal information that was already discarded by individuals and businesses has led many states to create statutes to require secure disposal of personal information in all its forms. In California, businesses are required to take "reasonable steps" to securely dispose of customer records containing personal information within their custody or control when the records are no longer needed.[51] Personal information here includes: name, signature, Social Security number, physical characteristics or description, address, telephone number, passport number, driver's

---

46. CAL. CIV. CODE § 56.
47. CAL. FIN. CODE § 4050.
48. CAL. CIV. CODE § 1798.79.
49. Cal. Civ. Code § 1785.10.
50. CAL. CIV. CODE § 1785.11.
51. CAL. CIV. CODE § 1798.80.

license or state ID card number, insurance policy number, education, employment, employment history, bank account number, credit card number, debit card number, or any other financial information, medical information, or health insurance information.

Because it has come to light that the digital storage now used in copy machines retains the copied images after the machine is sold or returned, states have started passing laws to require secure disposal of this equipment. Nevada's law[52] now requires, before a business or a data collector relinquishes control of such a copier or similar multifunction devices (including fax machines, printers, copiers, and scanners), and which uses a data storage device to store, reproduce, transmit, or receive data or images that may contain personal information, that it must destroy or encrypt any personal information contained therein using recognized standard "physical or technological" procedures.

M.   Data Breach Notification

Almost every state has adopted some form of data breach notification law, although there are significant differences in defining exactly what is a breach, when notification is required, and to whom notification is required. Under California law, government agencies[53] and businesses[54] are required to disclose a breach ("unauthorized acquisition of computerized data that compromises the security, confidentiality, or integrity") of unencrypted personal information using a pre-described set of information. Personal information is considered to be: Social Security number; driver's license number; financial account number numbers or credit or debit card numbers, in combination with any required security code, access code, or password that would permit access to an individual's financial account; medical information; or health insurance information.

N.   Encryption

To further increase the confidentiality of personal information, a few states have begun to mandate the use of encryption in certain

---

52. Nev. Rev. Stat. § 603A.215.
53. Cal. Civ. Code § 1798.29.
54. Cal. Civ. Code § 1798.82.

communications. In Nevada, the law requires that encryption be used when personal information is transmitted beyond a secure network or when its storage devices containing personal information are moved.[55]

O.   *Information Security*

To address the entire area of protection of personal information, states have begun to require either general or specific information security provisions in their laws. In California,[56] businesses (except financial institutions and health-care providers regulated elsewhere) are required to implement and maintain reasonable security procedures and practices appropriate to the nature of the information and to protect the personal information from unauthorized access, destruction, use, modification, or disclosure and require any applicable third parties to do the same. Massachusetts requires specific security provisions, such as authentication and access controls, up-to-date patching, use of network firewalls, personal information encryption for network transmissions or storage on portable devices, and malware protection.[57]

4.3   Child-Specific Laws and Cyberstatutes—Federal

The following laws are the principal federal statutes that address many of those risks that were described in Chapter 2. There are other federal statutes not covered here that address some of the offline behaviors of criminals, deal with the offline abuse of children, and provide assistance of various kinds to young victims. For example, there have been quite a few federal statutes prohibiting and then refining the prohibition of child pornography.[58] Discussed in this section are those statutes that deal directly with protecting

---

55. Nev. Rev. Stat. § 603A.
56. CAL. CIV. CODE § 1798.81.5.
57. Mass. 201 CMR 17.00.
58. *See, e.g.*, Protecting of Children Against Sexual Exploitation Act (1977); Child Protection Act (1984); Child Sexual Abuse and Pornography Act (1986); Child Protection and Obscenity Enforcement Act (1988); and Child Protection Restoration and Penalties Enhancement Act (1990).

children online and indirectly by addressing the certain types of conduct that influence online behaviors.

A. PROTECT Our Children Act[59]

The purpose of this act is to develop a national strategy for child exploitation prevention and interdiction (discussed in Chapter 3) and to help law enforcement investigate and prosecute child predators by assisting the Internet Crimes Against Children Task Force (also discussed in Chapter 3) and funding forensic labs. This includes banning any live video of sexual abuse images or using an altered version of an image of an identifiable child. It also requires any electronic communications service (ECS) or remote computing service (RCS) providers (see ECPA above) to report immediately to the CyberTipline when they become aware of any child pornography images and the details of when they were uploaded, transmitted, or received, but they are not required to monitor users or content. This information may be forwarded to foreign law enforcement as applicable depending on the source.

B. PROTECT Act[60]

The purpose of this statute includes preventing child abduction and sexual exploitation. Among the measures are stronger criminal penalties for sexual abuse and murder resulting from sexual abuse, kidnapping, and child sex tourism (both foreign and interstate and including attempt and conspiracy to do so). Attempt liability is also added for international parental kidnapping (see below for original statute). Investigations and prosecutions are enhanced by allowing interception of communications in child sexual offense investigations, removing the statute of limitation on these crimes, not allowing pretrial release of a suspect, and requiring the reporting of missing children up through the age of 21. The act also sets up a national coordinator of the AMBER Alert system and the CyberTipline (discussed in Chapter 3).

---

59. Providing Resources, Officers & Technology to Eradicate Cyber Threats to Our Children Act, Pub. L. 110–401 (2008).

60. Prosecutorial Remedies and Other Tools to End the Exploitation of Children Today Act, Pub. L. 108–21 (2003).

The act then describes how the Supreme Court's decision in *Ashcroft v. Free Speech Coalition*[61] has had a negative impact on prosecutions of child sexual abuse image producers by requiring proof that a real child is depicted in the abuse images (i.e., rather than a computer-generated depiction). It proposes a prohibition on obscene virtual child pornography depicting children engaged in the same conduct as is banned when abuse of real children is involved. This clause has withstood legal challenge, because obscene material in any form is prohibited.[62] It also prohibits extraterritorially all of the same acts to produce child sexual abuse images for distribution in the United States. The act also bans Internet domain names that are misleading and cause minors to view harmful material (Truth in Domain Names Act).

C.   *Adam Walsh Child Protection and Safety Act*[63]

The purpose of this statute is to "protect children from sexual exploitation and violent crime, to prevent child abuse and child pornography, and to promote Internet safety" through a series of acts combined to form this legislation. A significant part of this statute is the Sex Offender Registration and Notification Act (Adam Walsh was a six-year-old who was abducted and murdered in 1981) establishing a national Internet-viewable registration system (including DNA evidence) and expanding the definition of crimes for a child predator. Enhancing federal criminal law to further protect children from sexual and other violent attacks includes banning Internet sales of date-rape drugs and increasing many of the child-crime-related punishments, including minimum terms. There is also a provision for civil commitments for prisoners in federal custody after their sentences are completed if they are deemed likely to be unable to refrain from child molestation after release. This provision was upheld by the Supreme Court.[64]

To attack those who are using the Internet and the ease of production and processing available through new technologies to

---

61. 535 U.S. 234 (2002).
62. United States v. Whorley, Case No. 06-4288 (4th Cir. 2008).
63. Pub. L. 109–248 (2006).
64. United States v. Comstock, 130 S. Ct. 1949 (2010).

greatly increase the market for child pornography, and calling on federal government powers to regulate interstate and foreign commerce, additional provisions have been added to address "child exploitation enterprises." To protect children from becoming repeated victims of child pornography, producers are now required to keep records of every performer and present these at appropriate judicial forums, asset forfeiture is provided for in child exploitation and obscenity cases, and the production of obscene materials, as well as selling or transferring, is prohibited.

The Internet Safety Act defines "child exploitation enterprises" as when a person commits at least three separate felony incidents involving child exploitation offenses involving more than a single victim and committed those in concert with at least three other persons. The sentences involved are a minimum of 20 years. Also, the use of misleading words or imbedded images in the viewable or nonviewable content of a website to deceive a minor into viewing harmful material (or anyone into viewing obscene material) is prohibited.

D.   *Children's Internet Protection Act (CIPA)*[65]

The intent of this statute is to protect children from offensive content over the Internet on school and library computers. Schools or libraries that are recipients of funding under the E-Rate plan for Internet connections must be "monitoring the online activities of minors" and have an Internet safety policy that, for computers accessed by minors, includes technology protection measures that block or filter Internet access to visual images that are obscene,[66] child pornography,[67] or harmful to minors.[68] But to remain constitutional, the statute must require that the filters be lifted for any adult user upon request.[69] Also, the safety policy must address:

---

65. Pub. L. 106-554 (2000).
66. Defined at 18 U.S.C. § 1460.
67. Defined at 18 U.S.C. § 2556.
68. Defined at CIPA § 1703.
69. United States v. American Library Ass'n, Inc. et al., 539 U.S. 1194 (2003).

- access by minors to inappropriate matter on the Internet;[70]
- the safety and security of minors when using electronic mail, chat rooms, and other forms of direct electronic communications;
- unauthorized access, including so-called "hacking," and other unlawful activities by minors online;
- unauthorized disclosure, use, and dissemination of personal information regarding minors; and
- measures restricting minors' access to materials harmful to them.

The statute was revised by the Protecting Children in the 21st Century Act,[71] which added provisions that schools receiving this funding are required to educate minors on "appropriate online behavior, including interacting with other individuals on social networking websites and in chat rooms and cyberbullying awareness and response."

E. *Child Pornography Prevention Act (CPPA)*[72]

Based on significant findings by Congress that new computer technologies allowed child sexual abuse images that "appear to be children engaging in sexually explicit conduct that are virtually indistinguishable to the unsuspecting viewer from un-retouched photographic images of actual children engaging in sexually explicit conduct," this statute was intended to ban both real and computer-generated images that "appear[s] to be" or "convey[s] the impression" of children involved in sexual activity. The Supreme Court ruled that this expanded definition of child pornography was overbroad.[73] The Court stated that the statute used neither the *Miller* obscenity standard nor the *Ferber* child pornography standard (founded on the state's compelling interest to protect children). Being neither obscene nor the result of child sexual abuse, the speech covering virtual images was within the First Amendment protec-

---

70. Defined by Neighborhood Children's Internet Protection Act § 1732(2).
71. Pub. L. 110-385 (2008).
72. Pub. L. 104-208 (1996).
73. Ashcroft v. Free Speech Coalition, 535 U.S. 234 (2002).

tions and so the "appears to be" and "conveys the impression" clauses were unconstitutional.

F.   *Child Online Protection Act (COPA)*[74]

Congress intended that this statute provide the mechanism to protect children from materials on the Internet that "frustrate parental supervision or control." To do so, making materials harmful to minors available on the World Wide Web as part of a commercial activity is prohibited. Affirmative defenses include good-faith efforts to restrict access by minors. This was a second attempt by Congress after the Communications Decency Act[75] had its indecency provisions struck down as infringing on the First Amendment (also holding that the Internet should be regulated like the press instead of the broadcast industry, but leaving alone the § 230 ISP protections for customer-initiated content).[76] But this statute itself was challenged in court and, through a long procedural history, was repeatedly ruled to be in violation of the First Amendment, given that less restrictive means such as blocking or filtering software were available (and the act did not cover overseas materials or non-web (e.g., email) sources).[77]

G.   *Children's Online Privacy Protection Act (COPPA)*[78]

COPPA addresses the protection of the personal information collected from children. This includes information that is collected from children through requests, where children make such information publicly available (e.g., through chat rooms) or by tracking tools (e.g., cookies). There are a number of requirements for the operators of commercial websites and online services directed at children younger than 13 years of age (children 13 and over are covered under the unfair or deceptive practice restrictions of the FTC Act) or general websites with knowledge that such personal information is collected from children, whether foreign or U.S.-based, for commerce inside the United States. These website operators must:[79]

---

74. Pub. L. 105-277 (1998).
75. Pub. L. 104-104 (1996).
76. Reno v. ACLU et al., 521 U.S. 844 (1997).
77. Ashcroft v. ACLU et al., 542 U.S. 656 (2004).
78. Pub. L. 105-277 (1998).
79. Children's Online Privacy Protection Rule, 16 C.F.R. § 312.

- Post on the website home page, and each page where information is collected, a notice of what information is collected, how it is used, and any disclosure practices.
- Disclose to a parent the types of information collected from their child after using reasonable methods to ensure they are dealing with the child's parent, and allow the parent to stop use of collected data or collection of future data about the child.
- Not allow participation in online activities to require disclosure of more personal information from the child than is reasonably necessary.
- Implement reasonable procedures for protecting the "confidentiality, security, and integrity" of the child's personal information.
- Before collecting personal information from a child, make reasonable efforts to both notify the child's parent of the site's information practices and then receives verifiable consent from the parent.
- Base the type of verifiable consent on a sliding scale based on the proposed use (i.e., external use requires more rigorous verification than internal use).
- Offer parents the ability to let the operator collect and use the child's personal information without being required to disclose it to third parties.
- Allow exceptions for one-time requests, homework help, contests, etc.

The FTC reviews the enabling rule every five years, first in 2005, but made no changes. In 2010 another review was initiated, from which the FTC proposed the following changes:[80]

- Change the definition of personal information to include geolocation information, posted photos, video and audio of a child, and persistent identifiers that can permit the contacting of a specific individual, such as tracking cookies used for behavioral advertising.

---

80. FTC Press Release, FTC Seeks Comment on Proposed Revisions to Children's Online Privacy Protection Rule (Sept. 15, 2011).

- New forms of parental notice and verifiable consent.
- Improved security protections, including reasonable measures taken by the operator or third-party provider, retention of information only as long as required, and secure information disposal techniques.
- Clarifies the definition of "online services" currently covered by the COPPA Rule including "mobile applications that allow children to play network-connected games, engage in social networking activities, purchase goods or services online, receive behaviorally targeted advertisements, or interact with other content or services," plus Internet-enabled gaming platforms, voice-over-Internet protocol services, and Internet-enabled location based services.[81]

The FTC over the years has brought a series of actions under COPPA based on unfair and deceptive practices under the FTC Act.[82] For example, in addition to those enforcement actions discussed in Chapter 2, the FTC reached a settlement with a company that owns popular apparel brands and had been collecting personal information on the websites, including from children under the age of 13, in order to enter sweepstakes and receive brand updates.[83] In another settlement, the personal information of over 30,000 children under the age of 13 was collected on music-related websites.[84] The personal information on almost 2 million children under the age of 13 had been collected by the defendant in an enforcement action that was settled with a blog-hosting website.[85] All of these were done without appropriate parental consent. And most recently, the FTC settled with a children's social-networking site that allowed children as young as seven to register and provide personal information with-

---

81. FTC, *Children's Online Privacy Protection Rule,* 76 Fed. Reg. 59, 804 (Sep. 27, 2011).

82. 15 U.S.C. § 45.

83. United States v. Iconix Brand Group, Inc., Case No. 09-civ-8864 (S.D.N.Y. 2009).

84. United States v. Sony BMG Music Entertainment, Case No. 08-civ-10730 (S.D.N.Y. 2008).

85. United States v. Xanga.com Inc. et al., Case No. 06-civ-6853 (S.D.N.Y. 2006).

out parental consent.[86] The defendant was charged under COPPA with failing to provide notice on the website or directly to parents and not getting verifiable consent from parents, and under the FTC Act with deceptive acts because the representations the social networking site made were contrary to its practices.

H.   *Trafficking Victims Protection Act (TVPA)*[87]

Although it does not address electronic communications directly, this statute targets many of the risks described in Chapter 2, such as sexual exploitation involving activities related to prostitution, pornography, and sex tourism, and forced labor. The traffickers of children will purchase them "from poor families and sell them into prostitution or into various types of forced or bonded labor." The findings of Congress also state that victims "are often forced through physical violence to engage in sex acts or perform slavery-like labor." Sex trafficking of persons less than 18 years of age is considered a severe form of trafficking and special provisions apply. Efforts of the governments of countries receiving financial or security assistance to combat such trafficking must be assessed if those countries are a point of origin, transit, or destination for victims of severe forms of trafficking. Those found not to be making significant efforts to come into compliance with minimum standards can lose their assistance from the United States. Severe penalties are also prescribed for those involved with child sex trafficking and for forced labor. Products mined or manufactured by forced child labor violate the Tariff Act of 1930.[88] The Human Smuggling and Trafficking Center was established by the Intelligence Reform Act and Terrorism Prevention Act.[89]

I.   *International Child Kidnapping Act*[90]

This statute provides penalties for anyone who removes or attempts to remove a child from the United States or retains a child who has

---

86. United States v. Godwin dbaSkidekids.com, Case No. 11-civ-03846 (N.D. Ga. 2011).

87. Pub. L. 106-386 (2000).

88. 19 U.S.C. § 1307.

89. Pub. L. 108-458 (2004).

90. Pub. L. 103-173 (1993).

been taken outside the United States to obstruct parental rights. Although it does not target electronic communications directly, this is one of the risks mentioned in Chapter 2. There are exceptions for those acting under a valid court order or fleeing domestic violence. This statute is not supposed to detract from the procedures available under the Hague Convention on the Civil Aspects of International Parental Child Abduction (discussed in Chapter 3). The National Conference of Commissioners on Uniform State Laws has promulgated a model law on child abductions for states to bring conformity to state laws, to "deter both predecree and postdecree domestic and international child abductions by parents, persons acting on behalf of a parent or others."[91]

J. KIDS Act[92]

This legislation required that convicted sex offenders provide their Internet identifiers to sex offender registries. Internet identifiers are defined as "electronic mail addresses and other designations used for self-identification or routing in Internet communication or posting." With a secure system established by the government, the social networking websites can compare data from the National Sex Offender Registry with the Internet identifiers of users of the social networking websites. For any matches found, the social networking site may request further information and may deny use of their social networking site to the matched sex offender.

4.4 Child-Specific Laws and Cyberstatutes—States

In addition to federal statutes dealing with the Internet risks to children mentioned in Chapter 2, most U.S. states have passed laws addressing some of these risks. Beyond criminal statutes dealing with offline behaviors, states have passed laws dealing with electronic communications and children, in addition to the cybercrime and data protection laws discussed above, that are applicable to all age groups. The National Conference of State Legislatures has published websites that address each of these categories. To illustrate the types of laws

---

91. National Conference of Commissioners on Uniform State Laws, Uniform Child Abduction Prevention Act (2006).
92. Pub. L. 110-400 (2008).

that states have passed, the laws in California, a state often at the forefront of cybercrime and privacy legislation and litigation, will be again be used (and the state of Colorado also for the filtering laws). Italics are added where an electronic communication aspect is part of a more general provision.

A. Cyberharassment[93]

Under California criminal law, it is a crime for a person who threatens to commit an action that will result in death or great bodily injury to another person with the intent that the statement, made verbally, in writing, or *by means of an electronic communication device*, is to be taken as a threat, even if there is no intent of actually carrying it out, which is so unequivocal, unconditional, immediate, and specific as to convey to the person threatened a gravity of purpose and an immediate prospect of execution of the threat, and thereby causes that person reasonably to be in sustained fear for his or her own safety or for his or her immediate family's safety.[94]

It is a crime for a person who, with intent to place another person in reasonable fear for his or her safety or the safety of the other person's immediate family, by means of an electronic communication device (e.g., telephones, cell phones, computers, Internet web pages or sites, Internet phones, hybrid cellular/Internet/wireless devices, personal digital assistants (PDAs), video recorders, fax machines, pagers), and without consent of the other person, and for the purpose of imminently causing that other person unwanted physical contact, injury, or harassment, by a third party, electronically distributes, publishes, e-mails, hyperlinks, or makes available for downloading personal identifying information, including, but not limited to, a digital image of another person, or an electronic message of a harassing nature about another person, which would be likely to incite or produce that unlawful action.[95]

It is also a crime to for a person who, with intent to annoy, telephones or makes contact *by means of an electronic communi-*

93. NATIONAL CONFERENCE OF STATE LEGISLATURES, CYBERSTALKING, CYBERHARASSMENT AND CYBERBULLYING LAWS.

94. CAL. PENAL CODE § 422.

95. CAL. PENAL CODE § 653.2.

cation device with another and addresses to or about the other person any obscene language or addresses to the other person any threat to inflict injury to the person or property of the person addressed or any member of his or her family.[96]

B. Cyberbullying[97]

Under California's education code, schools are committed to reducing bullying, including acts that are committed personally or by means of an electronic act,[98] which is defined as the transmission of a communication, including, but not limited to, a message, text, sound, or image by means of an electronic device, including, but not limited to, a telephone, wireless telephone or other wireless communication device, computer, or pager.[99] Students can be suspended for acts of act of bullying, including those committed by means of an electronic act.[100]

C. Cyberstalking[101]

Under California civil law, stalking requires that the defendant engaged in a pattern of conduct with the intent to to follow, alarm, or harass the plaintiff, causing the plaintiff to reasonably fear for his or her safety or the safety of an immediate family member, and the defendant made a credible verbal or written threat, including that communicated *by means of an electronic communication device*, or a threat implied by a pattern of conduct, or a combination of verbal, written, or electronically communicated statements and conduct, made with the apparent ability to carry out the threat and the intent to place the plaintiff in reasonable fear for his or her safety, or the safety of an immediate family member, even after a demand to cease and abate this pattern of conduct.[102]

---

96. CAL. PENAL CODE § 653m.

97. NATIONAL CONFERENCE OF STATE LEGISLATURES, CYBERSTALKING, CYBERHARASSMENT AND CYBERBULLYING LAWS.

98. CAL. ED. CODE § 32270.

99. CAL. ED. CODE § 32261.

100. CAL. ED. CODE § 48900(r).

101. NATIONAL CONFERENCE OF STATE LEGISLATURES, CYBERSTALKING, CYBERHARASSMENT AND CYBERBULLYING LAWS.

102. CAL. CIVIL CODE § 1708.7.

Under California criminal law, a defendant is guilty who willfully, maliciously, and repeatedly follows or willfully and maliciously harasses (knowing and willful course of conduct directed at a specific person that seriously alarms, annoys, torments, or terrorizes the person, and that serves no legitimate purpose) another person and makes a credible verbal or written threat, including that communicated *by means of an electronic communication device*, or a threat implied by a pattern of conduct or a combination of verbal, written, or electronically communicated statements and conduct, made with the apparent ability to carry out the threat and the intent to place that person in reasonable fear for his or her safety, or the safety of his or her immediate family.[103]

D. *Electronic Solicitation*[104]

Under California criminal law, it is a crime for an adult stranger who is at least 21 years old to knowingly contact or communicate with a minor who is under 14 years old, knowing (or reasonably should know) that the minor is under 14 years old, for the purpose of persuading and luring, or transporting, or attempting to persuade and lure, or transport, that minor away from the minor's home or from any location known by the minor's parent, legal guardian, or custodian for any purpose without the express consent of the minor's parent or legal guardian, and with the intent to avoid the consent of the minor's parent or legal guardian.[105]

It is also a crime, except when done for legitimate scientific or educational purposes, for a person who, knowing (or reasonably should know) that a person is a minor, knowingly distributes, sends, causes to be sent, exhibits, or offers to distribute or exhibit by any means, any harmful matter to a minor with the intent of arousing, appealing to, or gratifying the lust or passions or sexual desires of that person or of a minor, and with the intent or for the purpose of seducing a minor.[106] It is a crime if a person, knowing that a person is a minor, knowingly distributes, sends, causes to be sent, exhibits,

---

103. Cal. Penal Code § 646.9.

104. National Conference of State Legislatures, Electronic Solicitation or Luring of Children.

105. Cal. Penal Code § 272(b).

106. Cal. Penal Code § 288.2(a).

or offers to distribute or exhibit by electronic mail, the Internet, or a commercial online service any harmful matter to a minor with the intent of arousing, appealing to, or gratifying the lust or passions or sexual desires of that person or of a minor and with the intent, or for the purpose of, seducing a minor.[107]

E.   Internet Filtering[108]

Under California's educational code,[109] public libraries that receive state funds and provide public access to the Internet need to have a policy regarding access by minors to the Internet and make it available to members of the public at every library branch. In Colorado, the state laws address both schools and libraries, in that to receive funding, school and public libraries must adopt policies, install software on publicly accessible computers, and select Internet service providers who use filters that limit the access of minors to material that is obscene or illegal.[110] Public libraries must implement Internet safety policies for minors' access.[111] Public schools need to adopt Internet safety policies for minors that include the operation of a technology protection measure that blocks images that are obscene, child pornography, or are harmful to children for each computer operated by the district that allows for access by a minor to the Internet.[112]

F.   Internet Supply-Chain Disclosures

In California, in an effort to ensure that slavery and human trafficking, this newly effective statute[113] requires that retailers and manufacturers in the state inspect and report on their supply chains. Specifically, those types of businesses of with gross receipts in excess of $100 million are required to provide consumers sufficient information to be able to "distinguish companies on the merits of

---

107. CAL. PENAL CODE § 288.2(b).
108. NATIONAL CONFERENCE OF STATE LEGISLATURES, LAWS RELATING TO FILTERING, BLOCKING AND USAGE POLICIES IN SCHOOLS AND LIBRARIES.
109. CAL. ED. CODE § 18030.5.
110. COLO. REV. STAT. § 24-90-404.
111. COLO. REV. STAT. § 24-90-603.
112. COLO. REV. STAT. § 22-87-103-104.
113. Cal., Transparency in Supply Chains Act of 2010.

their efforts to supply products free from the taint of slavery and trafficking." A conspicuous link on the retailer or manufacturer's website to the necessary information is required, which includes:

- Engaging in (preferably third-party) verification of product supply chains to evaluate and address risks of human trafficking and slavery.
- Conducting (preferably independent, unannounced) audits of suppliers to evaluate supplier compliance with company standards for trafficking and slavery in supply chains.
- Requiring direct suppliers to certify that materials incorporated into the product comply with the laws regarding slavery and human trafficking of the country or countries in which they are doing business.
- Maintaining internal accountability standards and procedures for employees or contractors failing to meet company standards regarding slavery and trafficking.
- Providing company employees and management with direct responsibility for supply chain management training on human trafficking and slavery, particularly with respect to mitigating risks within the supply chains of products.

G. *Teacher-Student Communications*[114]

The state of Missouri in 2011 passed the first law of its kind in the country restricting electronic communications between teachers and students. This statute, named after a 13-year-old student who was forced into a sexual relationship by a teacher many years older than her, requires school districts in the state to develop policies on the use of electronic media "and other mechanisms" for communications between students and school employees (including teachers). As revised, it focuses on preventing improper communications between staff members and students. It also requires schools to train employees to recognize signs of sexual abuse in children, "signals of potentially abusive relationships between children and adults," and on mandatory reporting requirements.

---

114. Mo., Amy Hestir Student Protection Act, S.B. 54 as revised by S.B. 1, Mo. REV. STAT. § 162.609 (2011).

Chapter 5

International Laws Protecting Children and the Internet

All of the risks that were discussed in Chapter 2 are global in nature. This is almost by definition, as the Internet is an international network, so these potential problems extend to every country. The way each country addresses these risks through statutes and programs will differ, reflecting the culture, values, leadership, and history of that nation. There have been and still are many international and regional efforts to harmonize national laws to make the prosecution of cybercriminals easier to accomplish no matter where they are located. But awareness of the problem and implementation of common statutory solutions are quite different, so it becomes important to understand the differences in applicable laws around the world. Awareness of the legal protections is not only necessary to address cybercrimes but also helps parents and lawyers make decisions about the use of certain online services, such as the countries parents will allow their child's personal data to be stored in.

To get an understanding of the types of laws, the major geographic regions of the world are presented, each starting with any regional frameworks and then the major national statutes. As in

125

Chapter 4, there are two significant areas of laws to be analyzed: those that apply generally to cybercrime and data protection and those that apply directly or indirectly to children's use of the Internet. The four major regions cover Europe, Asia/Pacific, the Americas outside the United States, and Africa/Middle East. This discussion starts with Europe due to the significant number of influential regional initiatives in this area. Due to the uniformity provided by EU regional directives, after the regional perspective only two European countries are discussed. The other global regions focus primarily on national laws. For brevity, the laws of subnational jurisdictions (i.e., provinces, states, territories) are not discussed. Some of the international data protection laws in this section are presented in greater detail in a recent book by the same author.[1]

In evaluating and comparing the statutes in the various regions and countries, it may be important to keep in mind how well these laws have kept up with the changes in technology. For example, if the national law criminalizes only the possession of child pornography but does not criminalize obtaining access to these child abuse images, then is the act of watching child abuse on streaming videos over the Internet a crime?[2]

POINTS FOR PARENTS
o   In Europe, major regional directives and conventions frame the national statutes.
o   Europe is a leader in implementing statutes protecting the rights of children online.
o   Laws in Asia/Pacific and the Americas reflect international influences and local norms.
o   Many countries across the world offer minimal statutory protection for children online.

---

1. THOMAS J. SHAW, ESQ., CLOUD COMPUTING FOR LAWYERS AND EXECUTIVES – A GLOBAL APPROACH, Ch. 3 (2011).

2. Suggested by presenter comments at SOP 441 Workshop – Framework for International Cooperation on Child Online Protection, Nairobi, Kenya (Sept. 2011).

5.1   Europe

A.   General Cybercrime and Data Protection Statutes—Regional

1.   Convention against Cybercrime[3]

To address the risks of cybercrime, the Council of Europe created the Convention of Cybercrime. Unlike the European Union (EU), the Council of Europe cannot mandate laws, only create conventions that individual member states may or may not ratify. As of the beginning of 2012, only 31[4] of the 47[5] member states of the Council of Europe had ratified the Convention. In addition, the Convention is open to non-member states; however, although several signed it, only the United States has ratified it, with reservations, as had a number of the European ratifying states. Fifteen of the signatories have never ratified it. Of the major European economies, notable non-ratifiers include Russia, Turkey, and Sweden.

The main chapters address those measures that should be taken at a national level and international cooperation. The chapter on measures to be taken at a national level has sections on substantive criminal law, procedural law, and jurisdiction. The following conduct is to be criminalized: illegal access, illegal interception, data interference, system interference, and misuse of devices, under the category of *Offences against the confidentiality, integrity and availability of computer data and systems.* Under the next category of *Computer-related offences* are computer-related forgery and computer-related fraud. The third category is *Content-related offences*, which includes offenses related to child pornography; and the final category is *Offences related to infringements of copyright and related rights.* There are penalties for attempting and aiding and abet-

---

3. Council of Europe, Convention on Cybercrime, CETS 185 (2001).

4. *Ratified*: Albania, Armenia, Azerbaijan, Bosnia and Herzegovina, Bulgaria, Croatia, Cyprus, Denmark, Estonia, Finland, France, Germany, Hungary, Iceland, Italy, Latvia, Lithuania, Moldova, Montenegro, Netherlands, Norway, Portugal, Romania, Serbia, Slovakia, Slovenia, Spain, Switzerland, the former Yugoslav Republic of Macedonia, Ukraine, United Kingdom.

5. *Not Ratified*: Andorra, Austria, Belgium, Czech Republic, Georgia, Greece, Ireland, Liechtenstein, Luxembourg, Malta, Monaco, Poland, Russia, San Marino, Sweden, Turkey.

ting. Corporations that commit these acts are to be held as liable as individuals.

Each of the following offenses requires that the perpetrator perform the act intentionally.

- *Illegal access*: This involves the access, without a legal right, to the whole or any part of a computer system. Additionally, there may be the added qualifications that the offense is committed by "infringing security measures" with the intent to obtain computer data or with some other "dishonest intent," or the access is to a computer system that is connected to another computer system.

- *Illegal interception*: The crime is for the interception, by "technical means," of non-public transmissions of computer data or programs without any legal right to do so. Additionally, there can be the requirement that the offense is committed with "dishonest intent" or the interception is to, from, or within a computer system that is connected to another computer system.

- *Data interference*: This is the damaging, deletion, deterioration, alteration, or suppression of computer data without the legal right to do so. Additionally, there can be a requirement that this conduct results in serious harm.

- *System interference*: This is the serious hindering of the functioning of a computer system without the legal right to do so by inputting, transmitting, damaging, deleting, deteriorating, altering, or suppressing computer data.

- *Misuse of devices*: When, for the purpose of committing one of the preceding offenses and without a legal right, a person possesses and/or is involved in the production, sale, procurement for use, import, distribution, or otherwise making available of: a device, including a computer program, designed or adapted primarily for the purpose of committing any of the offenses above or a computer password, access code, or similar data by which the whole or any part of a computer system is capable of being accessed.

- *Computer-related forgery*: Without a legal right to do so, it is criminal to be involved in the input, alteration, deletion, or suppression of computer data resulting in inauthentic data with the intent that it be considered or acted upon for legal purposes as if it were authentic, regardless whether or not the data is directly readable and intelligible. Additionally, the intent to defraud, or similar dishonest intent, can be required before criminal liability attaches.

- *Computer-related fraud*: Without a legal right to do so, it is criminal to cause the loss of property to another person by any input, alteration, deletion, or suppression of computer data, or any interference with the functioning of a computer system, with fraudulent or dishonest intent of procuring an economic benefit for oneself or for another person.

- *Child pornography*: For any material that visually depicts a minor engaged in sexually explicit conduct, a person appearing to be a minor engaged in sexually explicit conduct, or realistic images representing a minor engaged in sexually explicit conduct, all of the following conduct is criminal:
  - producing child pornography for the purpose of its distribution through a computer system;
  - offering or making available child pornography through a computer system;
  - distributing or transmitting child pornography through a computer system;
  - procuring child pornography through a computer system for oneself or for another person; and
  - possessing child pornography in a computer system or on a computer data storage medium.

  It is permissible to lower the age of a minor to not less than 16 years of age.

- *Infringements of copyright and related rights*: The infringement of copyright requires that acts be committed willfully, on a commercial scale, and by means of a computer system. It uses the infringement as pursuant to obligations undertaken under five major international agreements on copyrights: the

Rome Convention,[6] the Bern Convention,[7] the WCT,[8] the WPPT,[9] and TRIPS.[10] The infringement of moral rights, which give authors the ability to claim authorship and to prevent modifications or distortions of their work, is an exception.

In national procedural law, rules are needed to preserve stored computer data and network traffic data, to order production of this data from its custodian, to be able to search and seize stored computer data, and to capture real-time network traffic data and real-time content data. Member states should be able to exercise jurisdiction over perpetrators whose criminal conduct occurs in its territory, airplanes, or ships; by one of its nationals; or by an offender whom it chooses not to extradite based on his/her nationality.

International cooperation is highly encouraged in investigations, prosecutions, and the collections of electronic evidence. Mutual assistance should be provided, and for those countries that require criminality of the offense in both countries to offer such assistance (dual criminality), that should be deemed to exist. Parties may request expedited preservation of stored computer data, expedited disclosure of preserved traffic data, access to stored computer data, trans-border access to stored computer data, real-time collection of traffic data, or interception of content data. The offenses listed in the substantive law section above should be deemed to be listed offenses on the extradition treaties between member states, and when there is no such bilateral treaty, the Convention itself can serve as the legal basis for extradition for those offenses listed above.

There is some controversy as to whether the Convention, which is open to ratification by any state, should serve as a global standard. Reluctance to embrace the Convention as a global standard starts within Europe itself, where 15 of the 47 Council of Europe

---

6. International Convention for the Protection of Performers, Producers of Phonograms and Broadcasting Organisations (1961).

7. Paris Act of July 24, 1971, revising the Bern Convention for the Protection of Literary and Artistic Works (1886, last amended 1979).

8. WIPO Copyright Treaty (1996).

9. WIPO Performances and Phonograms Treaty (1996).

10. Agreement on Trade-Related Aspects of Intellectual Property Rights (1994).

member states still have not ratified it. There is also the concern that it does not cover many offenses that were not as highly visible when it was passed, such as identity theft, and is not easy to revise to deal with new threats. Finally, it may reflect the values and legal systems of Europe more than those of other countries in the global community. While often noted in regional and global declarations, the Convention has not been ratified outside of Europe (with the lone exception of the United States). There is also an additional protocol[11] to the Convention dealing with online racist and xenophobic acts (separated due to differing traditions regarding free speech across member states).

2. EU Framework Decision on Attacks against Information Systems[12]

This decision is to help harmonize national criminal laws related to attacks against information systems, especially from organized crime and terrorists. Specifically, the crimes are the illegal access to an information system, illegal system interference, and illegal data interference, plus attempt, aiding, and abetting. Member jurisdiction includes that over one of its nationals, for the benefit of a corporation headquartered in its territory, or an act committed in its territory, either by a person located in its territory (even if the information systems are outside its territory) or against information systems in its territory (even if the offender is outside its territory). Unlike the Council of Europe, the European Union can require its members to implement framework decisions and directives into local legislation. This framework decision was to have been implemented by member states by March 2007.

In 2010, the EU issued a proposed new Directive[13] that, among other provisions, would add to penalties for the use of malicious software like botnets or unlawfully obtained computer passwords.

---

11. Council of Europe, Additional Protocol to the Convention on Cybercrime, concerning the criminalisation of acts of a racist and xenophobic nature committed through computer systems, CETS 189 (2003).

12. EU, Council Framework Decision 2005/222/JHA of February 24, 2005, on attacks against information systems.

13. EU, Proposal for a Directive on attacks against information systems, repealing Framework Decision 2005/222/JHA (2010).

It would also criminalize the illegal interception of information systems. While these provisions were included in the Convention on Cybercrime, they were excluded from the 2005 Decision. It also raises penalties for the use of tools that impact a significant number of systems or do significant damage (measured by disruption of services, financial cost, or loss of personal data) and for committing crimes while concealing the perpetrator's real identity. As of early 2012, this updated directive has not yet been promulgated.

3.   Data Protection Directive[14]

This directive protects the personal information of natural persons (not corporations) in the EU during processing. "Processing" is any operation on personal data, such as "collecting, records, organization, storage, adaption or alteration, retrieval, consultation, use, disclosure by transmission, dissemination or otherwise making available, alignment or combination, blocking, erasure, or destruction." A data controller, who determines the "purposes and means" of processing, is required to adhere to these principles by ensuring that personal data must be:[15]

- processed fairly and lawfully;
- collected for specified, explicit, and legitimate purposes and not further processed in a way that is incompatible with those purposes;
- adequate, relevant, and not excessive in relation to the purposes for which they are collected and/or further processed;
- accurate and, where necessary, kept up to date; every reasonable step must be taken to ensure that data which are inaccurate or incomplete, having regard to the purposes for which they were collected or for which they are further processed, are erased or rectified; and
- kept in a form that permits identification of data subjects for no longer than is necessary for the purposes for which the data were collected or for which they are further processed.

---

14. EU, Directive 95/46/EC on the protection of individuals with regard to the processing of personal data and the free movement of such data.

15. *Id.* art. 6.

Personal data may only be processed with the consent of the data subject, with exceptions for performance of a contract, legal obligations or legitimate interests of the controller, vital interests of the data subject, or in the public interest,[16] among other prohibitions on the processing of sensitive data. The data subject has several rights, including receiving notice of the types of collection and other processing of his/her data, of access to and revision or blocking of incorrect data, to not be subject to decisions based on automated processing of the data, and to the confidentiality and security of her/his personal data. This is supplemented by protections for personal data processed during the investigation and prosecution of crimes.[17]

In 2010, the EU looked at the need for revising this directive.[18] It found that the core principles of the directive were still valid; however, the following issues needed to be addressed:

- assessing the impact of new technologies;
- enhancing the internal market dimension of data protection;
- addressing globalization and improving international data transfers;
- providing a stronger institutional arrangement for the effective enforcement of data protection rules; and
- improving the coherence of the data protection legal framework.

Included in the considerations for the way forward for data privacy is a focus on children: "introducing specific obligations for data controllers on the type of information to be provided and on the modalities for providing it, including in relation to *children*."

In early 2012, the EU issued a proposed revised framework for data privacy as a regulation.[19] The advantage of this being issued

---

16. *Id.* art. 7.

17. EU, Council Framework Decision 2008/977/JHA of November 27, 2008, on the protection of personal data processed in the framework of police and judicial cooperation in criminal matters.

18. EU COMMISSION, A COMPREHENSIVE APPROACH ON PERSONAL DATA PROTECTION IN THE EUROPEAN UNION (2010).

19. EU, Reg. __/2012/EU of January __, 2012, on the protection of individuals with regard to the processing of personal data and on the free movement of such data (General Data Protection Regulation).

as a regulation is its immediate effect (no need to wait for enabling legislation in each country) and its uniformity. There is also to be a directive on the processing by authorities of personal data in criminal investigations and prosecutions. The objectives of the regulation are to protect the personal data and allow the free movement of data within the EU. Followng are the key proposed changes:

- Applies to processing done on personal data in the EU or on the personal data of an EU resident wherever the processing is done.
- Express, opt-in consent is required for direct-marketing activities.
- A new right to be forgotten (have all data deleted on a data subject).
- The new right of data subject portability between ISPs.
- Data breach notification obligations for all data controllers.

4.   E-Privacy Directive[20]

This directive concerns data privacy on networks, including areas such as tracking cookies and spam. As amended,[21] it seeks to address the concerns that "[P]ublicly available electronic communications services over the Internet open new possibilities for users but also new risks for their personal data and privacy." Electronic communications providers are required to keep user communications and related traffic data confidential. Traffic and location data must be deleted or anonymized when no longer needed and can be used only for other purposes, such as marketing or value-added services, with the user's informed consent. Safeguards should be provided for unsolicited commercial marketing emails and messages, and prior consent may be required for bulk versions (spam). Disguising the identity of the sender should be prohibited. Spyware,

---

20. EU, Directive 2002/58/EC of July 12, 2002, concerning the processing of personal data and the protection of privacy in the electronic communications sector.

21. EU, Directive 2009/136/EC of November 25, 2009, amending . . . Directive 2002/58/EC concerning the processing of personal data and protection of privacy in the electronic communications sector and . . . .

web bugs, hidden identifiers, and other similar devices placed on a user's PC without her knowledge to gain access to user data or trace Internet activities or store hidden information should be allowed only with user consent and for legitimate purposes. Users should be notified of breaches of their personal data. Cookies should require knowledge of their existence and the right to refuse their placement on the user's access device.

5. Data Retention Directive[22]

This directive requires ISPs to retain certain traffic and location information on their electronic communication customer's network usage. This information could then potentially be used in the "prevention, investigation, detection, and prosecution of criminal offences." This directive continues the prohibition against unconsented processing of individuals' personal data and the need to continue to safeguard that under the DPD, while giving law enforcement the ability to examine the traffic and location data in regard to crimes. The data to be retained includes that which identifies the source and destination/recipient of a communication, the time and date of the communication, the type of communication, and the location for mobile device communications. Data should be retained for six months to two years and have the same type of safeguards as all data under the DPD. No content data is to be retained.

B. General Cybercrime and Data Protection Statutes—by Country

Because countries in Europe are required to implement laws described in EU directives and many have voluntarily ratified Council of Europe conventions, the major countries in Europe generally follow the rules as described above. But because local implementations can be different due to lack of regional directives and leeway given therein, the following is a brief look at two European countries, one common law (the UK) and one civil law (Germany), for the general cybercrime and data protection laws in each.

---

22. EU, Directive 2006/24/EC of March 15, 2006, on the retention of data generated or processed in connection with the provision of publicly available electronic communications services or of public communication networks and amending Directive 2002/58/EC.

1.   United Kingdom

The principal statute protecting computers in the UK is the Computer Misuse Act of 1990[23] as amended.[24] It prohibits access to a computer's materials without authorization with the intent to do so.[25] It is an offense to gain unauthorized access to a computer intending to commit or facilitate a further offense, even if such an act is impossible.[26] It is also criminal to, without authorization and knowledge thereof: (a) impair the operation of any computer; (b) prevent or hinder access to any program or data held in any computer; (c) impair the operation of any such program or the reliability of any such data; or (d) enable any of the things mentioned in paragraphs (a) to (c) above to be done.[27] It is also an offense if a person obtains, "makes, adapts, supplies or offers to supply" any article intending it to be used to commit or to assist in one of these unauthorized actions.[28] This law covers acts performed in the UK or to computers situated in the UK.[29]

The principal data protection law in the UK is the Data Protection Act.[30] As are most personal data privacy laws around the world, it is based on a set of privacy principles. The key principles regarding personal data are as follows:

- Must be fairly and lawfully processed and with data subject consent or an exception.
- Must only be used for the purpose for which it was collected and relevant to that purpose.
- Must not be disclosed to other parties without the data subject's consent.
- Individuals have a right of access and correct if factually incorrect.
- Must not be kept for any longer than is necessary and kept up to date.

---

23. UK, Cap. 18.
24. UK, Police and Justice Act (2006).
25. UK, Cap. 18 § 1.
26. *Id.* § 2.
27. *Id.* § 3.
28. *Id.* § 3A.
29. *Id.* § 5.
30. UK, Data Protection Act (1998).

- Must not be sent outside Europe without data subject consent or adequate protections.
- Must not be used for direct marketing.

In addition, data controllers/processors must register and have adequate security measures. The UK has a law on junk mail.[31]

2. Germany

Cybercrimes are punishable under the German Penal (or Criminal) Code (*Strafgesetzbuch* or *StGB*). Under the section for Data Espionage,[32] it is a crime to obtain data, either stored or during electronic transmission, without authorization that was "specially protected" by appropriate safeguards. It is also prohibited to unlawfully delete, suppress, alter, or render unusable or attempt to do so,[33] or to materially interfere with an organization's data processing by these acts or by destroying, damaging, removing, altering, or rendering unusable a data-processing system or network or attempting to do so.[34] Storing or using a forged document on a computer is a crime,[35] as is falsely using data processing,[36] or committing a computer-related fraud[37] for a personal material benefit through incorrect configuration of a program, use of incorrect or incomplete data, or unauthorized use of data.

Data is protected under the Federal Data Protection Act[38] (BDSG), which requires that there be a legal basis for any data processing done by data controllers/processers. The data subject has the rights to receive notice about processing and collection, and to access and revise, delete, or block his/her personal data. Data must

---

31. UK, Privacy and Electronic Communications Regs. (2003).
32. Germany, StGB § 202a.
33. *Id.* § 303a.
34. *Id.* § 303b.
35. *Id.* § 269.
36. *Id.* § 270.
37. *Id.* § 263a.
38. Germany, Federal Data Protection Act (*Bundesdatenschutzgesetz*, BDSG) (1990).

be collected lawfully and with consent and used only for the purposes for which it was collected. Germany has a spam statute.[39]

C.   Child-Specific Laws and Cyberstatutes—Regional

Following on from the UN Convention on the Rights of the Child and the need to implement these rights, the Convention on the Exercise of Children's Rights has been promulgated by the Council of Europe[40] to promote the rights and best interests of children. The rights of children in Europe, which the member states and parents should promote and protect, include the rights to be informed, to express their views in proceedings, and to appoint representatives. Beyond these procedural rights, there have quite a number of children-focused regional directives and guidance issued by the EU in its various structures over the years. For brevity, the section will cover only the most recent. There is also a self-regulatory/co-regulatory model used in Europe for the Internet, the basis for which is described below.

1.   Directive on Combating Sexual Abuse and Sexual Exploitation of Children and Child Pornography[41]

Superseding previous direction from the EU, this new directive deals with many areas of child exploitation, including "various forms of sexual abuse and sexual exploitation of children which are facilitated by the use of information and communication technology, such as the online solicitation of children for sexual purposes via social networking websites and chat room." It also deals with child sexual abuse images: "Knowingly obtaining access by means of information and communication technology to child pornography should be criminalized." In addition to criminalizing the above offenses, the directive also seeks to prohibit child sex

---

39. Germany, Act against Unfair Competition (*Gesetz gegen Unlauteren Wetbewerb*) § 7.

40. Council of Europe, European Convention on the Exercise of Children's Rights, CETS No. 160 (1996).

41. EU, Directive 2011/92 of Dec. 13, 2011, on Combatting the Sexual Abuse and Sexual Exploitation of Children and Child Pornography and Replacing Council Framework Decision 2004/68/JHA (2011).

tourism. Removal and blocking of child abuse images is also called for. It requires complying laws, regulations, and administrative provisions to be in place by the end of 2013 in all member states except Denmark.

The specific articles criminalize offenses concerning sexual abuse, sexual exploitation, child pornography, and solicitation, including attempting, aiding, and abetting. Measures should also be taken to eliminate advertising abuse and child sex tourism and remove and block images of child sexual abuse. Jurisdiction spans not only conduct committed in member territory or by one of their nationals, but also by member states for victims who are nationals or habitual residents, acts committed for the benefit of a corporation in its territory, or when the offender is a habitual resident. Jurisdiction is also to include those uses of information and communications technology to commit these offenses, whether or not it is based in their territory. Jurisdiction is also not to be subordinated to the condition that the acts are a criminal offense at the place where they were performed.

2. Convention on the Protection of Children against Sexual Exploitation and Sexual Abuse[42]

The objectives of this Council of Europe convention are to prevent and combat sexual exploitation and sexual abuse of children, protect the rights of child victims of sexual exploitation and sexual abuse, and promote national and international cooperation against sexual exploitation and sexual abuse of children. It encourages member states to raise the awareness of those in contact with children, to educate children as to the "risks of sexual exploitation and sexual abuse" and protection methods, and to gain participation from others, including industry and the media. Its substantive criminal law provisions cover sexual abuse, child prostitution, and child pornography; pornographic performances, viewing, and solicitation; and attempt, aiding, and abetting, as well as corporate liability. It also calls for the recording and storing of

---

42. Council of Europe, Convention on the Protection of Children against Sexual Exploitation and Sexual Abuse, CETS 201 (2007).

national data on convicted sexual offenders. As of early 2012, it has been ratified by only 17 of the 47 member states. It is further described in Chapter 3.

3.   Directive on Preventing and Combating Trafficking in Human Beings and Protecting Its Victims[43]

This directive is focused on updating the categories of crimes and victims involved in human trafficking and laying out appropriate sanctions for the perpetrators of these acts. It requires member states to criminalize "[t]he recruitment, transportation, transfer, harbouring or reception of persons, including the exchange or transfer of control over" persons including children. A number of provisions address the immediate and longer-term support and assistance required by child victims, especially those who are unaccompanied, including the need to shield them during criminal investigations and prosecutions. It requires complying laws, regulations, and administrative provisions to be in place by April 2013 in all member states except the UK and Denmark.

4.   Protecting Children in the Digital World[44]

Much of the approach to online protections for children, including mobile and social networks, is through a self-regulation model. As such, the following are not statutes, but regional recommendations. This 1998 recommendation[45] called on member states to work to-

43. EU, Directive 2011/36 of April 5, 2011, on Preventing and Combating Trafficking in Human Beings and Protecting Its Victims and Replacing Council Framework Decision 2002/629/JHA (2011).

44. European Commission, on the application of the Council Recommendation of September 24, 1998, concerning the protection of minors and human dignity and of the Recommendation of December 20, 2006, on the protection of minors and human dignity and on the right of reply in relation to the competitiveness of the European audiovisual and online information services industry - PROTECTING CHILDREN IN THE DIGITAL WORLD (2011).

45. EU, Council Recommendation 98/560/EC of September 24, 1998, on the development of the competitiveness of the European audiovisual and information services industry by promoting national frameworks aimed at achieving a comparable and effective level of protection of minors and human dignity.

ward implementing self-regulation frameworks that increased the protection of children using Internet online services. To create a climate of trust, they should also fight against illegal content in online services. It also calls for raising awareness among parents and educators to help children "make responsible use of" information services. It calls on industry to draw up codes of conduct to protect children. This was updated in 2006,[46] to account for changes to technology and media. It calls on member states to establish quality labels for service providers and the ability to report illicit or suspicious behavior on the Internet. It calls on industry to have content warning labels and filters.

This 2011 document reviews the status of the issues raised in the previous two documents above. It finds that self-regulatory codes of conduct are in place in 24 of 27 EU countries but at varying levels of protection. For hotlines, there are again differences in implementation across the region in the 19 members who have implemented notice and take-down procedures. Only 11 member states report that ISP codes of conduct in respect to children are "well-adapted to the new digital environment." Only 10 member states report the guidelines for operators and/or children on social networking sites, although the *Safer Social Networking Principles for the EU* (discussed in the next section) may help. Age rating and classification of content systems are considered effective in 12 states, while 13 states believe they need to improve. Twenty member states are using filtering systems and 25 use parental control systems. On-screen icons and/or acoustic warnings have proven helpful in warning parents about upcoming child-inappropriate content. Seventeen member states consider the age-rating systems for video games (e.g., PEGI and PEGI online, discussed in Chapters 3 and 6) satisfactory. Because of the often fragmentary nature of many of the measures to safeguard children online, the paper concludes by stating that "further action at European level may build on the best practices of the Member States and reach economies of scale for the ICT sector

---

46. EU, Recommendation 2006/952/EC of December 20, 2006, on the protection of minors and human dignity and on the right of reply in relation to the competitiveness of the European audiovisual and online information services industry.

that will help children to safely reap the benefits of the constantly evolving digital world."

5.   Safer Internet Programme[47]

To provide a legal basis and funding for many of the programs used to the protect children on the Internet, this EC decision has objectives of ensuring public awareness on safer use of online technologies, fighting against illegal content and harmful conduct online, promoting a safer online environment, and establishing a knowledge base, including investigation of online victimization of children. Some of these programs such as hotlines are discussed in Chapter 3. It has also led to voluntary programs with industry in Europe in the areas of Internet/online media,[48] mobile phones,[49] and social networking sites.[50] The new online collation will look at five areas: reporting tools for harmful content and contact, age-appropriate privacy settings, wider use of content classification, wider availability of parental controls, and effective take-down of child abuse material. The mobile phone framework focuses on access controls, raising awareness, commercial content classification, and illegal content. The social networking principles involve raising awareness, age-appropriate services, empowering users, ease of reporting inappropriate conduct or content, notification of illegal content or conduct, safe approaches to personal information and privacy, and the means to review illegal or prohibited content/conduct.

---

47. European Commission, Dec. No 1351/2008/EC of December 16, 2008, establishing a multiannual Community programme on protecting children using the internet and other communication technologies.

48. Twenty companies in the *Coalition to make a better and safer Internet for children* (2011).

49. Mobile and content providers, *European Framework on Safe Mobile Use by Younger Teenagers and Children* (2007).

50. Twenty providers of social networking services, *Safer Social Networking Principles for the EU* (2009).

D.   *Child-Specific Laws and Cyberstatutes—by Country*

1.   **United Kingdom**

One significant, although by no means the only, act addressing children in the UK is the Protection of Children Act.[51] This law seeks to "prevent the exploitation of children" through the creation, possession, or distribution of child abuse "indecent" images. This includes publishing an advertisement about these images and applies to individuals and corporations. In this law, "child" means one under the age of 16. The trafficking of children is banned inter alia under the Sexual Offenses Act.[52] Cyberbullying may be addressed through a number of different laws.[53]

2.   **Germany**

As explained above, crimes in Germany are covered under the Criminal (Penal) Code. Regarding child sexual abuse images, it is prohibited to disseminate, publicly display, make accessible, produce, obtain, advertise, or import or export these images, or make such use possible by another or attempt to do so.[54] It is also criminal to sexually abuse a child with the intent of producing child pornography.[55] Child sex tourism involving its nationals is a crime as well,[56] as is trafficking of children for sexual purposes.[57] A law intended to filter child abuse images on websites was passed[58] but has not been successful due to free speech concerns and is being withdrawn.[59]

5.2   Asia/Pacific

Unlike Europe, Asia/Pacific tends to take a less regional, more individual country approach. With that said, there are some regional

---

51.   UK, Protection of Children Act (1978).

52.   UK, Sexual Offences Act (2003).

53.   UK, Malicious Communications Act (1988), Protection from Harassment Act (1997), Communications Act (2003).

54.   Germany, StGB § 184(3).

55.   *Id.* § 176a(2).

56.   *Id.* § 176 and § 182.

57.   *Id.* § 180b.

58.   Germany, Access Impediment Act (2009).

59.   *German Web Blocking Law Repealed*, EDRI (Dec. 2011).

efforts that involve voluntary forums. The APEC (which is not just composed of Asia/Pacific countries) has undertaken some activities as described in Chapter 3, but these are not directives for statutes or regulations. So it is more important to see what the key countries have implemented locally. The countries included in this section are China, South Korea, and Japan as the leading economies in the region and in Northeast Asia; India as a leading economy in South Asia; Australia as a leading economy in Australasia; Indonesia as a leading economy in Southeast Asia; and Hong Kong and Singapore as typical regional headquarter locations for multinational organizations projecting into China and ASEAN, respectively. Importantly, unlike other regions where the selected countries may be the only relevant examples, in Asia additional countries—New Zealand, Taiwan, Malaysia, and Thailand—have relevant laws and are omitted only for reasons of space. For more details on the data privacy laws in the region, see previous writings by the author.[60]

A.   General Cybercrime and Data Protection Statutes

1.   Australia

Australia is a federal system and so has federal as well as state/territory laws. For cybercrimes, the rules are in the criminal code as amended by the Cybercrime Act.[61] This act details the following serious computer offenses: (1) unauthorized access to data, unauthorized modification of data, or unauthorized impairment of electronic communications to or from a computer, using either a telecommunications service or not, with intent to commit a serious offense;[62] (2) unauthorized modification of data in a computer that causes impairment of access to that or other data in any computer or impairs the reliability, security, or operation of any data on any computer or telecom services in Australia;[63] and (3) unauthorized

---

60. Thomas J. Shaw, Esq., *Asia-Pacific Data Privacy Laws: Model Corporate Privacy Principles*, IAPP PRIVACY ADVISOR (March 2010).

61. Australia, Cybercrime Act, An Act to amend the law relating to computer offenses and for other purposes (No. 160 of 2001).

62. Australia, CRIMINAL CODE § 477.1.

63. *Id.* § 477.2.

impairing of an electronic communication to or from a computer in Australia or over a telecom service.[64] Additional offenses include unauthorized access to or modification of restricted data,[65] unauthorized impairment of data held on a computer disk or credit card,[66] and the possession or control of or the production, supply, or obtaining of data with the intention to commit or facilitate one of the above offenses.[67] There has been a recent legislative attempt to fill gaps in Australia's cybercrime laws by adopting the Council of Europe's Cybercrime Convention (described above), but it has not yet passed.[68]

In addition to a law addressing junk mail,[69] Australia has a data protection law that is based on the National Privacy Principles.[70] These principles concern limitations and legality of collection, use, and disclosure of personal data; ensuring data quality; providing reasonable data security; openness and the right of access and correction to personal data; the non-use of identifiers; the right of anonymity; transborder data flows that ensure that off-shored data has the same protections as on-shore; and special protections for sensitive information. The act is violated by breaching any of the National Privacy Principles or an approved privacy code.

2. Japan

Japan's laws on cybercrime include the Unauthorized Computer Access Law;[71] the new cybercrime law making the creating, distributing, or storing of a computer virus or sending pornographic images via spam to random people a crime;[72] and provisions in the penal code on computer data and systems.[73] The first of these three

---

64. *Id.* § 477.3.
65. *Id.* § 478.1.
66. *Id.* § 478.2.
67. *Id.* § 478.3–.4.
68. Australia, Cybercrime Legislation Amendment Bill (2011).
69. Australia, Spam Act (No. 129 of 2003).
70. Australia, Federal Privacy Act (No. 119 of 1998).
71. Japan, Unauthorized Computer Access Law (No. 128 of 1999).
72. Japan, Act for Partial Revision of the Penal Code to deal with the sophistication of information processing, etc. (No. 24 of 2011).
73. Japan, Penal Code (No. 45 of 1907, amended 1987).

laws prohibits unauthorized access to a computer over a telecom network by using the access code of another or using commands or other information to evade the security control mechanism[74] or to facilitate by providing such an access code.[75]

Under the penal code, it is unlawful to commit forgery with the intent to deceive others concerning a legal right.[76] Intentional interference with a computer system used for a business transaction is also prohibited.[77] It is crime to profit from the entering of fraudulent information or instructions into a computer system[78] or to destroy the electronic information of another.[79]

Japan's data protection law requires that personal data be specified and then limited to that use, that collection be lawful, that the data be accurate, that there be appropriate security controls and supervision of employees and third parties, that use of third parties requires consent of the data subjects, and the rights of access, correction, and notice.[80] Japan also regulates junk mail.[81]

3.   China

In China, the protection against cybercrimes is found in its criminal code. Unauthorized access to computer systems with certain types of information is illegal.[82] Sabotaging computer systems by deleting, altering, adding to, or interfering and thereby causing abnormal operation of those systems is illegal, as is unauthorized modifying, deleting, or adding of data or application programs, or intentionally creating or distributing a computer virus that affects the operation of computer systems.[83] It is prohibited to use a computer for crimes such as financial fraud, theft, corruption, misap-

---

74. Unauthorized Computer Access Law, art. 3.

75. *Id.* art. 3.

76. Japan, PENAL CODE, art. 161 bis.

77. *Id.* art. 234 bis.

78. *Id.* art. 246 bis.

79. *Id.* art. 259 bis.

80. Japan, Act on the Protection of Personal Information (2003).

81. Japan, Law on Regulation of Transmission of Specified Electronic Mail (2002).

82. China, CRIMINAL CODE, art. 285.

83. *Id.* art. 286.

propriation of public funds, or stealing state secrets, or for other crimes.[84] In addition, all of the following acts on the Internet are criminalized:[85]

- Selling defective products or making false claims on commodities and services
- Damaging other people's business reputation and product reputation
- Infringing upon other people's rights to intellectual property
- Fabricating and spreading false information to influence securities and futures trading and the disruption of the financial market
- Insulting other people or fabricating stories to slander others
- Illegally intercepting, changing, or deleting other people's e-mail or other data information, thus infringing upon other people's freedom of communication
- Engaging in theft, fraud, and burglary

China has no comprehensive data protection law. Instead, there are a variety of different national and provincial laws across criminal law, tort law, industry regulations, and consumer protection statutes that make up this quilt of privacy protections.[86] China prohibits junk mail through regulations.[87] China recently announced that illegally obtaining, buying, or selling data from networks or providing hacking tools are to be considered crimes.[88]

---

84. *Id.* art. 287.

85. China, The Decision of the Standing Committee of the National People's Congress on Maintaining Internet Security (2000).

86. *See* THOMAS J. SHAW, ESQ., CLOUD COMPUTING FOR LAWYERS AND EXECUTIVES – A GLOBAL APPROACH (2011), Ch. 3.3, and for recent updates *see* Thomas Shaw, *2011 (1H) Information Law Updates – Cases, Statutes and Standards*, INFORMATION SECURITY AND PRIVACY NEWS (newsltr. of the ABA Sec. Science & Technology Law), Vol. 2 Issue 4 (Autumn 2011) and Thomas Shaw, *2011 (2H) Information Law Updates – Cases, Statutes and Standards*, INFORMATION SECURITY AND PRIVACY NEWS (newsltr. of the ABA Sec. Science & Technology Law), Vol. 3 Issue 1 (Winter 2012).

87. China, Regulations on Internet Email Services (2006).

88. Xinhua, China issues legal interpretation to tighten grip on hacking (Aug. 29, 2011).

4.   India

India cybercrime law is based on the Information Technology Act.[89] It is a crime in India to do the following acts to a computer, computer system (including removable storage), or computer network:[90]

- Gain unauthorized access or facilitate another in doing so
- Download or copy data stored therein
- Introduce malware
- Cause any damage (destroy, alter, delete, add, modify, or rearrange any computer resource by any means), including to computer programs
- Cause disruptions
- Cause denial of access to authorized persons
- Tamper and cause services to be charged to the wrong person's account

It is also a crime to knowingly or intentionally conceal, destroy, or alter, or cause another to conceal, destroy, or alter, any computer source code used for a computer, computer program, computer system, or computer network.[91] Hacking is also prohibited, if one knows that such hacking will likely cause damage, destroy, delete, or alter any information residing in a computer resource or diminish its value or utility, or affect it injuriously by any means.[92]

India's data protection law is relatively recent and is based on privacy principles that include limitations on personal data collection and use, rights of access and correction, notice, and transfer and written consent requirements for sensitive information.[93]

5.   Singapore

Cybercrimes are prohibited under the Computer Misuse Act of 1990.[94] It is a crime to gain unauthorized access to a computer program or

---

89. India, Information Technology Act (2000).

90. *Id.* § 43.

91. *Id.* § 65.

92. *Id.* § 66.

93. India, Ministry of Communications and Information Technology, INFORMATION TECHNOLOGY (REASONABLE SECURITY PRACTICES AND PROCEDURES AND SENSITIVE PERSONAL DATA OR INFORMATION) RULES (2011).

94. Singapore, Cap. 50A.

data or causing data thereof.[95] It is a crime to obtain access (authorized or unauthorized) to a computer with the intent to commit or facilitate an offense involving property, fraud, dishonesty, or bodily harm.[96] Unauthorized modification (temporary or permanent) to the contents of a computer is illegal,[97] as is unauthorized interception or use of computer service.[98] The unauthorized interference, interruption, or obstruction with the lawful use or action that "impedes or prevents access to, or impairs the usefulness or effectiveness of, any program or data stored in a computer"[99] or the unauthorized disclosure of access codes for gain or illegal purposes are all illegal.[100]

Singapore has historically had a voluntary data privacy scheme.[101] This code had the following data privacy principles: accountability (for third-party outsourcers), purpose of collection, consent to processing, fair and legal collection, limited use, disclosure and retention, accuracy, appropriate safeguards, openness (notice), access and correction, and complaint process. In 2012, a new data protection law is supposed to be passed based on changes outlined by the government.[102] Singapore has a spam email law.[103]

6.   Hong Kong

Hong Kong, although part of China, is a Special Administrative Region with its own laws and legal traditions. Cybercrimes are penalized through the Computer Crimes Ordinance,[104] which modified several existing ordinances. For example, it is a crime to unlawfully damage or destroy any program or data held in a computer or in a computer storage medium or to misuse a computer so as to cause it to function differently than planned, to alter or erase any program or

---

95. *Id.* § 3.
96. *Id.* § 4.
97. *Id.* § 5.
98. *Id.* § 6.
99. *Id.* § 7.
100. *Id.* § 8.
101. Singapore, Model Data Protection Code for the Private Sector (2003).
102. Singapore Ministry of Information, Communication and the Arts, *Proposed Consumer Data Protection Regime for Singapore* (Sept. 2011).
103. Singapore, Spam Control Act (2007).
104. Hong Kong, Computer Crimes Ordinance (1993).

data held in a computer or in a computer storage medium, or to add any program or data to the contents of a computer or of a computer storage medium.[105] It is a criminal offense to use a telecom network to gain unauthorized access to any program or data in a computer.[106] It is prohibited for any person to obtain access to a computer with intent to commit an offense, deceive, cause loss to another, or obtain dishonest gain for himself or another.[107]

Trespassing into a building with the intent to do any of these is also a crime:

(a) unlawfully causing a computer in the building to function other than as it has been established by or on behalf of its owner to function, notwithstanding that the unlawful action may not impair the operation of the computer or a program held in the computer or the reliability of data held in the computer;

(b) unlawfully altering or erasing any program, or data, held in a computer in the building or in a computer storage medium in the building; or

(c) unlawfully adding any program or data to the contents of a computer in the building or a computer storage medium in the building.[108]

Hong Kong's data protection law is the Personal Data (Privacy) Ordinance of 1997.[109] It gives the data subject the right of access to and correction of his/her personal data held by a data user. Matching procedures require consent, and although still not in operation, data transferred outside Hong Kong requires consent or the same procedures in the receiving country. Data subjects can opt out of any direct marketing. The six data protection principles for this ordinance include restrictions on manner and use of data collection, continued accuracy of the data and retention only as long as necessary, use only for the purpose collected, practical security measures,

---

105. Hong Kong, Cap. 200 §§ 59–60.
106. *Id.* Cap. 106 § 27A.
107. *Id.* Cap. 200 § 161.
108. *Id.* Cap. 210 § 11.
109. *Id.* Cap. 486.

notice to the user of the data held and the data user's policies/procedures, and the access to data mentioned above. Proposed amendments include bans on cross-marketing and oversight of subcontractors handling personal data.[110] Junk mail is prohibited by the Unsolicited Electronic Messages Ordinance of 2007.[111]

7. (Republic of) South Korea

In South Korea, making fraudulent modifications to data using a computer for personal gain is a crime.[112] It is also prohibited to gain unauthorized access to information on a network or to distribute or interfere with computer networks and systems.[113] Information stored on networks should not be intercepted or disclosed.[114] South Korea has a full data protection law[115] that has recently been revised.[116] The privacy principles include: consent to collection of personal information limited to what is necessary, and that information should not be disclosed without consent, should be kept accurate, and should be destroyed when no longer needed. The revised act includes data breach notification rules and consent requirements for sensitive information. Junk mail is regulated through the original data protection law and subsequent revisions and regulations.

8. Indonesia

Cybercrimes are prohibited under the e-commerce law.[117] This includes transmitting or otherwise making electronic information accessible without authorization under a variety of circumstances.[118] It is also prohibited to gain unlawful access to computers, including

---

110. Hong Kong, Personal Data (Privacy) (Amendment) Bill 2011.

111. *Id.* Cap. 593.

112. Republic of Korea, Criminal Code, art. 347-2.

113. Republic of Korea, Act on Promotion of Information and Communications Network Utilization and Information Projection, art. 48 (2001).

114. *Id.* art. 49.

115. Republic of Korea, Act on Promotion of Information and Communication Network Utilization and Information Protection (2001).

116. Republic of Korea, Personal Information Protection Act (2011).

117. Indonesia, Law Concerning Electronic Information and Transactions (*Tentang Informasi Dan Transaksi Elektronik*) (No. 11 of 2008).

118. *Id.* art. 27–29.

hacking, or to intercept private communications.[119] It is a crime to interfere with data by altering, transmitting, deleting, etc., or interfering with a system.[120] It is prohibited to "produce, sell, cause to be used, import, distribute, provide, or own" programs or hardware that accomplishes any of these crimes or are targeted at defeating security access codes or to commit forgery through alteration of electronic data.[121] Data privacy is also protected under this law, with any use of electronically stored personal data requiring the consent of the data subject and the rights of access to one's own data.[122]

B.   Child-Specific Laws and Cyberstatutes

1.   Australia

Australia has a series of provisions addressing child pornography, online solicitation, and similar offenses in its criminal code. It is a crime to use a telecom service to access, transmit to one's self or another, make available, publish, distribute, advertise, promote, or solicit child pornography[123] or child abuse ("torture, cruelty or physical abuse") material[124] or to possess, control, produce, supply or obtain, for use through a telecom service, child pornography[125] or child abuse material.[126] It is also a crime for an ISP with knowledge that its service can "be used to access particular material that the person has reasonable grounds to believe is child pornography or child abuse material and they do not report it to the police within a reasonable time period."[127] It is also a crime, using telecom services, for an adult (aged 18+) to have sexual relations with a child (under the age of 16),[128] to procure a child for sexual relations,[129]

---

119. *Id.* art. 30–31.
120. *Id.* art. 32–33.
121. *Id.* art. 34–35.
122. *Id.* art. 26.
123. Australia, Criminal Code, § 474.19.
124. *Id.* § 474.22.
125. *Id.* § 474.20.
126. *Id.* § 474.23.
127. *Id.* § 474.24.
128. *Id.* § 474.25A.
129. *Id.* § 474.26.

to groom a child for sexual activity,[130] or to transmit incident material to a child.[131] It is also an offense to use a telecom service for suicide-related material.[132] Trafficking children is a crime.[133]

2. Japan

To protect children on the Internet, Japan has implemented the Act on Provision of Environment for Safe and Secure Internet Use for Young People.[134] This statute concerns raising awareness of children and the filtering of harmful content by ISPs. Some examples of what is considered harmful content include: information in which the provider thereof directly and expressly offers to undertake or mediate, or induces, a crime or an act that violates criminal laws and regulations, or information that directly and expressly induces a suicide; obscene depiction of sexual conduct or genitals, etc., of humans or any other information that considerably excites or stimulates sexual desire; or grisly depiction of a scene of murder, execution, abuse, etc., or any other information having extremely cruel content. The basic intent is to increase children's ability to deal with harmful content, while at the same time reducing the likelihood that they will encounter it by filtering.[135] The filtering software includes dissemination into the home for Internet viewing there.[136] Internet filtering capabilities shall be provided by mobile phone operators,[137] ISPs,[138] equipment manufacturers,[139] and server administrators.[140]

---

130. *Id.* § 474.27.
131. *Id.* § 474.27A.
132. *Id.* § 474.29.
133. *Id.* § 271.
134. Japan, Act on Provision of Environment for Safe and Secure Internet Use for Young People (No. 79 of 2008).
135. *Id.* art. 3.
136. *Id.* art. 14.
137. *Id.* art. 17.
138. *Id.* art. 18.
139. *Id.* art. 19.
140. *Id.* art. 21.

It is a crime to distribute, sell, or publicly display an obscene image,[141] while child pornography is banned by statute.[142] It is a crime to distribute, sell, commercially lend, or display in public (including on the Internet) child pornography or to produce, possess, transport, import, or export in support of those acts,[143] even if done by Japanese nationals outside Japan, including over telecom networks.[144] But the possession of child pornography with no intent to distribute is not a crime in Japan. Japan recorded the highest number of child pornography cases in 2011, which it attributes to online file-sharing services, after it clamped down on online video viewing by working with ISPs.[145] Trafficking a child for the purpose of child prostitution or child pornography is a crime, as is transnational kidnapping by enticement or force.[146] Abuse of a child by having him/her perform any kind of sexual act is prohibited.[147]

In addition, to address problems with Internet dating ("matching") services, Japan has passed a statute to protect children who become involved from criminal activity.[148] Operators must verify that children are not registered on the site.[149] They are also fined if children are solicited for sex through the site or for compensated dating.[150]

3. China

The general welfare of children is initially addressed in a separate law.[151] While child pornography is not expressly banned, the pro-

---

141. Japan, PENAL CODE, art. 175.

142. Japan, Act on Punishment of Activities Relating to Child Prostitution and Child Pornography & for Protecting Children (No. 52 of 1999, amended 2003).

143. *Id.* art. 7.

144. *Id.* art. 10.

145. *Child porn cases on the rise*, JAPAN TODAY (Feb. 17, 2012).

146. Japan, Act on Punishment of Activities Relating to Child Prostitution and Child Pornography & for Protecting Children (No. 52 of 1999, amended 2003), art. 8.

147. Japan, Child Abuse Prevention Law, art. 3 (No. 82 of 2000).

148. Japan, Law Concerning Regulations of Acts of Soliciting Children through Matching Business via Internet (No. 83 of 2003).

149. *Id.* art. 7.

150. *Id.* art. 16.

151. China, Law on the Protection of Minors (1991, amended 2006).

ducing, reproducing, publishing, selling, or disseminating obscene materials with the purpose of making profits is banned,[152] and distributing these will be severely punished.[153] It is criminal to establish a pornographic website or provide links to pornographic sites on the Internet to spread such information.[154] This was further clarified in a later promulgation from the Supreme People's Court.[155] Trafficking of a child is a crime in China.[156]

4. India

It is a crime in India to publish or transmit, or cause to be published in electronic form, any material that is lascivious or appeals to prurient interests or if its effect is such as to tend to deprave and corrupt persons who are likely, having regard to all relevant circumstances, to read, see, or hear the matter contained therein.[157] An amendments act prohibits creation, collection, browsing, downloading, advertising, exchanging, publishing, or distributing child pornography.[158] It also bans online solicitation and the facilitating or recording of online child sexual abuse.[159]

5. Singapore

Singapore alone among the countries discussed herein has not signed or ratified the Optional Protocol to the Convention on the Rights of the Child discussed in Chapter 3. Singapore supports children through the Children and Young Persons Act.[160] It is a criminal offense to engage in an "obscene or indecent act" with any child (less than 14

---

152. China, CRIMINAL CODE, art. 363.

153. *Id.* art. 364.

154. China, The Decision of the Standing Committee of the National People's Congress on Maintaining Internet Security (2000).

155. China, Interpretation on Several Issues Regarding the Implementation of Laws in Dealing with Criminal Cases Involving the Production, Duplication, Publication, Sale & Dissemination of Pornographic Electronic Information Using Internet, Mobile Communications Terminals, Radio Stations (2004).

156. *Id.* art. 240.

157. India, Information Technology Act § 67.

158. India, Information Technology (Amendments) Act (2008) § 67B.

159. *Id.*

160. Singapore, Cap. 38.

years old) or young person (less than 16 years old).[161] It is against the law to traffic in children[162] or to import a child into the country under false pretenses.[163] There are prohibitions against child prostitution,[164] child sex tourism,[165] and cybergrooming[166] under the penal code. The country does not specifically have laws that prohibit child pornography but has prohibitions against obscene and objectionable depictions under the Undesirable Publications Act.[167] The Media Development of Singapore Authority Act[168] provides the MDA the authority to regulate ISPs, and, under its Internet Code of Practice, it prohibits depicting "a person who is, or appears to be, under 16 years of age in sexual activity, in a sexually provocative manner or in any other offensive manner."[169] Online solicitation of a minor is also a criminal offense.[170] In addition, there have been voluntary industry efforts to protect the young from inappropriate content on mobile devices, in images, games, and chat rooms.[171]

6.   Hong Kong

Hong Kong prohibits child abuse images through the Prevention of Child Pornography Ordinance (2003).[172] It is an offense to print, make, produce, reproduce, copy, import or export, publish, advertise, or possess child abuse images.[173]

7.   (Republic of) South Korea

South Korea bans child pornography through the Internet as well

---

161. *Id.* § 7.
162. *Id.* § 12.
163. *Id.* § 13.
164. Singapore, Penal Code § 376B.
165. *Id.* § 376C-D.
166. *Id.* § 376E.
167. Singapore, Cap. 338.
168. Singapore, Cap. 172.
169. Singapore MDA, Internet Code of Practice 4(2)(d).
170. Singapore, Penal Code § 376E.
171. Local telecom providers, *Voluntary Content Code for Self-Regulation of Mobile Content* (2006).
172. Hong Kong, Cap. 579.
173. *Id.* § 3.

as its possession.[174] This includes the acts of production, import and export, displaying, distributing, and selling. Also prohibited is trafficking children, domestically or internationally, knowing they will be used in child pornography. Korea also restricts access by minor to harmful content and has a identity verification system for minors online.[175]

8.   Indonesia

Indonesian law prohibits child pornography, through the Internet or any means of communication, as well as possession of child pornography.[176]

5.3   Americas

The Americas (except the United States) comprise countries that have a number of different legal traditions. The countries discussed here include Canada and Mexico representing North America and Brazil and Argentina representing South America. Canada is a common-law country with an English and French legal influence; Mexico is a civil-law country with Spanish and French legal influences; and Argentina and Brazil both have a habeas data tradition in data protections but quite differing statutory implementations. With the most extensive legal framework, Canada is presented first. While there are some similarities, with these countries it is more important to look to the national differences and perhaps the international influences on each.

There are at least two regional efforts within this area. One is the Memorandum of Montevideo,[177] which calls on Latin-American (and Caribbean) nations, educational institutions, law enforcement, and industry to protect the privacy of children online through

174. Republic of Korea, Act on Protecting Youth from Sexual Exploitation (2000).

175. Korea, Act on Promotion of Information and Communications Network Utilization and Information Protection (2007).

176. Indonesia, Law on Pornography and Pornographic Acts (*Rancangan Undang-Undang Anti Pornografi dan Pornoaksi*) (No. 44 of 2008).

177. Memorandum on the Protection of Personal Data and Privacy in Internet Social Networks, Specifically in Relation to Children and Adolescents (2009).

a series of recommendations focusing on keeping their personal information secure and eliminating child pornography. The second is cybercrimes efforts under the Organization of American States (OAS), including the Inter-American Cooperation Portal on Cyber-Crime[178] and the Working Group on Cybercrime under the ministers of justice or attorney-generals across the region (REMJA), which is a forum for regional cooperation to prevent, investigate, and prosecute cybercrime, following on from the Comprehensive Inter-American Cybersecurity Strategy.[179]

A.   General Cybercrime and Data Protection Statutes

1.   Canada

Cybercrime is prohibited under the Canadian penal code. It is an offense to fraudulently[180] obtain a computer service, intercept any function of a computer system, use a computer system with intent to commit mischief in relation to data or a computer system, or use, possess, traffic in, or permit another person to have access to a computer password that would enable a person to commit an offense. It is also a crime to make, possess, sell, offer for sale, or distribute "any instrument or device" that is "primarily useful" for committing one of these offenses.[181] Creating mischief in relation to data is to willfully destroy or alter data; render data meaningless, useless, or ineffective; interfere with the lawful use of data; or deny access to data to any person who is entitled to access.[182]

Data protection is under the Personal Information Protection and Electronic Documents Act (PIPEDA).[183] The privacy principles in this statute include: accountability for personal data under an organization's control; disclosing the purpose of collection; obtaining consent to process personal data; collection must be fair and

178. *See* www.oas.org/juridico/english/cyber.htm.
179. OAS, A Comprehensive Inter-American Cybersecurity Strategy: A Multidimensional and Multidisciplinary Approach to Creating a Culture of Cybersecurity, General Assembly Resolution AG/RES. 2004 (XXXIV-O/04).
180. Canada, PENAL CODE § 342.1.
181. *Id.* § 342.2.
182. *Id.* § 430.1.1.
183. Canada, S.C. 2000, Ch. 5.

lawful and limited to necessary information; use is limited to the reason collected and personal data should be retained only as long as necessary; data needs to be accurate; appropriate safeguards need to be implemented; and the data subject has rights of notice, access, and correction, and a process for challenging compliance.

Junk mail is prohibited by the Fighting Internet and Wireless Spam Act 2010[184] and changes it makes to provisions of PIPEDA. PIPEDA is amended to prohibit the collection of personal information by means of unauthorized access to computer systems and the unauthorized compiling of lists of electronic addresses.[185] It prohibits the sending of commercial emails unless it identifies the sender and recipients must be able to contact the sender for at least 60 days and can unsubscribe, excepting emails used in the normal course of business transactions.[186] It is prohibited to alter the transmission data of an email so it is delivered to a different address than intended by the sender.[187] It is prohibited to install a computer program on another's computer during the course of commercial transaction or have that program send emails from the other user's computer.[188]

Express permission must be sought if a person intends that the installed computer program will cause the computer system to operate in a manner contrary to the reasonable expectations of the owner/user.[189] For example:

- collect personal information stored on the computer system;
- interfere with the owner's or an authorized user's control of the computer system;
- change or interfere with settings, preferences or commands already installed or stored on the computer system without the knowledge of the owner or an authorized user of the computer system;

---

184. Canada, An Act to . . . Regulating Certain Activities that Discourage Reliance on Electronic Means of Carrying Out Commercial Activities . . . , S.C. 2010, Ch. 23.

185. *Id.* § 82.

186. *Id.* § 6.

187. *Id.* § 7.

188. *Id.* § 8.

189. *Id.* § 10(5).

- change or interfere with data that is stored on the computer system in a manner that obstructs, interrupts, or interferes with lawful access to or use of that data by the owner or an authorized user of the computer system;
- cause the computer system to communicate with another computer system, or other device, without the authorization of the owner or an authorized user of the computer system; or
- install a computer program that may be activated by a third party without the knowledge of the owner or an authorized user of the computer system.

This does not apply to the following types of programs:[190]

- Cookies
- HTML code
- Java scripts
- Operating systems
- Programs that work only with previously consented-to programs

2. Mexico

Under Mexico's penal code, certain types of cybercrimes are prohibited: the unauthorized copying, modification, destruction, or loss of information from a computer system that is protected by security measures,[191] including those of the government[192] and financial institutions.[193] The Mexican data privacy law[194] principles require legally collected personal data, consent to processing and written consent for sensitive personal data, that data must be accurate and retained no longer than needed, that processing must be limited to the purpose of collection, oversight of outsourcers, and the rights to notice and access, rectify, cancel, object, and consent to transfers to third parties. There is some protection from

---

190. *Id.* § 10(8).
191. Mexico, PENAL CODE (*Código Penal Federal*), art. 211 bis 1.
192. *Id.* art. 211 bis 2.
193. *Id.* art. 211 bis 4.
194. Mexico, The Federal Law on Protection of Personal Data held by Private Parties (*Ley Federal de Protección de Datos Personales en Posesesión de los Particulares*) (2010).

junk email under the consumer protection statutes that allow recipients to opt out of receiving advertising notices.[195]

3. Brazil

Under Brazilian law, a public servant may not perform an unauthorized modification of information or programs or enter false data into a public system for personal benefit.[196] Hacking, among other conduct, would be prohibited under a proposed cybercrimes law,[197] such as obtaining access through a breach of security to a computer network, communication device, or computing system that is protected by access restrictions. It would also penalize unauthorized transfer or disclosure of protected information from computer systems, deleting the information of others, disseminating malware, and fraud or forgery by computer.

4. Argentina

The data protection act[198] in Argentina also contains prohibitions on certain cybercrimes. The following acts are prohibited under this act: knowingly and unlawfully violating data confidentiality and security data systems, breaking in any way into a personal data bank, or disclosing to third parties information registered in a personal data bank that should be kept secret by provision of law.[199] After the passing of a cybercrime law,[200] the penal code has many prohibitions, such as for illegal access,[201] illegal interception,[202] interference with data,[203] interference with systems,[204] and computer fraud.[205]

---

195. Mexico, Federal Consumer Protection Law (*Ley Federal de Protección al Consumido*), art. 76 bis VI (2000).

196. Brazil, Law no. 9983 of 2000, art. 313.

197. Brazil, Proposed Law no. 84/99.

198. Argentina, Personal Data Protection Act (*Ley de Habeas Data y Protección de Datos Personales*) (No. 25.326 of 2000).

199. Argentina, CRIMINAL CODE (*Código Penal*), § 157 bis.

200. Argentina, The Act on Cybercrimes (*Leyes de Delitos Informaticos*) (No. 26.388 of 2008).

201. Argentina, CRIMINAL CODE, § 153 bis, 157.

202. *Id.* § 153.

203. *Id.* §§ 183–84.

204. *Id.* §§ 183–84,197.

205. *Id.* §§ 172–73.

The privacy principles in the data protection act include lawful and not excessive collection; personal data should be used for its collected purpose; data must be kept accurate; the data owner has the right of access; and the data should be destroyed when it is no longer necessary.[206] Processing requires consent; owners must receive notice; sensitive data receives special controls; and appropriate security measures are required.[207] International transfer requires consent, and data owners have the rights of access, notice, and rectification.[208] While there is no separate junk-mail law, provisions of the data protection act can be used to stop spammers[209] (a data owner can request the withdrawal or blocking of his name (opt-out) from data banks used for promotional, commercial, or advertising purposes).

B.   Child-Specific Laws and Cyberstatutes

1.   Canada

The creation, printing, publishing, or possessing of child pornography for the purpose of publication; transmitting, making available, distribution, selling, advertising, importing, exporting, or possessing of child pornography for the purpose of transmission; making available, distribution, sale, advertising or exportation, possessing, or accessing of child pornography is banned in Canada under the penal code.[210] Judges can require child pornography to be deleted from the hosting website and the poster of such identified.[211] The reporting of child pornography by ISPs with knowledge or reasonable grounds to believe in the presence of such on websites or in emails is now mandatory.[212] It is also a crime to lure a child for sexual offenses over the Internet.[213] Recently introduced legislation would add offenses for providing sexually explicit ma-

---

206. Argentina, Personal Data Protection Act §§ 3–4.

207. *Id.* §§ 5–9.

208. *Id.* §§ 12–16.

209. *Id.* § 27(3).

210. Canada, PENAL CODE § 163.1.

211. *Id.* § 164.1.

212. Canada, An Act respecting the mandatory reporting of Internet child pornography by persons who provide an Internet service, S.C. 2011 Ch. 4.

213. Canada, PENAL CODE § 172.1.

terials to a child for the purpose of committing a sexual offense against the child and to use a telecom or computer system to arrange for the committing of a sexual offense against a child.[214]

2.   Mexico

It is prohibited to provide pornography to children.[215] Inducing a child to be filmed for child pornography, including via transmission over computer networks, is banned under the penal code, as is the commercial production, distributing, selling, buying, storing, advertising, transmitting, importing, or exporting of any child pornography.[216] The non-commercial buying, leasing, or possession of child pornography is also a crime.[217] The acts to promote, publicize, invite, facilitate, or manage child sex tourism, traveling inside the country or internationally, are criminal,[218] as is the performing of sexual acts with children during such tours.[219]

3.   Brazil

Child pornography is banned by law,[220] but the law was recently expanded.[221] It is prohibited to produce, sell, publish, transmit over the Internet, or publicize child pornography or to facilitate, recruit, or coerce the participation of a child in such. Acquisition and possession of child pornography is also criminal. Using digital editing techniques to simulate child pornography is also punishable. The solicitation of children for sexual acts or posing by any form of communication including the Internet is banned, as is presenting them with pornography for the same reasons.

---

214. Canada, Protecting Children from Sexual Predators Act, Bill C-54 (2011).
215. Mexico, PENAL CODE, art. 200.
216. *Id.* art. 202.
217. *Id.* art. 202 bis.
218. *Id.* art. 203.
219. *Id.* art. 203 bis.
220. Brazil, Law no. 8069 of 1990, art. 240–41.
221. Brazil, Law no. 11829 of 2008.

4.   Argentina

Commercial use of child pornography is banned under the penal code, but not possession or distribution through the Internet.[222] Children also have the right to not be subject to any form of economic exploitation, torture, sexual exploitation, trafficking, or abduction.[223]

5.4   Africa and Middle East

The implementation of these types of laws in Africa and the Middle East ranges from more robust (e.g., South Africa's child pornography law, Israel's data protection law) to almost nonexistent (many examples in the region). To highlight what is possible, three of the countries in this large region that have passed such statutes are presented: South Africa, Israel, and Turkey. Due to their long histories, large geography, and various political changes in recent memory, it is not possible to find regional trends yet in these statutes, so each country should be analyzed on its own.

A.   *General Cybercrime and Data Protection Statutes*

1.   South Africa

In South Africa, it is a crime to gain unauthorized access to, interfere with access to, intercept, or interfere with data.[224] It is also a crime for someone who "produces, sells, offers to sell, procures for use, designs, adapts for use, distributes or possesses" or uses a device or computer program whose purpose is to overcome the security mechanisms protecting data. Fraud and forgery using a computer is also banned.[225]

South African privacy law requires a data controller to have express written consent for the collection, processing, or disclosure

---

222. Argentina, PENAL CODE, § 128.

223. Argentina, Law for Protection of the Rights of Children and Adolescents (*Ley de protección integral de los derechos de las niñas, niños y adolescents*), art. 9 (No. 26.061 of 2005).

224. South Africa, Electronic Communications and Transactions Act § 86 (No. 25 of 2002).

225. *Id.* § 87.

of a data subject's personal information.[226] Only necessary information must be collected; collectors must provide notice; the information must not be used for any other purpose; and it must not be disclosed to third parties. All activity must be logged, and it must be deleted when it is no longer required.[227]

2.   Israel

Under the Computers Law,[228] it is a crime to, without authorization, damage, delete, or disrupt a computer or its programs or information.[229] Creation of software that creates or directly creates information that misleads (fraudulent) is criminal.[230] It is also a crime to access information on a computer without authorization[231] and, further, to do so to commit another crime[232] or to create or distribute a computer virus.[233] Unlawful disruption of a computer, its data and programs, including misappropriating or deleting its information, is tortious.[234]

Israeli data privacy law protects both the rights of privacy and data in databases.[235] Data subjects have the rights of notice, inspection, and amendment to their own personal data.[236] Israel is considered to be one of the few countries outside the EU to possess an adequate data protection law by the EU Article 29 Working Party (for international data transfers).[237]

---

226. South Africa, Electronic Communications and Transactions Act § 51.

227. *Id.*

228. Israel, Computers Law (1995).

229. *Id.* Ch. B.2.

230. *Id.* Ch. B.3.

231. *Id.* Ch. B.4.

232. *Id.* Ch. B.5.

233. *Id.* Ch. B.6.

234. *Id.* Ch. B.7.

235. Israel, Privacy Protection Act (No. 5741 of 1981).

236. *Id.* §§ 11,13,14.

237. Article 29 Data Protection Working Party, Opinion 6/2009 on the level of protection of personal data in Israel.

3.   Turkey

Under Turkish criminal code, it is prohibited to use, copy, or obtain data or programs without authorization from a computer system.[238] It is also prohibited to interfere with data or a computer system, either for personal benefit or to commit a forgery.[239] Turkey does not yet have a dedicated privacy law, as there are limited protections in the civil and criminal codes and telecom regulations, but there are certain safeguards for the collection and processing of data and the requirement of consent from the e-signature law.[240]

B.   *Child-Specific Laws and Cyberstatutes*

1.   South Africa

Child pornography is banned in South Africa under two statutes. Under the Sexual Offenses Act,[241] it is crime to display child pornography to an adult or child. It is also a crime to display child pornography to a child to encourage him or her to engage in a sexual act or to an adult to encourage him or her to perform a sexual act with a child[242] or to use a child in child pornography.[243] Under the Films and Publications Act,[244] it is an offense to produce, possess, distribute, import, export, broadcast, distribute, or advertise child pornography.[245] Further, ISPs are required to take "all reasonable steps to prevent the use of their services for the hosting or distribution of child pornography" and prevent access to child pornography.[246] Those with knowledge of child pornography, including that received via email, must report it to the appropriate authorities.

---

238. Turkey, Criminal Code, art. 525.

239. *Id.*

240. Turkey, E-Signature Law (No. 5070 of 2004).

241. South Africa, Criminal Law (Sexual Offences and Related Matters) Amendment Act (2007).

242. *Id.* §§ 10,18,19.

243. *Id.* § 20.

244. South Africa, Films and Publications Act (1996).

245. *Id.* § 27.

246. *Id.* § 27A.

2. Israel

Sexual exploitation of minors is prohibited under the penal code.[247] The advertising of child pornography is also prohibited.[248]

3. Turkey

Child pornography and sexual exploitation of children is banned by law.[249] The use of the Internet to do so is also prohibited, and blocking orders will be issued by Turkish courts.[250]

---

247. Israel, Penal Law § 345 (No. 5737 of 1977).

248. *Id.* § 214.

249. Turkey, PENAL CODE, art. 103.

250. Turkey, Regulation of Publications on the Internet and Suppression of Crimes Committed by Means of Such Publication, art. 8 (No. 5652 of 2007).

Chapter 6

Best Practices to Protect Children and the Internet

The statutes discussed in the preceding two chapters provide legal protections and possible avenues for criminalization and recovery, but this is only one part in the larger process that must be undertaken to protect children on the Internet. There are a number of processes, safeguarding techniques, and stakeholders involved to implement a truly comprehensive approach to addressing Internet risks for children. The appropriate starting point is with the risks discussed in Chapter 2. We will apply a risk assessment approach to those risks so that the various stakeholders—attorneys, parents, schools, organizations, and children—can assess the risks relevant to their roles. Once the risks are understood, the appropriate safeguards can be determined and implemented to keep children safe online.

Before understanding the risk assessment and reduction strategies, the roles of the various stakeholders must be clear. The role of the lawyer here is to understand the global scale of legal protections available to clients and the appropriate interfaces with law enforcement, prosecutors, and regulators. Lawyers will also assist clients in responding to any risks that have manifested themselves and require legal advice. Before that, lawyers should take the responsibility for advising their clients on the risk assessment process and the appropriate risk reduction techniques. This may be a new role for some—providing proactive advice on situations that may never occur—but should be akin to estate planning or other proactive legal services. Clients will be the other stakeholders—parents and their children, the schools (districts, principals, teachers), and organizations that are holding the personal data of children. How the lawyer advises each group of stakeholders will overlap with advice to the other groups but in total should cover all aspects of protecting the child.

This chapter starts with the analysis the lawyer must perform on the global legal protections available for children. The risk assessment process is next explained, including how each of the various stakeholders should be involved. The succeeding sections will explain the actions that each stakeholder must take to assess risk and implement appropriate safeguards.

POINTS FOR PARENTS

o   Risks assessment are necessary to identify and manage the risks to children online.
o   Each stakeholder has a unique role in assessing and avoiding the risks to children online.
o   Parents and children must work together to identify the risks and find safeguards.
o   Schools and organizations must proactively address reducing online risk to children.

6.1   Global Legal Analysis

A lawyer must know which legal protections are implicated by which risks in children's use of the Internet. The best approach is to understand the risks as they were explained in Chapter 2, match them to the types of criminal or civil legal protections, and then determine which countries around the world may be involved, so that the lawyer can then identify which statutes and which provisions are within the scope of their client's needs. When using the Internet, one has entered a global arena, where the laws from around the world will be implicated. Exactly which laws will be used will be part of a later analysis, as explained in Chapter 3. If a lawyer is performing a proactive risk assessment for her clients, then this global legal analysis will occur in advance of risks manifesting themselves, in which case the lawyer must determine the countries most likely to be involved. If this is in response to risk that has already manifested itself, the countries involved will be more easily defined.

The first step in this process is to return to the risks in Chapter 2 and make sure they are fully understood. They are listed here again for convenience.

- Child abuse images (child pornography)
- Online contact and cybergrooming
- Offline contact and harmful conduct
- Harmful content/violent video games
- Cyberharassment/cyberbullying
- Child prostitution/child sex tourism
- Loss of physical freedom
- Invasion of privacy
- Identity theft
- Financial crimes

Each of these risks maps to certain types of statutes discussed in Chapters 4 and 5. In Figure 6-1 (page 172), while each type of statute is listed only once, it may apply to more than one risk. For example, the provisions of spam laws apply not only to the risks of child abuse images but also to online contact, online games, invasion of privacy, identity theft, and financial crimes.

For each type of statute, it is appropriate to determine the best practices example to use to when evaluating actual statutory provisions. For best practice example laws, it would be optimal to use the most comprehensive statutes in each area globally, but as technology has advanced, gaps have opened under even the most comprehensive of laws. In addition, there may not always be agreement on which laws meet that standard—for example, in areas such as data privacy. The most appropriate technique then is to start with the provisions of the most comprehensive laws available and supplement them as necessary.

For cybercrimes, the Council of Europe Convention on Cybercrime has been held out as a leading standard but, due to its age and lack of revisions, it may be better supplemented by later writings. The International Telecommunication Union (ITU) has

Figure 6-1

Risks to Children	Type of Statute
Child Abuse Images (Child Pornography)	• Child Pornography • Spam (Junk Mail)
Online Contact and Cybergrooming	• Online Solicitation
Offline Contact and Harmful Conduct	• Cyberstalking • Sex Offender Registry
Harmful Content/ Violent Video Games	• Pornography/Hate Speech • Library-School Filtering • Content/Game Rating Systems
Cyberharassment/ Cyberbullying	• Cyberbullying • Cyberharassment
Child Prostitution/ Child Sex Tourism	• Child Sex Tourism • Child Prostitution • Child Sexual Abuse
Loss of Physical Freedom	• International Abduction • Child Trafficking • Child Labor
Invasion of Privacy	• Illegal Access/Interception • Data/System Interference • Misuse of Devices
Identity Theft	• Identity Theft/Computer Fraud • Phishing/Breach Notification • Data Protection/Destruction
Financial Crimes	• Consumer Protection • Data Privacy • Online Tracking

created a list of cybercrimes that supplements the Convention. For child pornography, the International Center for Missing and Exploited Children (ICMEC) has created a model set of laws. For data privacy, the OECD's original privacy principles are a useful starting point. For other laws, there are various examples that can be used, but in all cases identifying core principles in each area should be the main focus. This discussion will focus only on identifying offending conduct, not on the types of penalties, rules for prosecutions, or investigatory techniques.

The steps that the lawyer should take in understand the totality of the protections available to children online under a global legal analysis can be depicted as in the following diagram. The applicable risks from the first step are the output of the risk assessments explained in the following sections.

A. *Child Pornography*

Depending on the countries involved, there may be limited help from statutes around the world. A global review by the ICMEC found that of the 196 countries reviewed, only 45 have sufficient child pornography legislation and 89 have no specific child pornography laws. Drawing on both the ICMEC's model legislation[1] and the Council of Europe's CETS 201[2] suggests that child pornography laws should have provisions that accomplish the following::

- Define "child" (maximum age) and "child pornography" (to include at least real and simulated acts and availability on all types of media).
- Criminalize child pornography possession and all actions related to it, such as production, distribution, sale, purchase, lending, referrals, and advertising.
- Criminalize use of pornography to groom children.
- Criminalize inchoate crimes related to child pornography.
- Penalize parents/guardians who acquiesce to their child's participation.
- Criminalize Internet access, downloading, and distribution of these abuse images.
- Require ISP reporting and removal of known child pornography images.

---

1. INTERNATIONAL CENTRE FOR MISSING & EXPLOITED CHILDREN, CHILD PORNOGRAPHY: MODEL LEGISLATION AND GLOBAL REVIEW (2010).

2. Council of Europe, Convention on the Protection of Children against Sexual Exploitation and Sexual Abuse, CETS No. 201 (2007).

- Criminalize recruiting or coercing a child into participating in pornographic performances or causing a child to participate in such performances.
- Criminalize knowingly attending pornographic performances involving the participation of children.

B.　*Spam (Junk Mail)*

Spam is often used to draw children into many of the other areas of risk (e.g., pornography, ID theft). There is no model law on spam, but the ITU did attempt to draft an analysis of how to approach spam law drafting at the last Worls Summit on Information Society (WSIS) conference.[3] That document plus existing junk-mail statutes suggest that spam laws should have provisions that do the following:

- Define the medium (email, mobile phones, SMS, etc.).
- Define the requirement for a commercial purpose.
- Define whether unsolicited recipients must first opt-in.
- Define whether existing customers are excluded.
- Define where there is a "bulk" transmission requirement.
- Prohibit unauthorized use of another's computer to send such emails.
- Require that sexually oriented emails have a warning label.
- Penalize the linking of junk emails to child pornography.
- Provide an ability to unsubscribe.
- Provide contact information that stays valid for a period of time.
- Require that the message subject not be misleading.
- Penalize any attempts to hide the sender's name and origination.

C.　*Online Solicitation*

Statutes banning online solicitation do not yet have a model law. CETS 201 does require member states to prohibit such conduct,[4] as

---

　　3.　ITU, A Comparative Analysis of Spam Laws: The Quest for a Model Law (2005).
　　4.　CETS 201, art. 23.

do U.S. state and some country statutes. Online solicitation and grooming legal provisions should require:

- banning the online proposal for an offline meeting made by an adult to a child;
- prohibiting the offline meeting between the adult and the solicited child for illegal purposes;
- banning luring a child away from his/her home;
- penalizing the subverting of the ability to consent for the child's parent or guardian; and
- prohibiting the provision of pornography to children for the purpose of grooming them for sexual purposes.

D. *Cyberstalking*

Laws banning cyberstalking are relatively new and would more typically be found as extensions to existing laws on offline stalking. From existing laws, cyberstalking provisions should specify:

- the pattern of conduct that defines cyberstalking;
- whether offline conduct is required;
- the type of threats and the access and network media in scope;
- whether the actual ability to carry out the threats is required;
- whether a demand to cease and desist is required and when;
- levels of severity; and
- the differences between cyberstalking and cyberbullying/ harassment.

E. *Sex Offender Registry*

Due to higher recidivism rates for child sex offenders (four times higher[5]) and numerous high-profile crimes,[6] laws registering convicted child sex offenders and notifying those in proximity to their residences are increasing. From existing laws, the provisions should define:

---

5. BUREAU OF JUSTICE STATISTICS, RECIDIVISM OF SEX OFFENDERS RELEASED FROM PRISON (2003).

6. Sex Offender Registration and Notification Act § 102.

- the offenses for which a sex offender shall be registered and jurisdictions;
- a registry system, including the data to be entered;
- the availability on the Internet of such information;
- any Internet user IDs used by a sex offender for matching by social networking and other children-focused Internet sites;
- a community notification system, including who will be notified and with what media; and
- the verification system and process to ensure compliance.

F.   Harmful Content

Perhaps here more than in any area, it is difficult to define a model law, due to differences in national attitudes toward free speech rights and the control that national governments have over Internet filtering. For those countries that centralize the Internet access, specific statutory requirements for banning harmful content may be less necessary than for those in an open Internet environment. Also, the views on prohibiting adult pornography and restricting various types of hate speech differ widely. The provisions that these laws, if they exist, such as CETS 189, should define:

- the content that is considered harmful to children;
- whether the provision of such content is a crime;
- the systems that are in place to regulate such content from the Internet;
- the role of adult pornography in general;
- prohibiting its provision to children; and
- hate speech and restrictions on its dissemination, including racist or xenophobic materials, threats, and insults,

G.   Library/School Filtering

Statutes may require that those institutions most closely affiliated with children, public schools and libraries, make extra efforts to block harmful content from the Internet for PCs to which children have access. From existing statutes, these laws should require:

- the type of content that must be blocked;
- the techniques appropriate to perform this filtering;

- details of the Internet safety policies required by the libraries and schools;
- additional requirements for ISPs used by libraries and schools;
- monitoring required of children when using the PCs of the school or library;
- the requirements for adult use of the same PCs; and
- awareness training.

H. Content-/Game-Rating Systems

Although not technically statutes, these rating and age-verification systems are used to keep children away from harmful content. The content-rating system is used, for example, in the front of pornography sites to ensure that children cannot enter. These can use differing techniques to block the access of children, such as by using a third-party verifiable age check or a token that children may not have, such as the requirement for a credit card, or by using age information held by the credit card company.

The game-rating system should be based on a standard similar to the PEGI/PEGI Online systems. The Pan-European Game Information age-rating system provides labels that help parents in Europe "make informed decisions on buying computer games." It uses a series of labels based on the ages at which children can safely play an interactive game. There are five labels, for ages 3, 7, 12, 16, and 18. PEGI 3 is considered suitable for all ages, with possible violence in a comical context. All characters are clearly fantasy, and there are no scary sounds or pictures or bad language used. PEGI 7 is like a PEGI 3, with some sounds or scenes that might be considered frightening.

PEGI 12 labels have slightly more graphic violence toward fantasy characters or non-graphic violence toward human-looking characters. Nudity may be slightly more graphic, and bad language must be mild and not sexual expletives. PEGI 16 applies to games that depict violence or sexual activity that looks like real life. Crimes, tobacco, and drugs can be shown, or more extreme bad language is possible. PEGI 18 is the adult level, with extreme violence. Packaging depicts which of these characteristics caused the age rating:

violence, bad language, fear, drugs, sexual, discrimination, gambling, and online gameplay with other people.

Online games that are small can receive a PEGI OK label, meaning all ages can play, which requires that it does not contain any of the characteristics list above. PEGI Online requires online gaming sites to follow the PEGI Online Safety Code to receive the PEGI Online logo. This system requires that games are age-rated under the PEGI system, that there be a mechanism to report inappropriate content, that they make reasonable efforts to prohibit and remove "illegal, offensive, racist, degrading, corrupting, threatening, or obscene" content, have a coherent privacy policy, and have a responsible adverting policy.

I.   Cyberbullying/Cyberharassment

These laws are relatively new, so the provisions can most easily be drawn from existing leading statutes, as discussed in Chapter 4. These statutes should have provisions that define:

- the differences between cyberharassment and cyberbullying;
- the types of electronic media within scope (or any media);
- the types of personal information that can be used to harass or bully online;
- the types of actions that are considered cyberharassment or cyberbullying;
- the impact of the threats on the intended victim(s);
- the differences between direct communication to the victim and communicating to third parties about the victim; and
- differing levels of severity.

J.   Child Sex Tourism

These types of laws are becoming more prevalent in response to the use of the Internet to facilitate these tours. From existing laws, these laws should have provisions that criminalize:

- the behavior of its nationals wherever they commit these acts;
- those acts committed within its territory;
- arranging, promoting, and guiding such tours;

- all illegal acts committed with children on such tours;
- use of the Internet in planning such tours; and
- any illicit video or audio captured during such tours for use in promoting the tours or in possessing or distributing child pornography.

K. *Child Prostitution/Child Sexual Abuse*

Generally condemned by statute in most countries and specially addressed in the Council of Europe Convention, these laws should at least define the age of a "child" and criminalize:

- procuring of sexual acts with a child;
- sale of or profiting from sexual acts with children;
- use of the Internet in any sexual acts involving children;
- recruiting a child into child prostitution;
- all forms of child sexual abuse;
- the use of force, threats, or other forms of coercion in these acts; and
- parents/guardians who acquiesce to their child's participation.

L. *International Abduction*

The laws against international familial child abduction should include at least the following provisions:
- Criminalize abducting a child from her/his country of habitual residence
- Criminalize retaining a child outside her/his country of habitual residence
- A requirement to obey the legal orders from the country of the child's habitual residence
- Penalize the use of undue influence on a child to perpetrate the crime
- Penalize the use of the Internet to communicate with children to facilitate the abduction and thereby subvert the consent of the custodial parent
- Exceptions for demonstrated spousal or child abuse

M. Child Trafficking/Child Labor

Children are trafficked for a number of reasons, many having to do with sexual exploitation but also with the exploitation of their labor. These statutes should include:

- criminalization of child trafficking for sexual, forced labor, or any others reasons;
- criminalization of abduction, coercion, or misrepresentations leading children to be subject to trafficking;
- criminalization of child trafficking whether the country is a source, destination, or transit;
- definition of a child for labor purposes; and
- prohibitions on purchasing products known to be produced/mined with child labor.

N. Illegal Access/Interception/Acquisition

Provisions for these crimes come from both the Council of Europe Convention on Cybercrime and more recent reports from ITU.[7] Illegal access statutes should:

- criminalize the unauthorized access to any part of a computer system;
- require these acts to be committed intentionally;
- define whether the act must require defeating security measures;
- define whether intent to obtain computer data or other dishonest intent is required;
- define whether data must be obtained, modified, or damaged; and
- define whether the acts must be in relation to a computer system that is connected to another computer system.

Illegal interception/acquisition laws should:

- criminalize the unauthorized interception of non-public transmissions of computer data;

---

7. ITU, *Global Strategic Report* (2010).

- criminalize the unauthorized acquisition of non-public computer data;
- require these acts to be committed intentionally;
- require the use of technical means;
- define whether the data or transmission must be protected by security measures;
- define whether dishonest intent is required; and
- define whether the acts must be in relation to a computer system that is connected to another computer system.

O.   Data/System Interference

Provisions for these crimes also come from both the Council of Europe Convention on Cybercrime and reports from the ITU. In addition, because data interference implicates the creation and use of malware, some of the state statutes discussed in Chapter 4 are appropriate. Data interference statutes should:

- criminalize the unauthorized damaging, deletion, deterioration, alteration, or suppression of computer data and programs;
- criminalize hindering the functioning of an information system by rendering computer data inaccessible;
- require these acts to be committed intentionally;
- define whether the act must result in serious harm; and
- criminalize the creation and/or distribution of malware.

System interference laws should:

- criminalize the serious hindering (without right) of the functioning of a computer system by inputting, transmitting, damaging, deleting, deteriorating, altering, or suppressing computer data; and
- require these acts to be committed intentionally.

P.   Misuse of Devices

Provisions for these crimes also come from both the Council of Europe Convention on Cybercrime and reports from the ITU. Data interference provisions should:

- require these acts to be committed intentionally;
- require that the acts be unauthorized;
- criminalize the production, sale, procurement for use, import, or distribution, with the intent it be used to commit one of the above offenses, a device, including a computer program, designed or adapted primarily for the purpose of committing any of the offenses, or a computer password, access code, or similar data by which the whole or any part of a computer system is capable of being accessed;
- criminalize the possession of the device or computer password described above; and
- define whether a certain number of such items be possessed before criminal liability attaches.

Q.   Identity Theft/Computer Fraud

Identity theft statutes have become more prevalent and are being addressed at both global and national levels. In combination with these are statutes based on computer fraud, the likely result of an identity theft. Based on actual statutes and global reports, the identify theft statute should:

- criminalize the false impersonation of another to convert money or property;
- criminalize the use of that information without consent for any unlawful purpose;
- criminalize the acquisition, transfer, or retention of the personal identifying information or document of another with the intent to defraud;
- criminalize the production, transfers, or possession of false document-making tools;
- criminalize the use of a computer system to transfer, possess, or use a means of personal identifying information or document of another with the intent to commit or to aid or abet a crime; and
- define personal identifying information and document.

The computer fraud statute should:

- criminalize the loss of property from any input, alteration, deletion or suppression of computer data or any interference with the functioning of a computer system, with fraudulent or dishonest intent to obtain unwarranted economic benefit; and
- require these acts to be committed intentionally.

R. Phishing

Phishing laws are relatively new and should be viewed as a preparatory activity to identity theft and financial crimes. Based on actual laws, these statutes should:

- criminalize solicitation of certain information through fraudulently pretending to be real business;
- define the Internet-based techniques used to perform phishing activities; and
- define the type of information for which phishing is prohibited.

S. Breach Notification

Breach notification laws are based on the type of information, who is notified, and when notification is necessary. From actual laws, these statutes should specify:

- the definition of a data breach;
- the type of information that requires breach notification;
- the circumstances of potential harm that require breach notification;
- who is notified and in what time frame;
- the information provided in a breach notification; and
- the methods of communicating a breach notification.

T. Data Protection/Destruction

Data protection statutes are those narrowly focused on access to a certain type of information that can be used in identity theft, such as U.S. Social Security numbers. Data destruction statutes focus on ensuring that personal data cannot be used by identity thieves after it is discarded. From actual statutes, they should:

- define the specific types of data that they are protecting;
- define the actions that data custodians must take to protect personal data;
- define the data destruction standards that must be employed;
- define the types of data storage devices in scope; and
- penalize failure to properly protect or destroy personal data.

U. Consumer Protection

This area covers a number of different consumer protection areas, from unfair and deceptive practices such as those covered by the FTC Act discussed in Chapter 4 to consumer credit reporting laws. From actual statutes, credit-reporting provisions should include defining:

- the types of organizations that must protect credit information;
- how consumers can access their own credit information;
- how consumer can dispute and update disputed information;
- how consumers can freeze future credit reports; and
- the type of information that can be contained in credit reports.

V. Data Privacy

There are quite a number of different data privacy approaches. In the United States, at a federal level this includes GLBA and HIPAA, while many nations have general data protection laws, as described in Chapter 5. From actual statutes, these laws should define:

- the privacy principles that they adhere to and data subject rights;
- the types of data protected by the statute;
- the practices that accompany each of those principles, such as privacy notices;
- the rules on consent;

- the rules on third-party disclosure;
- the risk assessment processes required; and
- the safeguards required around the protected data.

W. Online Tracking

Online tracking statutes are relatively new, while spyware statutes have been around longer. From these actual statutes, online tracking statutes should include:

- defining what type of tracking data is held;
- what media (e.g., Internet, mobile devices);
- whether consumers opt-in or opt-out of processing such data; and
- what notice to consumers is required and what information should be included.

Spyware statutes should:

- criminalize the unauthorized copying of software onto another's computer that performs prohibited acts;
- define the prohibited acts;
- define the deception required to copy the software or perform the acts; and
- define the deception required to make other software not perform its usual tasks.

Online behavioral advertising guidelines created by the FTC for the tracking of consumer's online activities over time include these four principles,[8] which it supplemented in a later report that calls for a Do-Not-Track mechanism[9] (shown as the fifth principle below).

- Transparency of tracking and consumer control over tracking data use
- Reasonable security and limited data retention
- Affirmative express consent for material changes to existing privacy promises

---

8. FTC, SELF-REGULATORY PRINCIPLES FOR ONLINE BEHAVIORAL ADVERTISING (2009).

9. FTC, PROTECTING CONSUMER PRIVACY IN AN ERA OF RAPID CHANGE—A PROPOSED FRAMEWORK FOR BUSINESS AND POLICYMAKERS (2010).

- Affirmative express consent to (or prohibition against) using sensitive data for behavioral advertising
- Uniform and comprehensive consumer choice mechanism for online behavioral advertising ("Do Not Track")

6.2   Risk Assessments

A.   Stakeholder Roles

To understand the risks that exist in a child's Internet life, a risk assessment methodology must be employed. With that methodology, the various threats and vulnerabilities can be analyzed by those in the roles related to safeguarding a child's online experiences. Starting with those farthest away from the child physically are the organizations that offer online services to and store the data of children. Next are the schools and libraries that interact with the child offline but provide the entry point and guidance for the child's online experience. Then there are the child's parents or legal guardians (hereafter "parents"), who have the overall responsibility for their children's online experiences and will provide most of the monitoring and additional guidance for their children. The children themselves have a role first as safe learners and light users of the Internet and then increasingly as heavier users, experimenters, and perhaps mentors of online technology.

The lawyer's role is to be the one knowledgeable in the legal protections, in the risk assessment process, and in proactively and reactively advising his parent and child clients. Although parents will have the ultimate responsibility for their children's online experience, they will not have the legal knowledge, and may not have the technology or risk assessment knowledge, required to truly keep their children safe. This is also true for many organizations and schools, who, due to limited budgets, other demands, and changing technology, are not able to assess the complete risks to all children or, more specifically, to individual children. While each stakeholder has a role to play in assessing risk and designing appropriate safeguards, the lawyer should take the lead role in protecting children's involvement with the Internet. In the best case, this process is a preventive set of actions; in the medium case, it is a planned, reactive set of actions to a still-safe situation that has already occurred; and in the worst case, it is responding to a no-longer safe situation where criminal conduct may have already taken place. To stay in the green zone of the best case, it is important for all of the stakeholders to work together to proactively assess the risks and make their plan of action.

B.   Scope of Risk Assessment

In very general terms, there are two broad categories of children's risks from the Internet. The first is that the child may become a victim of Internet usage, even though he/she is not an Internet user. These children may become victims of child sex tourism, prostitution, trafficking, sexual abuse, child labor, and (partly) child pornography. Their becoming a victim was not related to their own use of the Internet but due to the use of the Internet by others to facilitate the crimes for which the child is the unwilling target. As such, the risk assessment would focus on the perpetrator's use of the Internet, which is an issue for law enforcement and so is outside the scope of this book.

The second general category of children's risk on the Internet is for those children who become a victim (or an aggressor) because they are Internet users. These are the children who fall prey to child pornography, cybergrooming, offline contact, harmful content, violent or harmful video games, cyberharassment, cyberbullying, cyberstalking, international child abduction, invasion of privacy, identity theft, or financial crimes. They may also be on the other side of certain types of behavior (i.e., as the aggressor). The risk assessment discussed next applies to this category of children.

When assessing risk of a child's use of the Internet, it is important to define the scope of the risk assessment exercise before utilizing the methodology. Within the general area of children's use of the Internet, there are many aspects to defining the scope of an individual child's use. Here is a list of initial questions that will begin to set the boundaries on the scope needed for the assessment:

- Where does the child use the Internet?
- What Internet services does the child use?
- How and by whom is the child's Internet use monitored?

- Does the child use any mobile devices to access the Internet?
- Does the child belong to any Internet groups?
- Does the child have a mobile phone?
- Does the child have access to a credit card or other financial device or data?
- Is the child in a stable family environment with constant oversight?
- How many hours per day does the child spend online?
- Has the child experienced previous problems on the Internet?

C. Risk Assessment Methodology

When assessing risk, there must be a general methodology used within which certain factors that are specific to the subject matter are evaluated. An established international standard for assessing risk in the field of information security is from the International Organization for Standardization (ISO). The ISO 27005 risk assessment methodology[10] is relatively straightforward and can be adapted to this situation. Six steps are used: context establishment, risk assessment, risk treatment, risk acceptance, risk communication, and risk monitoring and review.

The context management step involves three principal actions. The first two are setting the scope and defining the roles, both of which were discussed above. The other is setting the basic criteria used in a later step for accepting risk. It is important to understand that all risk cannot be eliminated, as the cost is too high—either in financial terms or in the opportunity costs of avoiding the activity. So all of the roles involved with use of the Internet must accept some amount of risk associated with those activities.

Risk itself is made up of a number of components. Risks are a product of the threats, vulnerabilities, the likelihood of occurrence of a threat exploiting a vulnerability, and the impacts of such occurrence. The threats most typically are defined as those forces external to a child's environment that may have a negative impact. Threats can come from bad actors, such as sexual predators, identity thieves,

---

10. ISO/IEC 27005, INFORMATION TECHNOLOGY—SECURITY TECHNIQUES—INFORMATION SECURITY RISK MANAGEMENT (2008).

or cyberbullies, or from different aspects of technology, such as malware, child pornography, or violent games. Vulnerabilities are most easily understood as things about children or their environment that make the threats easier to accomplish. Examples of this include risk-taking behavior, use of unprotected computers, and lack of oversight by those responsible for the child's Internet safety.

Once the risks are derived from matching the threats with the vulnerabilities, the likelihood and the impact must be analyzed. The likelihood is simply the numerical percent chance that the risk will manifest itself and affect the child. To make this easier to define, it is sometimes described in a category of high, medium, or low likelihood. The impact is what happens to a child and her world when the risk does manifest itself. This is subjective but can be described in some cases in financial terms, in other cases in reputational terms, in terms of physical safety, or for the effect on a child's mental and emotional state.

In the second step, risk assessment, a number of discrete actions are required. Before making a list of the threats, one must first think in terms of what could be threatened. For a child involved with the Internet, this could include any of the following:

- physical safety
- emotional well-being and development
- personal dignity
- social standing and reputation
- financial assets (parents' and child's)
- identity
- trust in computers and technology
- trust in others
- parents' emotional well-being and time
- privacy and personal information (parents' and child's)
- credit (parents' and child's)
- personal freedom
- access to both parents
- right to freedom of express and to anonymity
- right of freedom of association and to an education

Once the "assets" that could be impacted by the threats are understood, then the threats themselves must be delineated. Individual threats will be listed below according to the role responsible for them, but a few points about threats: First, threats may be based on either intentional or accidental conduct. So the threat assessment process needs to consider not only the bad actor but the less culpable actor, who may be a peer of the child, who did not intend to cause such a result. Second, threats should be considered in their untreated state, i.e., without any risk treatments applied. This allows for true appreciation of the seriousness of the threat and also allows for reconsideration of the risk treatment being used. Threats can be identified from the online activities inventory, described in Chapter 7.

After threats have been identified, then vulnerabilities will need to be identified. Vulnerabilities are something that will change over time and in differing circumstances. Children who change residences, switch schools, survive a divorce, are promoted a grade, or join different activities at school will now have potentially different vulnerabilities. So the vulnerabilities need to be reassessed on a regular basis and after each significant change to their activities and circumstances. Vulnerabilities that do not have corresponding threats (e.g., a child who eats pizza while online) do not need to be addressed with the subsequent risk treatments. Individual vulnerabilities will be listed below according to the role responsible for them.

When the impacts and likelihood of threats are determined, the risks can be ranked according to the likely impact. It may be easiest to understand this through an example. Numbers will be assigned as follows: high = 3, medium = 2, low = 1. If a risk has a high probability of occurring (3) and a high impact (x3), then it has a likely impact of 9. If a high-impact risk (3) has a low likelihood of occurrence (x1), then its likely impact is only 3. And if a low impact (1) has a low likelihood of occurrence (x1), then its likely impact is only 1. And so on, thereby ranking all of the risks in the order of their likely impact on the child (and parent).

The resulting list of likely risk occurrences is ranked and risk treatments can be derived and applied. There are a number of different risk treatment responses to risks: risks can be avoided, they can be insured, they can be outsourced, they can be reduced by various processes or technologies, or they can be retained. Avoidance is not partaking in the activity from which the risk arises. Insurance would be used in cases of financial assets or personal loss, personal information, or identity. Outsourcing would be tasking someone else to perform an online activity for the child or parent (e.g., having an older child print or type certain homework assignments for a younger child or download them onto a less-exposed computer). Retaining the risk is basically not doing anything beyond making a conscious decision based on full awareness that no further actions will be taken about that risk.

The final risk treatment option is to reduce a risk by applying some new technology (e.g., child-monitoring software or antivirus or blocking software) or new way of doing things (e.g., requiring adult presence when online activities occur or not allowing access from a friend's house). This option is the most typical and beneficial, as it allows the child to still partake in the Internet and derive the benefits therein but puts up safeguards that protect that activity. The vast majority of the suggested risk treatments in the following sections are the implementation of safeguards to reduce risks ("controls"). Controls are typically categorized as preventive, detective, corrective, deterrent, or containment/recovery.

The final three steps in the risk assessment process involve risk acceptance, risk communication, and risk monitoring and review. Risk acceptance is the acceptance of the overall amount of risk involved in all the activities of the child (as opposed to retaining a single risk). There will always be some amount of risk to be accepted at the end of the process and it is best to proactively understand that. Risk communication involves the process of ensuring that all stakeholders understand the risks and the risk treatments undertaken. Risk monitoring and review require that all stakeholders understand that this is not just to be implemented and left alone but requires regular monitoring to ensure that the safeguards are working as expected and are reviewed and revised periodically as appropriate. Those who want to look beyond current risks can refer to ENISA's guide to emerging and future risk.[11] For an additional

---

11. ENISA, EFR (Emerging and Future Risk) Framework Handbook (2009).

risk assessment methodology, one is produced by the U.S. government.[12] Those wanting a wider needs evaluation of their child beyond the Internet can use an approach from the United Kingdom.[13]

Any risk assessment first requires the scope to be set, the roles of the participants to be defined, and assets that need protection to be identified. Then the iterative process begins, by making an inventory of the child's online activities (discussed in Chapter 7). It proceeds through each set of actions until it comes back around to updating the online activities inventory and starting the cycle of the process anew.

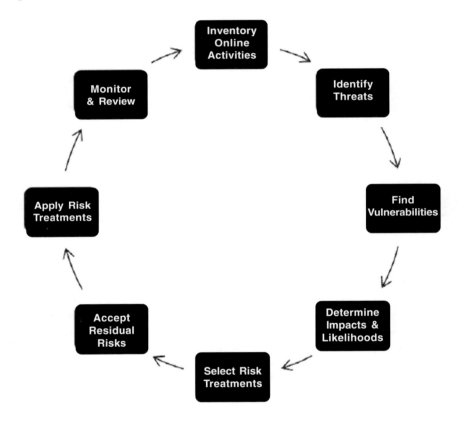

12. NIST, SP 800-30 Rev. 1, GUIDE FOR CONDUCTING RISK ASSESSMENTS (2011).

13. Children's Workforce Development Council, *Common Assessment Framework for children and young people* (2009).

6.3   Children and Parents

The risks to children from the Internet are most easily understood by categorizing them according to where they may encounter these threats. Children will encounter the Internet at home, at their school or library, and everywhere else. The risks change in these different locations not because the Internet is any different but because others factors will vary, such as the level of supervision, the type of access device used, the applications and services available, the types and strengths of procedural and technological protection implemented, and the degree of personal safety. The threats and vulnerabilities are not mutually exclusive across these locations, so only the incremental risks will be shown for the latter two locations.

When assessing the risks and creating risk treatment plans, parents must work together with their child. There are various approaches for parents in getting their child's cooperation. It is important to remember the different perspectives of both parties in this relationship, as one study showed that even when using both open and restrictive techniques to safeguard their child's Internet use, children and parents often reported significantly different levels of the child's compliance with certain usage rules.[14] For example, 57 percent of parents reported that children were not allowed to enter data into online forms, but only 20 percent of the children said that was a parental rule.

A.   At Home

Children at home would seem to be in the safest, most stable environment. While that is true of some homes, in others stability may be lacking, or oversight may be insufficient. But even in the most stable of homes the parent-child dynamic may not always lead to a greater actual level of safety. In a study on children's online safety that asked the children directly,[15] 40 percent said they rarely speak about what they do online with their parents because they do not seem to take an interest; 73 percent said they have access to the

---

14. LSE, *Regulating the internet at home: contrasting the perspectives of children and parents* (2006).

15. International Youth Advisory Congress online survey of 764 children aged 11–17, London (July 2008).

Internet whenever they want, with no restrictions on what they view; and 44 percent said they had come across images or content they thought were inappropriate for their age. Online safety cannot be assumed or taken for granted even in the most loving families, and so all must go through the same rigorous risk assessment process.

1.   Threats

The threats to children at home in using the Internet will include many of the external threats that exist no matter where they use the Internet. Such threats include the following:

- Online predators who cybergroom children for child pornography
- Online predators looking for offline sexual contacts with children
- Online predators searching for new child abuse images to trade
- Online predators who lurk in chat rooms or online game websites
- Data mining or profiling by online predators to identify vulnerable children
- Cyberstalkers who piece together physical location information from many sources to find children offline
- Criminals who want to steal the identity of children
- Online predators who communicate with children without parent's knowledge
- Criminals who steal financial information from children
- Online vendors, legitimate and otherwise, who advertise/sell directly to children
- Online tracking-history collectors
- Data collected by spyware and malware
- Online game producers who do not adequately screen their products
- Online vendors who do not provide adequate age-verification processes
- ISPs who do not adequately filter child abuse images
- Viewing of violent or sexual imagery or inappropriate language in video games

- Viewing adult or child pornography, hate speech, or other harmful content
- Communications leading to being abducted and internationally transported away from their habitual residence
- Having their privacy invaded through illegal access to their computer or interception of their communications
- Compromise of authentication information through specialized methods/tools
- Having their system or data interfered with by malware
- Having their system used to facilitate distributed denial-of-service (DDoS) attacks or forward junk mail

2.   Vulnerabilities

These concern the factors within the child's home environment that make the Internet riskier, including actions of the child and the parents. They include:

- unstable home environment/lack of parental supervision;
- lack of knowledge of risks by the supervising parent;
- inconsistent review of the child's Internet use by the supervising parent;
- excess risk taking by the child;
- prioritizing social relationships over Internet safety (30 percent of teens in a recent survey admitted that they have shared an online password with friends);[16]
- inadequate or inappropriately implemented software safeguards;
- using new technologies without implementing safeguards (e.g., wireless without encryption); and
- the child's use of age-inappropriate applications, services, or devices.

3.   Treatments

Treating these risks will be unique to each situation, but there are a number of potential responses. Of course, any risk may be retained or avoided, so this list looks primarily at risk reduction tech-

---

16. Pew Research Center, *Teens, Kindness and Cruelty on Social Network Sites* (2011).

niques. Some of these risk reduction techniques will be technology-based, while others will be process-based. This list applies especially to the youngest of children. As children mature and their knowledge and demonstrated abilities with handling the Internet increase, some of these controls can be eased. For those parents overly concerned about privacy issues (or whose children protest too much about the same), there is no answer that works in all situations, so each parent must decide where to draw the line on privacy issues with their own children.

When designing and implementing these safeguards, parents will need to be more open with their children based on the type of safeguards to be implemented. While parents clearly do not want to give out their administrator passwords (even though it is the child who may be more technically sophisticated), they do want their children to have at least the same level of understanding about key concepts. For example, both parents and children need to have the same definitions for the personal information that they do not want disclosed to others on the Internet. Is it first name, last name, both names, all parts of an address or just the street address, their school grade, or just their name, all numbers, or just financial account numbers?

Most important, there must be trust and open communications between parents and children. All technology has limits; the Internet has many, many different access points; and even those caregivers with the best of intentions make mistakes. As such, children will need not only to be educated on how to deal with situations for which they were not trained, but also to be able to confide in their parents to help them. Parents and children will need to have a series of mutually agreed-to rules that can withstand the limitations of technology and humans. In the end, each child will have to be able to deal with the risks of the Internet that squeeze through all of the safeguards set up to keep him/her out. Just to start out on the right path: the more things are done in the open by both parents and children, the more trust is built.

As a final point, is it important to recall the role of technology in the mix of risk treatments. Three key points are regarding this role are: "Technology can play a role but should not be the sole input to improved safety for minors online. The most effective technology solution is likely a combination of technologies. Any and every technology solution has its limitations."[17] The possible risk treatments follow.

- Ensure that every computer and Internet access computer-like device (e.g., iPads) has at least the following:
    o Parental monitoring software
    o Logging of all Internet activity of the child
    o Administrator passwords known only to the parent
    o Separate user IDs and passwords for parents and children
    o Pop-up ad blockers
    o Blocking and deletion of Internet cookies, including Flash cookies
    o Browser add-ins to block web beacons or other tracking technologies
    o URL blocking (only proactively accepted websites can be viewed)
    o Spam email filters to block and delete such mails
    o Antivirus/malware/antispyware software with automated threat signature downloads
    o Password vault techniques for any passwords stored on the computer
    o Use of child-safe search engines or locking of search engine safety controls
    o Encryption used for any personal information maintained on the computer
    o Encryption and other techniques used for any wireless access
    o Legitimate certificate authorities in browsers
    o Up-to-date (and automated) system software patches
    o Personal firewalls
    o Blocking of unused ports
    o Disabled webcam and wireless access when not monitored and used

---

17. U.S. INTERNET SAFETY TECHNICAL TASKFORCE, ENHANCING CHILD SAFETY & ONLINE TECHNOLOGIES (2008).

- Regular parental review of child's online activity, including computers and mobile phones, to check for unknown email addresses or phone numbers.

- Periodically do a general and wide-ranging search of the Internet to see what information about your child is available online and follow up on any data for which the source cannot be verified, requesting deletions where appropriate.

- Age-appropriate education of children on Internet safety, including how to report situations where they feel uncomfortable.

- Other Internet safety actions:
    o   Use the Do-Not-Track features in web browsers and other tools to block online tracking, despite some early limitations with these capabilities.[18]
    o   Consider opting out of receiving ads (e.g., networkadvertising.org).
    o   Unsubscribe from any unwanted non-junk advertising lists.
    o   Use ISPs or Internet email services that filter spam.
    o   Use network firewalls that limit IP addresses, ports, and MAC IDs.
    o   Consider necessity of using webcam features.
    o   Set age-appropriate financial and site limits for legitimate purchases of music and software.

- For any social networking sites children belong to:
    o   Never "friend" any person they do not know in the real world.
    o   Do not upload any information that would cause embarrassment if it became public.
    o   Don't put real personal information in profiles.
    o   Lock your profiles so only known friends can view them.
    o   Use all appropriate privacy settings available on the SNS.
    o   Know where to find the panic button.

---

18. CMU CyLab, *Why Johnny Can't Opt Out: A Usability Evaluation of Tools to Limit Online Behavioral Advertising* (2011).

- o Consider using kid-safe SNS or sites following the Safer Social Networking Principles.

- For file-sharing or photo/video-sharing sites:
  - o Never enter personal information that would allow tracing.
  - o Do not upload images that could not be shared with your grandmother.
  - o Do not download files except from trusted sources.
  - o Do not allow public posting of photos/videos of children under a certain age.
  - o Use available content restriction controls.

- For email accounts:
  - o Do not allow children under a certain age to have their own email or SMS accounts and then use non-name-specific user IDs.
  - o Monitor the user ID of received/sent emails for older children's email accounts.
  - o Set up content filters as appropriate.
  - o Don't give out email address to anyone but family and real friends.
  - o Use a generic name for the user ID that does not include a child's name.

- For mobile phones:
  - o For younger children, limit the numbers they can call to known persons.
  - o Employ GPS services that allow for location tracking of children.
  - o Use the telecom provider's spam and content-blocking packages.
  - o Use child-safe search engines or lock search engine safety controls.
  - o Give mobile phone number only to family and limited numbers of real friends.
  - o Consider necessity of Internet browsing access on mobile phone.
  - o Apply the same limits to texting as to email.
  - o Consider blocking photo sending/receiving features.

- For chat rooms/IM services:
    - o Allow children to join only approved chat rooms/IM services.
    - o Never provide personally identifiable information.
    - o Only friends known offline should be added to buddy lists.
    - o Send and receive only from those on buddy list.
    - o Never respond to requests to "tell me about your problems."

- For online games including game consoles:
    - o Use only games that follow a rating system (e.g., PEGI).
    - o Restrict access to online and offline games as appropriate.
    - o Limit amount of time spent playing daily.
    - o Set financial limits for purchasing as appropriate.
    - o Never provide personally identifiable information.

- Blogs:
    - o Consider the need to have a blog.
    - o Do not enter personal information.
    - o Do not enter any inappropriate comments and identifications of others.
    - o Use whatever privacy settings are available on the blogging site.

- Personal information:
    - o Such information should never be provided by a child to any website.
    - o Such information should never be provided by a child to any contact on the Internet.
    - o Parents should always be aware of which websites have personal information of their child.
    - o Parents have read and approved the privacy policies of any website storing their child's personal information.
    - o Do not carry personal information on memory sticks or portable devices.

- Credit history:
    - o Parents' and child's credit histories are checked at least annually.

o   Fraud alerts or freezes are placed as appropriate.

- Safe Internet use techniques are always followed:
  o   Strong passwords are always created.
  o   Passwords are never shared.
  o   User IDs are not based on the child's name.
  o   Spam emails are not to be opened.
  o   Attachments in unknown sender emails should not be opened.
  o   Spam or unknown sender emails should never be replied or linked to.
  o   No interactions with websites whose digital certificate is invalid and who are not pre-verified by applicable vendor software products.

B.   At School

The school environment is a combination of online and offline risks. This environment tends to magnify certain threats that are present in the non-school environment. It also introduces additional vulnerabilities due to the different access points, technical and procedural controls, and types and quantity of supervision. The threats and vulnerabilities shown here are not unique to the school environment, but this is where they are more likely to manifest themselves. When identifying potential risks, there are several things that parents can do beyond what the school itself does. These should not include "I trust my kid" without more.

1.   Threats

- Posting of inappropriate content about the child by the child
- Posting of inappropriate content about the child by peers
- Cyberharassment or cyberbullying of children by their peers
- Disclosure of confidential access codes to peers
- Theft of removable media or computer equipment with confidential information
- Retrieval of discarded confidential information
- Exposure to unvetted applications/academic services targeting children

2.   Vulnerabilities

- Less rigorous computer safeguards than in the home environment
- Periods of unsupervised Internet access
- Unvetted applications/academic services targeting children
- Physical contact with cyberbullies or cyberharassers
- Peer and other social pressures
- Children not understanding the implications of posting compromising images of themselves online

3.   Treatments

- Assess safeguards in the school environment and react accordingly.
    - o   Work with the school on risk reduction techniques.
    - o   Have your child avoid this risk by not being involved with the school activity.
    - o   Increase your child's awareness levels.
    - o   Move the activity from the school to the home environment.
- Never disclose passwords protecting confidential information to any peer.
- Utilize school policies regarding cyberharassment/cyberbullying.
- Block senders of cyberharassing messages.
- Ensure that all personal information is properly discarded.
- Educate children on the implications of publishing inappropriate self-images.
- Develop an appropriate response to cyberharassment/cyberbullying but report it to your parent and save.
- Follow acceptable use policies for student use of school equipment.

C.   *Elsewhere*

The universe of "elsewhere" becomes larger as the child gets older. Initially it may just include places where the parent goes also, such as a friend's houses and activities usually related to school. But older children will go to friends' houses by themselves, to school activities by themselves, to activities outside school, or perhaps on overnight trips. In addition, older children are more likely to have access to mobile phones or computers at Internet cafés. According to one study,[19] 22 percent of children go online at friends' houses, where there may be fewer safeguards (it has since risen to 51 percent[20] and 70 percent[21] in more recent studies). Beyond that, older children are more mobile and can more easily meet online contacts offline.

1. Threats

- Offline meetings with online predators
- Offline meetings with noncustodial parent intending abduction
- Detection of child's location using geolocation service data
- Interception of personal data/traffic data in wireless communications
- Interception of personal data by keyloggers or similar data-stealing devices
- Theft of data left from public access devices or by shoulder-surfing

2. Vulnerabilities

- Use of possibly less rigorously protected computers or public computers
- Use of possibly less secure networks
- Increase in risky online behavior outside supervision of parents and school
- Less safe physical environment
- Access to mobile devices possible when driving
- Loss of protection when removed from custodial parent

---

19. Symantec, *Norton Online Living Report 09* (2009).
20. EU, RISKS AND SAFETY ON THE INTERNET – THE PERSPECTIVE OF EUROPEAN CHILDREN (2010).
21. CCI, RISKS AND SAFETY FOR AUSTRALIAN CHILDREN ON THE INTERNET (2011).

3. Treatments

- Prohibition against entering or transmitting confidential information outside home
- Understanding of safeguards available at each location accessing the Internet
- Limits on use of mobile phones (services, hours, data transferred, and contacts)
- Prohibition (or supervision) of meeting unknown online contacts offline
- Open communications regarding contacts with both parents
- Processes for use of publicly accessible devices
- Prohibition on use of mobile devices when performing adult activities (e.g., driving)

6.4 Organizations Impacting Children

A. Schools

Schools have a dual role, dealing with children online both as facilitators of certain Internet-based educational services/websites and as mentors of their cybersafety skills, and then acting more like a private-sector firm in being a custodian for the personal data of children. Schools also have to intervene in certain behaviors involving students, such as accusations of cyberbullying or cyberharassment. Schools may also be under a requirement to safeguard the physical safety of students as well and legally liable if it fails to do so.[22] So the roles played by the schools are diverse but nonetheless require that they carry out each with equal diligence to ensure that children on the Internet are protected. In addition, schools provide library services that may have additional protection obligations, or these services may be carried out by public libraries under similar obligations. Only risks beyond what has already been discussed are presented.

---

22. Jane Doe v. Covington Country School District, Case No. 09-60406 (5th Cir. 2011).

1. **Threats**
   - Breach of confidential information held by schools
   - School allowing access to inappropriate websites or content
   - Misuse of school devices or online applications
   - Hijacking of school websites or other online communications media
   - Offsite online speech of students will harm the reputation of the school
   - Teachers, administrators, or staff will become the target of cyberbaiting or cyberharassment
   - Teachers will become inappropriately involved with students online
   - Violation of statutes, regulations, or policies in not keeping parents informed of collection and processing of their child's personal information

2. **Vulnerabilities**
   - Teacher, administrators, or staff not properly trained to address required roles
   - Insufficient clarity or dissemination of school policies for handling children on the Internet
   - Insufficient information security or privacy policies or poorly designed or implemented controls
   - Lack of appropriate technology controls on student-accessible computers, including student-to-student handoff
   - Lack of secure network or website controls
   - Storage/transmission of large amounts of personal data on students
   - Unclear policies related to student off-campus speech and conduct
   - Insufficient or untimely online safety training of students by school
   - Lack of sufficient understanding of legal obligations to students and parents
   - Ineffective implementation of controls by teachers and staff
   - Inadequate communications channels from the school to parents

3. Treatments

- Implement a full information security program to include information security polices, risk management, and applicable security controls.
- Design and implement appropriate controls for student-accessible devices, including audit of privileges and resources used.
- Disseminate and train all school employees on online use policies.
- Design and disseminate to all parents a school privacy policy regarding use of their personal data, including by all agents/subcontractors of the school.
- Add a social media policy to cover teachers' interactions with students.
- Implement a data breach response plan.
- Add acceptable use policy covering school assets and Internet use to student handbook.
- Assess privacy policies of all websites/Internet services used by students to perform assignments or that are accessible from the school environment.
- Allow parents to consent to all collection and processing of their children's personal information and all websites used in scholastic assignments.
- Inform parents of all Internet services used, including any that allow direct communications to or between students.
- Periodically review for compliance with all security and privacy obligations.

B. *Private Sector*

These organizations come in many different varieties—from those that deal directly with children, such as online game companies, advertisers, and providers of children's applications and services, to those who do not deal directly with children, such as IT and back-office processing firms who handle children's personal information. The private-sector organizations will have obligations to children and their parents under statute, by direct contract/terms of use, or via an online privacy policy. All of these organizations would be expected to have a full information security and privacy program (more fully described in other books by the author as mentioned above), so this section will discuss only those incremental issues related to children's use of their product or services.

1. Threats

- Personal information of children will be unlawfully collected or processed.
- Personal information of children will be lost or stolen or improperly disposed.
- Children will be allowed access to age-inappropriate content.
- Children will be allowed access to age-inappropriate services or games.
- Parents do not provide appropriate informed consent.
- Child-related statutes or voluntary codes of conduct are violated.
- Online predators will take advantage of their services to victimize children.

2. Vulnerabilities

- Insufficient information security or privacy policies or poorly designed or implemented controls
- Insufficient auditing of customer usage/tracking of personal data processing
- Insufficient risk management procedures to detect online predators
- Large databases of confidential personal information about child customers
- Inadequate records-retention policies and/or records-destruction techniques
- Age-verification tools and processes that do not perform adequately
- Processes to seek parental consent that are not well understood or implemented
- Lack of awareness of legal obligations or countries where child customers reside

3. **Treatments**

- Implement a full information security program to include information security polices, risk management, and applicable security controls.
- Design and implement appropriate controls for student personal information, including the use of encryption.
- Review and revise online privacy policy for personal information of children.
- Review and revise age-verification tools and processes.
- Review and revise parental consent mechanisms.
- Implement a data breach response plan.
- Determine all countries where child customers are located.
- Review compliance with all statutory, regulatory, and professional code security and privacy obligations globally.

Chapter 7

Starting and Conclusion

Keeping children safe in their involvement with the Internet requires constant diligence. This book has so far presented the risks of children's online participation, methodologies for assessing the presence of these risks, the types of risk treatments available (i.e., the legal protections and the technical and process safeguards), and the varied kinds of assistance available from governmental agencies and from public-private partnership activities. These have been presented from the perspective of children in both active and passive relationships with the Internet and based on where the child gains online access. In addition, those entities dealing with children, such as schools and private-sector organizations, have their own risk assessment and treatment requirements.

The stakeholders in protecting children online—the lawyers, parents, schools, and organizations—will need to have a place to start their involvement. Some, such as private-sector organizations that provide services to children, will already be heavily involved in meeting their legal compliance mandates for protecting children and their personal information. Parents and their lawyers may be closer to the beginning, never having considered the need to take a systematic approach to protecting their (or their client's) children online. Schools will likely fall somewhere in the middle, having taking some steps to protect children but needing to do more. This chapter discusses how on each of these major stakeholders can identify the steps they need to take to get started and stay on course in protecting children on the Internet, before closing with some final thoughts.

POINTS FOR PARENTS

o   Know how to inventory the child's online activities to start the risk assessment.
o   Understand the role of lawyers and what to request if some expectations are unfulfilled.
o   Understand the role of schools and what to request if some expectations are unfulfilled.
o   Understand the role of organizations and what activities to check for.

7.1   Getting and Staying Started—Parents

To get started protecting their child online, it is important for parents to understand the steps to take through the whole process. This will include understanding all the technologies that children use to access the Internet and all the technologies and processes that can be used to protect them while they are there. But first parents need to think about their relationship with their child. Do they have all of the necessary lines of trust built for the necessary rules and boundaries to be set on the child's Internet use and then for the child to honor those rules, even if the parent is not available to monitor those activities? Will the child seek out the parent when he encounters online predators or cyberharassment? Will the child use knowledge of new technologies to educate the parent or to make an end run around the existing limitations? The parent's role is vital, as "the strongest protective factor for children [is] actively engaged parents who share Internet experiences with their children and are willing to talk about the issues involved."[1]

When there is sufficient confidence in the parent-child relationship, the first thing to do is to take an inventory of all of the ways that the child uses the Internet. This could be as easy as utilizing a spread-

---

1. UNICEF, *Child Safety Online – Global challenges and strategies* (Dec. 2011).

sheet that lists the hardware, software, websites, services, and applications involved with each different use of the Internet, as follows. Remember that mobile phone networks, which are treated in this book as being part of the Internet, may actually be private networks.

Activity	Access Device	Location	Software	Website URL	Application
Math Quizzes	Class PC	School	Mozilla	quizzy.com.au	Quizzydizzy
Science Research	Library PC	School	Mozilla	Various sites	None
Email	Cell phone	Mobile	Gmail	atnt.com	MyMail
SNS	Laptop	Home	Safari	treetop.co.uk	Leaves
Online Games	Game console	Home	Safari	borg.com.sg	Borg7of17

From this inventory list, parents have obtained all kinds of valuable information. First, the list of activities provides the statement of scope for our risk assessment process. The risks that children are exposed to on the Internet are directly related to the activities in which they are involved. From this simple example, the child is involved in a class activity for taking math quizzes. This activity requires accessing a commercial Internet site and an application on that site. So there would need to be a risk assessment of the characteristics of the website itself, such as the validity of its digital certificate and its rating by one of the independent software verification services (e.g., those available as part of malware software packages). Also, does the website use cookies? And what information is stated in its posted privacy policy?

On this website, the application used would need to be understood. Does it collect personal information? If so, what information is collected, and how is it protected? Does it use encrypted transmission to collect the information based on sufficient algorithms? How are parents provided the opportunity to give express informed consent to any collection of their child's personal information? After the information is collected, how is it processed during its entire life cycle? What types of information security and privacy controls are in place? Is the data ever moved outside the country of collection? Is it ever provided to marketers, even those that are affiliated? Are there definite deletion dates and safe methods used for all personal data collected from children, including that stored on backup tapes or in mirrored-data locations? Is the data ever displayed on a screen (e.g., showing the full name or address of the child)? Does the application allow for child-to-child contact? These are just some of the questions that should be answered by schools before they would ever allow a child to utilize a commercial website to collect information and provide online services to a student.

This activity also shows that the child used a browser to access the application. Is the browser itself sufficiently secured? Is it up-to-date with all security patches? Does it block cookies and pop-ups? Are certain URLs blocked from being accessed by this browser? Does the browser allow for the initiation of mobile code? Are all appropriate security and privacy settings set instead of defaults taken upon installation? Can browser settings be modified by any user at this computer? Can the browser itself be changed to another type? There are also questions to ask about the computer itself, such as whether its security patches and operating system are up-to-date; if anti-virus, anti-spyware, and identity theft controls are in place; and the type of network security controls used for the LAN and WAN it is attached to.

The second activity listed is science research from the school library. This introduces several new elements for the risk assessment. The research will require visiting an undefined number of sites. It may also require the use of a search engine. For each site visited, how can it be verified in advance that it is child-safe? If there is a URL blacklist/whitelist that excludes sites needed by the student, will the site be unblocked for the child? Is the search engine child-safe, not displaying search results that are inappropriate for children? If so, how are the levels of appropriateness determined for each age group that might be using the computers, and how is that implemented in a multi-age-level environment? Also, as this is a library computer, does it have the same rigorous controls as the computer in the classroom?

The third activity involves email, so this introduces a new set of assessment criteria. These include whether the child has her own unique email ID or shares one with a parent. If the child has hei own user ID, what types of controls are placed on the email account, such as the amount of data that can be transmitted, whether files or attachments are allowed, if only certain addresses can be sent to or received from, or whether new addresses can be added to the contact list by the child? Are the junk-mail filters turned on and the prohibition not to respond to any such messages clear? This is a mobile phone, which raises the issue of potential unsupervised use. Have the parent and child set ground rules for use of the mobile phone? Are these ground rules reinforced by limitations on talk minutes, the use of text messaging, and the use of the camera in the phone? What uses have the GPS capabilities in the phone been put to (can the parent locate the child at any time)? Does the child have a one-button way to summon help?

The fourth activity involves a social network site (SNS). Is the SNS a very popular one in that country or is it one dedicated to children? If it is not dedicated to children, then what type of controls does it provide for children (e.g., age restrictions on registration, specific privacy controls related to children's data and verifiable consent by parents, limitations on certain activities)? Does the SNS make the child's profile private by default, as well as the location of any items that he may have uploaded? Have the parent and child reached agreement on those types of items that can be uploaded, any approval process required, the limitation of "friends" to friends known offline, and the use of any messaging or chat capabilities?

Because this is a home computer, all of the questions listed above about the computer and its operating software and the browser are relevant, with the difference that the parent is solely responsible for ensuring that these all provide appropriate levels of safeguards for the child. New items of assessment include the local and wide area networks used in the home, the use of any wireless networks, and the ISP chosen by the family. Can the local wired and wireless routers be configured to block on port ID, IP addresses, MAC IDs, etc., and require password access? Does the ISP offer a family package that is kid-safe? Does it block harmful content at varying levels that can be set by the parents based on a user ID? Are all network configuration settings revised by parents able to be locked?

The fifth activity involves online games. Are all games that are played online preapproved by the parent? Is there a rating system available that describes the content of the game? Do multi-player game sites that allow messaging provide controls that allow the locking down of a contact list and the blocking of messages from certain user IDs? Do they also provide a simple mechanism to report abuse? Are there controls for any financial transactions? Is there some type of monitoring software that can inform the parent of the activity on the game site and set appropriate limits on time of day and also total daily hours of use?

This simple example provides a starting point for parents in the online activities risk assessment process, including what kinds of questions to ask and what some of the appropriate risk treatments might be. Parents should always feel that they are in control of the process, even when some of the technology seems new, confusing, and overwhelming. When recently surveyed on whether they thought technology helped or hurt them in being a good parent, 59 percent claimed that technology made it more difficult to be a good parent.[2] For guidance on technology, parents can ask their child, who probably is closer to the latest trends, for help, with the understanding that the child may know how to do really cool things without necessarily understanding the best way to monitor herself. The parents can also talk to the IT staff at the child's school for additional help, but they may be limited to discussing only the equipment and services provided by the school. So the best recommendation for an advisor who can provide a complete solution is to engage a technology lawyer, who should be able to fill in both technology and legal understanding gaps and assess and explain the risks involved.

Sometimes one of a child's online activities will become an area of risk before there is time to adequately identify it proactively. As such, there may be a need for a technique to address immediate risks that might have arisen. Online solicitation is one area where the need

---

2. *Why parents help their children to lie to Facebook about age*, FIRST MONDAY Vol.16, No. 11 (Nov. 7, 2011).

for be able to assess the current situation is important. The following is a list of potential clues for parents and children that a child may be being cybergroomed by a predator:[3]

> "If someone . . .
> - Asks for identifying personal information about you or someone else, especially early on in the relationship
> - Is interested in exactly where you are, and who is with you or near you
> - Wants you to keep your 'relationship' a secret from others
> - Tells you things which make you feel uncomfortable
> - Asks about your sexual experience, or how you feel about doing certain sexual things
> - Is interested in what you are wearing, or wear to school or bed
> - Wants to know if you have a boyfriend or girlfriend
> - Is interested in your schedule, and when you will be alone or not with your parents or other caregivers
> - Wants to communicate with you at unusual hours, when everyone else is in bed or not home
> - Is interested to know if you are unhappy or lonely, and whether you get enough attention or get along with your parents or caregivers
> - Wants to meet with you alone or in secret
> - Wants to send you a mobile phone so they can talk with you
> - Wants you to send them pictures of you or of other people, and/or wants to send you pictures of themselves
> - Wants you to go to websites that contain pornography
> - Is much older than you and wants to be friends
> - Gets angry at you and tries to get you to 'make up with them'
> - Wants to send you gifts that you think are expensive or are of a very personal nature
> - Asks you to move your webcam so they can see certain things

---

3. Edited example from NetSafe New Zealand.

- Somehow seems to already know things about you that you have not told them."

7.2 Getting and Staying Started—Schools

Schools have a difficult set of obligations, but with that said, they need to more fully take on their responsibilities to parents and children by better risk-assessing the Internet activities of children at their schools. School personnel may too readily believe the posted privacy policies of commercial websites and Internet application providers without doing a deeper analysis to understand if that trust is totally warranted. As custodians of children's personal data, identities, and physical safety, and as mentors in their learning and personal development, schools should provide best-practice examples of safeguarding all activities in which they involve students. Just as schools would not consider taking the class on the school bus to a dangerous location without knowing full well what the safeguards were, they should apply the same diligence to making sure students avoid the unsafe aspects of Internet use.

Individual schools will be at varying degrees of commitment to students' online learning experiences. Suffice it to say that all schools will eventually arrive at the point where they must fully embrace online learning opportunities. The benefits offered to schools to facilitate learning are plentiful (e.g., unlimited research, graphical and audio representations of difficult subjects, iterative and fun testing techniques, online communities with other students, timely interactions with teachers, repeat viewing of class lectures, etc.) and low-cost. Within their respective budgets and abilities, schools fully committed to the Internet as a learning resource not only deepen the academic and social experiences of children but provide valuable online competence skills.

To get to the point where they can strongly support the beneficial aspects of the Internet, schools just as strongly face the downsides of learning with the Internet. At a minimum, this means that schools must also do a similar inventory of every type of Internet capability and service that they offer to students or require students use to complete school assignments.

Activity	Grade	Software	Website URL	Application
Math Quizzes	3-6	Mozilla	quizzy.com.au	Quizzydizzy
Science Research	All grades	Mozilla	Various sites	None
Teacher-student email	7-12	Gmail	gmail.com	SchoolMail
Student blog	10-12	Docs	kidsblogg.co.uk	Blogware
Reading Assistant	1-4	Mozilla	rassist.com.hk	ReadAssist

Once this inventory has been created, then an assessment of each service offered or assigned to students must be undertaken. With each activity, it is assumed that it is grade-appropriate. For the first activity, the school IT team and the sponsoring teacher/department should risk-assess this website and application for its commitment to student privacy. This assessment should include both reviewing the privacy notice on the website, any privacy or information security commitments in the standard contract or terms of use, and whatever additional information can be gleaned from questionnaires, interviews, emails, or phone calls with the organization hosting this application and website (the application provider and the operator of the website may be separate organizations requiring two assessments).

That risk assessment must determine at least if the personal information of children is adequately protected, if sufficient notice has been provided to parents about personal information collected and processed, and if sufficient procedures are in place to ensure that this service does not introduce any of the risks described in Chapter 2. How the website itself is protected from various threats must be assessed, as well as unresolved vulnerabilities. The audience of the application or service, how that audience is strictly controlled, and what the providing organization does to monitor and handle people outside that target audience must also be assessed. It is best to avoid relying on general platitudes from the organization ("we make reasonable efforts to protect children and their data") and ask more precise questions. Should a school utilize a service whose sponsoring organization cannot be fully risk-assessed?

With the second activity, which involves using an Internet browser to scan various sites, the focus shifts to the information security controls the schools has in place. It should go without saying that every school should have a rigorous information security and privacy program in place, including information security and privacy policies, risk assessment and treatment procedures, and information security controls. For browsers accessing the Internet, that includes much of what was mentioned above in the student's home computer risk treatment section. All of the appropriate safeguards should be in place at the computer, local server, network, proxy server, and firewall levels. These should include appropriate tools to block/filter inappropriate websites, content filters as appropriate for students by grade level, and malware/spyware protections. All school computers that students may use as Internet devices must also be assessed, looking to either compliance with a standardized configuration or a thin client format that assists in closing off access to local storage and USB/local port access.

The third activity allows communications between students and teachers. The assessment should be partly technical and partly policy/ procedure. The confidentiality of the messages in transit and storage, the limitation on use of attachments, the filters against junk mail, and the use of the predefined contacts list are all part of the technical evaluation. The policy/procedure evaluation requires clear rules about what types of communications are allowed between students and teachers; the standards for subject lines, name usage, and content; the expectations for the time to reply; whether group lists will be allowed; and what topics will be appropriate. There should be a policy in the student handbook as part of the appropriate-use guidelines of IT equipment but also an additional handout and review for any Internet-using class as well. Further guidelines for teachers on their Internet communications with students should be promulgated to all school employees.

The fourth activity gets into a potentially tricky area of student postings on a school website. While the technical assessment aspects of this include controlling who can update the blog and limiting access to who is able to view the blog, again the procedural aspects are important. There must be clear rules about how blog posters will be identified (anonymity is preferable for privacy reasons but not for accountability and perhaps peer relation reasons), if blog posts must be reviewed/accepted/rejected before they can be posted, and acceptable topics and content. Harassment or any kinds of bias against others is obviously unacceptable. The decision as to where this blog is hosted (school servers, hosted servers) and the risk assessment of that site must also occur.

The fifth activity is for another learning application used by students on a commercial site, but there are a few additional considerations. The age of the students here is younger, so the assessment must take into consideration risks that may be more (or less) prevalent in this age group. Also, the service is being provided from a domain in a different country. While merely indicative, the hosting of the student's personal information is now likely in a different location with different privacy laws. So the assessment should understand the impact to students' risk profiles for the new privacy and perhaps cybercrime laws. See Appendix C for a quick startup risk assessment process that teachers can utilize for websites or services that they identify as appropriate to use in teaching their students.

Beyond applications and services available to students on the Internet and the Internet access devices and networks used by students, personal information about the student is also collected and maintained by the school itself. This information is used in a variety of back-office applications, such as those for grade reporting, evaluations, activities and class schedules, disciplinary actions, possibly medical situations, and financial billing. The school should provide notice to parents of how the personal information of children and the financial information of parents is being processed and protected and its retention periods and eventual deletion.

Schools must also have vigorous polices for both students and faculty covering online activity both at school and outside school. Some of the risk activities, such as cyberharassment or cyberbullying, have offline components that manifest themselves on the school premises. School policies must address both aspects. The policies also must deal with issues of off-site Internet speech that interferes with the running of the school. And school policies have to address issues related to students on the Internet and teachers, such as "friending" between teachers and students or cyberbaiting of teachers by students. Teachers themselves may use the Internet in an inappropriate manner that reflects poorly on the school.[4]

The following, at a minimum, should be included in the privacy, information security, social networking, Internet usage, and other IT-related policies that schools must implement.

- A statement of commitment to safeguarding the privacy of students and the situations in which students should not have an expectation of privacy
- Descriptions of the applicable laws this policy endeavors to comply with
- Definition of what is included in students' personal information
- Types of information that are collected from and about students
- How the information is used, for what purposes, and by whom
- How long each type of information is retained
- How information is destroyed and/or anonymized
- An explanation of how informed consent is obtained from parents, including when such consent is required
- Description of the privacy notice provided to parents
- Any differences in policy provisions based on the ages of the students
- Any differences for sensitive information (including the definition thereof)
- Any disclosures of students' information to third parties and the reasons why, including legal obligations, statistical purposes, etc.
- Disclosures of students' information to parents and ages of emancipation
- Rights of access and update by parents and/or students
- Information security policies and procedures
- Requirements for any third-party outsourcers
- The geographic location of the student personal data

---

4. *Judge: Facebook post should cost job of NJ teacher*, Yahoo! News (Nov. 9, 2011).

- Use of third-party networks, websites, or applications
- Use of any website cookie or other tracking tools
- Use of school websites, blogs, chat rooms, etc., and acceptable usage
- Use of external websites, blogs, SNS, etc., from school and acceptable usage
- Use of school online tools for teacher-student interactions and acceptable usage
- Definitions and responses to cyberharassment/cyberbullying/cyberbaiting
- Internet-filtering goals and content targets
- Privacy complaint procedures and policy review and updating criteria

7.3 Getting and Staying Started—Organizations

Organizations should already be fully capable and cognizant of their obligations to protect the safety of children and their personal information. These organizations should already have implemented rigorous information security and privacy programs, should have sufficient privacy policies on their website, should know how to seek informed consent from parents, should have sufficient threat assessment processes, should have regular independent third-party reviews of their controls, and should know all of the statutes and regulations that they must comply with globally. But as there is a cost to all of this, some commercial organizations providing services or applications to children may not have implemented sufficient safeguards to protect children online.

The details of the programs these organizations should undertake are covered by the author in other books,[5] so this section will focus only on the aspects that are unique to providing services to children. These protections have to include not only techniques for proactively addressing the potential abuse of their applications or services by online predators or financial criminals, but also close

---

5. THOMAS J. SHAW, ESQ., CLOUD COMPUTING FOR LAWYERS AND EXECUTIVES – A GLOBAL APPROACH (2011); and THOMAS J. SHAW, ESQ. INFORMATION SECURITY AND PRIVACY – A PRACTICAL GUIDE FOR GLOBAL EXECUTIVES, LAWYERS AND TECHNOLOGISTS (2011).

ties to appropriate law enforcement agencies to be able to respond quickly as potential crimes arise. These organizations must ensure that they do not introduce new online risks to their children customers, that they protect children's identities and personal information, that they safeguard parents' rights to protect their own child, and that they keep all stakeholders appropriately informed.

As a simplified example, the following is extracted from the posted privacy policy of a well-known commercial provider of testing and skill-development tools for children available through the Internet. This website allows children to compete against one another during testing. The privacy policy covers a number of key points and descriptions:

- Children are allowed to compete against one another but are not allowed to communicate directly with each other.
- First names are displayed but not full names.
- The personal information of children is protected as required by named statutes in several countries.
- The type of information collected is precisely described.
- Only necessary information is collected.
- The type of consent required is specified.
- Teachers are allowed to provide consent for children.
- It describes in detail how the collected personal information is used.
- Users have the right to ensure that their personal information is accurate or to have it deleted.
- There is a commitment to keep the personal information confidential.
- Reasonable information security safeguards are employed.
- Sharing of information internally may occur within affiliated companies.
- There are limited exceptions for disclosure to third parties.
- Third parties are committed to follow the same confidentiality rules.
- International location of data is specified..
- Data retention periods are specified..
- Website tracking activities (all anonymous) on the server are described, as is the placement of cookies on the user's computer.

- Organization has the right to update the privacy policy at any time without notice.
- Privacy contacts are listed for the organization and various user countries.

By way of contrast, another well-known provider of educational services to children also posts a privacy policy. The services provided to children here do not require the display of children's names or provide for any interaction between children, so, as expected, the privacy policy is shorter. It starts out by stating that it is the end user's responsibility for any interception of data that occurs over the Internet. The organization takes responsibility for all reasonable measures to safeguard the privacy and safety of its users. While the site may collect personal information, it will not collect sensitive personal information without consent. The site will not disclose (or sell) personal information. The site may use cookies to collect statistical information. It may collect personal information from children without explicitly stating that parental consent is required. There is no reference to any statutes.

7.4   Getting and Staying Started—Lawyers

As mentioned previously, lawyers are those best positioned to bring all of this together. Children, parents, schools, and organizations will all have their particular focus on using or proving the services available on the Internet and their respective roles but will not have an all-pervasive view. Due to the broad range of legal protections addressing the various Internet risks (as discussed in Chapters 4, 5, and 6) and the technology and process safeguards used, only the technology-skilled lawyer can adequately advise upon all relevant aspects. Even then, the lawyer must keep up with the ever-changing technologies used by children, the burgeoning services on offer to children over the Internet, and the myriad legal protections available across the globe. The skills needed to keep children safe on the Internet are continually expanding.

In a typical scenario, a lawyer may be approached by a potential client who has been victimized by the conduct of others on the Internet. This may be concerning, for example, a child who has had her identity stolen. After understanding the background facts and circumstances, the lawyer can advise the parents and child on steps to take to freeze their credit, to contact all financial institutions that have accepted the fraudulent identity, and also to contact the appropriate law enforcement agencies. The lawyer can assist the victim through the criminal investigation aspects and look to any civil remedies available. Similarly for financial crimes, which may also involve the assets of the parents, the lawyer can help clients to stop any future activity against the financial accounts, assist as appropriate with the criminal investigation, and pursue civil remedies in whatever jurisdictions are required. Invasion of privacy has both a criminal and civil aspect, which may require the lawyer to communicate with the other party if a civil matter or with the police if a criminal matter.

The response to cases where the child has become involved in cybergrooming and possible offline contact will depend on how far the matter has developed but will involve law enforcement and the collection of evidence. The viewing of harmful content and child abuse images should be reported to the appropriate tipline and ISP and to the police to the extent it involves direct contact. Cyberharassment and cyberbullying may require the lawyer to deal with both criminal investigations and civil lawsuits and communications with the other party. The victims of child abuse, child pornography, child prostitution, child sex tourism, child labor, and international child abduction will also require legal assistance, which may go not only to the multi-country prosecution of their offenders but also for the legal protections they have under the laws of their current jurisdiction and potentially that of their abuser.

The lawyer will also be called upon to guide the proactive and reactive risk assessments of a child's online environment. This requires a thorough understanding of risk management techniques, of which at least those mentioned in Chapter 6 should be fully understood. There are myriad skills that a lawyer must possess to deal with the all of the global legal protections, risk assessments, risk treatments, and other responses that may be needed. In addition, the lawyer may be called upon to assist the school, from the perspectives of both what is appropriate for the school as an institution and what is best for children and their parents. And the lawyer will have a key role is overseeing the legal, risk, and security assessment and compliance activities for organizations that provide services to children over the Internet.

The lawyer must possess a global mind-set and understanding. As is repeated often in this book, the Internet is part of the global village, and so it is much more than likely that a lawyer will get involved in legal issues well beyond her or his jurisdiction. That means having a basic understanding of the types of legal regimes used around the world and techniques for how to "skill up" in the laws of those jurisdictions as required by the particular circumstances of each matter. It is not enough to offload these onto local counsel in each country, as someone has to bring all of these disparate laws together for the client, as was explained in Chapter 6. Understanding the multi-country legal analysis for Internet conduct also is essential. Lawyers focusing on this area of law will need to understand the legal theories dealing with cybercrimes, with data protection laws, and with Internet-related conduct that victimizes children. And those lawyers will, of course, need to understand the viewpoint and rights of the child, at all the differing age levels and with all of the curiosities that make up childhood.

7.5   Concluding Thoughts

I wrote this book because I was interested in discovering and moving to action all of those items that would keep my own child safe on the Internet as she grows up. I have found that there are even more items of concern for parents and lawyers than I had previously known. I have also found that there are so many resources around the world dedicated to dealing with the risks I outlined in Chapter 2. I have created a small list of these resources in Appendix A, which I hope will be of benefit to parents and children online and lawyers who have parents and children as clients. This list should be viewed as only a jumping-off point, as each HTML link provided will lead to many other valuable links to sites that provide further information and guidance.

Just as no set of client circumstances is the same as any others, there is no one set of safeguards for children on the Internet that works for every child. Parents and lawyers are going to have to address the unique circumstances of each case. Is the child a victim of a cybercrime, is the child a victim of child sexual abuse perpetrated through the Internet, or is the child an aggressor against another child online? Has the parent also been victimized, or is the parent or other adult the offender? Is the offender reachable or even known? Which jurisdiction's legal protections apply, and how should law enforcement be involved across these locations? What services of the many public or public-private partnerships should be used? To what extent is this a criminal matter, a civil matter, or just a family matter? Or is it a matter between peers or between teacher and student? What is the proper forum to resolve the issues, a courtroom or a schoolhouse? Is this a reactive situation where the online incidents have already occurred or are currently occurring, or is it a proactive precautionary endeavor?

All children deserve to be safe. Use of the Internet does not change that basic expectation. Enshrined in international, national, and local laws are the rights of children to grow up free of abuse in its many forms, to privacy, and to many other basic freedoms. On top of that is the necessity for children to be involved in the global learning community, so that they are able to fully partake in the flat world of the 21st century. More than ever, the skills taught in both the content and the usage of learning systems and capabilities offered over the Internet are what children will need as the most basic foundation for the world to come. Denying that to any child ensures that they will be left behind. Victimizing children through the Internet, in their roles as either active or passive participants, threatens to push them outside the sphere of possible success in life, not to mention impugning their basic human rights. The diminishment of childhood, with all of its possibilities, threatens not only the present but the future of all humanity.

It is my fervent hope that all of the stakeholders involved in children's experiences with the Internet will endeavor to better understand their roles and more actively pursue them, to the benefit of all children. Hopefully, each of these stakeholders will find a sufficient starting point from the guidance herein. To make it easier to get started for lawyers, Appendix B has a list of the global statutes discussed here, mapped to the risks listed in Chapter 2. These legal protections are the fall-back point if the risk treatment technical and process controls are not effective for any reason. The more that parents, schools, organizations, and lawyers, and children themselves, are made aware of the risks online, that vigorous risk assessments are performed for all Internet access and activities, and that strong risk treatments are put into place, the safer children will be in all aspects of their involvement with the Internet. That is the mandate to all of us—to protect the sanctity of childhood.

Selected Internet Child Safety Resources Available Online

Global

- International Center for Missing & Exploited Children
- Child Protection Partnership

United States

- NetSmartz Workshop
- National Center for Missing & Exploited Children
- **i**-SAFE
- Project Safe Childhood
- Stop Bullying
- OnGuard Online

European Union

- EU Kids Online project
- Safer Internet plus programme
- Insafe
- UK Council for Child Internet Safety
- Think U Know
- Childnet International
- (Germany) *Das Netz für Kids*

Asia-Pacific
- (Australia) Cybersmart
- (Japan) Yahoo! Kids
- (New Zealand) NetSafe
- (Singapore) Parents Advisory Group for the Internet
- (Hong Kong) Privacy Zone for Youngsters
- (India) Indian Child

Americas
- (Canada) The Door that's not Locked
- (Argentina) Internet Segura para los niños
- (Brazil) SaferNet Brasil
- (Mexico) La Asociación Mexicana de Internet

Africa/Middle East
- (Israel) Kids and Internet
- Arab Safety Internet Portal
- (South Africa) FPB Pro Child
- (Egypt) TE Data

Laws and Conventions Addressing Internet Risks for Children

The following table matches the laws and conventions discussed in Chapters 3, 4, and 5 to the risks identified in Chapter 2. This table is merely illustrative, as every applicable law in each region is not listed (e.g., harassment is against the law in most countries but there may not be a named cyberharassment statute), nor is every country described (only two countries per region are included). Co-regulatory or self-regulatory schemes, common in the area of harmful content, are not shown, but enabling statutes may be. This focuses on those countries and laws that were prominently covered in Chapters 4 and 5, to which the reader should refer for further details. The U.S. statutes are shown once but may apply to a number of the risks. The names of the statutes have been abbreviated or, for Europe, more familiar directive and treaty series numbers have been used. Criminal codes may include both national and state/province/territory laws.

Risk	Global	U.S.	EU	Asia/Pacific	Americas
Child Abuse Images (Child Pornography)	UN Convention Rights of the Child; UN Optional Protocol; ILO Convention 182	PROTECT Our Children Act; Adam Walsh Act; CIPA; CAN-SPAM; State laws: junk mail, filtering	CETS 201; CETS 185; EU Directive 2002/58; EU Directive 2011/92; Protection of Children Act (UK); StGB (Germany)	Criminal Code (Australia); Spam Act (Australia); Child Prostitution & Pornography Act (Japan); Regulation of Specified E-Mail (Japan)	Penal Code (Canada); Fighting Spam Act (Canada); Penal Code (Argentina)
Online Contact and Cybergrooming		KIDS Act; Protection of Children from Sexual Predators Act; State laws: Electronic solicitation	CETS 201; EU Directive 2011/92; Sexual Offense Act (UK)	Criminal Code (Australia); Law Concerning Regulations of Acts of Soliciting Children through Matching Business via Internet (Japan)	Penal Code (Canada)
Offline Contact and Harmful Conduct	UN Convention Rights of the Child	PROTECT Act; Adam Walsh Act; State laws: cyberstalking	CETS 201; Sexual Offense Act (UK);	Criminal Code (Australia);	Penal Code (Argentina)
Harmful Content/ Violent Video Games		CAN-SPAM; CIPA; State laws: Internet filtering	PEGI/PEGI Online; EC Directive 2007/65; Interstate Treaty on the protection of minors (*Jugendmedienschutz-Staatsvertrag*) (Germany)	Safe and Secure Internet Act (Japan); Broadcasting Services Amendment (Online Services) Act (Australia)	

Risk	Global	U.S.	EU	Asia/Pacific	Americas
Cyberharassment/ Cyberbullying		State laws: cyberbullying, cyber-harassment	Harassment Act (UK)	Criminal Code (Australia)	Penal Code (Canada)
Child Prostitution / Child Sex Tourism	UN Convention Rights of the Child; UN Optional Protocol; ILO Convention 182	PROTECT Act	CETS 201; EU Directive 2011/92; StGB (Germany)	Criminal Code (Australia); Child Prostitution & Pornography Act (Japan)	Penal Code (Canada); Penal Code (Argentina)
Loss of Physical Freedom	UN Convention Rights of the Child; UN Optional Protocol; Hague Adoption Convention; Hague Abduction Convention; ILO Convention 182; Palermo Protocol	PROTECT Act; TVPA; Intl. Child Kidnapping Act	CETS 201; EU Directive 2011/36; Sexual Offense Act (UK)	Criminal Code (Australia); Child Prostitution & Pornography Act (Japan)	Penal Code (Canada); Penal Code (Argentina)
Invasion of Privacy	UN Convention Rights of the Child	CFAA; HIPAA/HITECH; FERPA; ECPA; State laws: hacking, malware, privacy, encryption, infosec	EU FD 2005/222; CETS 185; Computer Misuse Act (UK); StGB Data Espionage (Germany)	Cybercrime Act (Australia); Unauthorized Computer Access Law (Japan)	Penal Code (Canada); Act on Cybercrimes (Argentina)

Risk	Global	U.S.	EU	Asia/Pacific	Americas
Identity Theft	UN Convention on Rights of the Child; OECD Guidelines on the Protection of Privacy and Transborder Flows of Personal Data	COPPA; Identity Theft Act; SSN Protection Act; State laws: phishing, identity theft, SSN protection, spyware, secure disposal, data breach	EU Directive 2002/58; EU Directive 95/46; Data Protection Act (UK); Data Protection Act (Germany)	Federal Privacy Act (Australia); Protection of Personal Information Act (Japan)	PIPEDA (Canada); Personal Data Protection Act (Argentina)
Financial Crimes		GLBA; FCRA/FACTA; Wire Fraud Statute; State laws: consumer credit, online tracking	CETS 185; EU Directive 95/46	Criminal Code (Australia); Criminal Code (Japan)	Penal Code (Canada); Act on Cybercrimes (Argentina)

Quick Startup for Schools—Short-form Internet Website/Service Risk Assessment by Teachers

Teachers are the primary drivers behind identifying new Internet websites and services that would benefit the children they teach. At the same time, teachers are occupied with many other tasks in developing and delivering their lessons. To assist teachers to drive use of the Internet in planning their educational delivery, the following short-form risk assessment of proposed websites/services can be used. It requires that teachers initiate the process when they find a website/service that they would like to use. It asks five questions that they must answer before then routing the form to the IT department for a more thorough information security and privacy assessment. It must be understood that this is an abbreviated, bare-minimum approach to get teachers and the IT department started and working collaboratively. Over time, more robust assessments by the initiating teachers will become natural. The evaluation by the IT department has many factors not shown in detail here but described in Chapters 6 and 7.

Internet Website/Service Risk Assessment by Teachers

The following questions identify risks to children in using the Internet. The objective of this process is to encourage more and deeper use of the Internet as part of our school's curriculum while protecting children. The teacher should complete the teacher section of the assessment. The school's IT department will then complete the IT section of the assessment. Upon approval by the IT department manager and/or administration and addition of the website/web service to our Internet filter list, the website or web service/application can be used in the curriculum. Please complete and route this form electronically to maintain the requested hyperlinks.

I. **Teacher's Assessment**
    A. Fill in the following information about each website or web service/application:

    •   Website Name: _____

    •   Website URL: _____

    •   Privacy Policy URL: _____

    B. What information is being collected from our children?
    C. Are our school's children able to communicate with children from outside our school or with adults through this website or service?
    D. Are the names of our children visible on the Internet when they use this website?
    E. Does this website allow advertising to children or have links to third-party sites?

II. **IT Department Assessment**
    F. Does the website's privacy policy meet our minimum standards for data collection?
    G. Does the website's privacy policy meet our minimum standards for data use?
    H. Does the website's privacy policy meet our minimum standards for retention/deletion?

I. Does the website's privacy policy meet our minimum standards limiting third-party use, geographic location services, and tracking technologies?

J. Do the website's information security controls, including encryption, appear sufficient?

III. IT Manager/Administration Approval

_____

Table of Authorities

Global

United States

State Laws

California

Cal. Civ. Code § 1798.80, 107
Cal. Civ. Code § 1798.81.5, 109
Cal. Civ. Code § 1798.82, 108
Cal. Civ. Code § 1798.85, 103
Cal. Civ. Code § 56, 107
 Cal. Civ. Code § 3344, 100
Cal. Civil Code § 1708.7, 120
Cal. Const. art 1, 100
Cal. Ed. Code § 18030.5, 122
Cal. Ed. Code § 32261, 120
Cal. Ed. Code § 32270, 120
Cal. Ed. Code § 48900(r), 120
Cal. Fin. Code § 4050, 107
Cal. Penal Code § 272(b), 121
Cal. Penal Code § 288.2(a), 121
Cal. Penal Code § 288.2(b), 122
Cal. Penal Code § 422, 119
Cal. Penal Code § 502(c)(8) , 102
Cal. Penal Code § 502, 101
Cal. Penal Code § 530, 104
Cal. Penal Code § 646.9, 121
Cal. Penal Code § 653.2, 119
Cal. Penal Code § 653m, 120
Cal. S.B. 761 (2011), 105
Cal. Veh. Code § 1808, 106
Cal., Transparency in Supply Chains Act of 2010, 122
Consumer Protection Against Computer Spyware Act, Cal. Bus & Prof. Code § 22947, 104
Online Privacy Protection Act, Cal. Bus. & Prof. Code § 22575, 106

Colorado
Colo. Rev. Stat. § 18-5.5-102(f), 102
Colo. Rev. Stat. § 22-87-103-104, 122
Colo. Rev. Stat. § 24-72.3-102, 103
Colo. Rev. Stat. § 24-90-404, 122
Colo. Rev. Stat. § 24-90-603, 122
Colo. Rev. Stat. § 4-3-506, 103

Africa and the Middle East

Asia/Pacific

Table of Cases

Index

253